DECOLONIZING DISCIPLINE

Perceptions on Truth and Reconciliation
ISSN 2371-347X

3 *Decolonizing Discipline: Children, Corporal Punishment, Christian Theologies, and Reconciliation,* edited by Valerie E. Michaelson and Joan E. Durrant

2 *Pathways of Reconciliation: Indigenous and Settler Approaches to Implementing the TRC's Calls to Action,* edited by Aimée Craft and Paulette Regan

1 *A Knock on the Door: The Essential History of Residential Schools from the Truth and Reconciliation Commission of Canada,* with a foreword by Phil Fontaine

DECOLONIZING DISCIPLINE

Children, Corporal Punishment, Christian Theologies, and Reconciliation

Edited by
Valerie E. Michaelson and Joan E. Durrant

UMP
UNIVERSITY OF MANITOBA PRESS

Decolonizing Discipline: Children, Corporal Punishment, Christian Theologies, and Reconciliation

24 23 22 21 20 1 2 3 4 5

University of Manitoba Press
Winnipeg, Manitoba, Canada
Treaty 1 Territory
uofmpress.ca

Cataloguing data available from Library and Archives Canada
Perceptions on Truth and Reconciliation, ISSN 2371-347X ; 3
ISBN 978-0-88755-865-8 (PAPER)
ISBN 978-0-88755-867-2 (PDF)
ISBN 978-0-88755-866-5 (EPUB)
ISBN 978-0-88755-918-1 (BOUND)

Cover design Kirk Warren
Interior design by Karen Armstrong

Printed in Canada

This book has been published with the help of a grant from the Federation for the Humanities and Social Sciences, through the Awards to Scholarly Publications Program, using funds provided by the Social Sciences and Humanities Research Council of Canada.

The University of Manitoba Press acknowledges the financial support for its publication program provided by the Government of Canada through the Canada Book Fund, the Canada Council for the Arts, the Manitoba Department of Sport, Culture, and Heritage, the Manitoba Arts Council, and the Manitoba Book Publishing Tax Credit.

Funded by the Government of Canada | Canada

The road we travel is equal in importance to the destination we seek. There are no shortcuts. When it comes to truth and reconciliation, we are all forced to go the distance.

— Justice Murray Sinclair, Chair, Truth and Reconciliation Commission of Canada

Let us resolve to make a difference by putting children first. If reconciliation does not live in the hearts of children, it does not exist at all.

— Dr. Cindy Blackstock

Whoever welcomes a child like this in my name welcomes me.

— Jesus

CONTENTS

In Memory of Clarence Hale, 1959–2020

Clarence Hale was the heart of this book. He shared his story here so that others could understand the devastating impact of violence on a child's soul. Experiences of racism and violence characterized his childhood, yet he grew into a man who courageously reclaimed his selfhood and his dignity as he broke the cycle of violence that had shaped his life. Through his generosity in sharing his own journey, Clarence became a catalyst of healing for countless others. He was an inspiration to his family, his faith community, and many in the world of AA. For those who knew him, Clarence embodied kindness, forgiveness, and reconciliation. He asked for little and gave so much—especially to children.

On 17 July 2020, Clarence was fishing with his wife Shirley, as he so often did. The canoe capsized and Clarence drowned. He was sixty-one years old.

We honour his memory, and all the goodness that he gave to this world. We are grateful to have known him.

ACKNOWLEDGEMENTS

We first acknowledge that this book emerged from a gathering that took place on the traditional lands of the Anishinaabe and Haudenosaunee peoples. Its chapters were written by contributors from across this land, which is known as Turtle Island by many of the Original Peoples who have lived on and cared for it from time immemorial. We acknowledge the enduring presence of the land and waters, creatures, earth and sky, First Nations, Inuit, Métis, and all other peoples. We are grateful for all those who care for the land and for all living creatures.[1]

In 2015, the Truth and Reconciliation Commission of Canada (TRC) released its summary report and Calls to Action, documenting how the past 150 years of Canada's relationship with Indigenous Peoples have been characterized by broken treaties, by physical, sexual, emotional, and cultural violence, and by the "destructive dynamics"[2] of an oppressive colonial system. Yet in the Calls to Action of the TRC, we have been given the opportunity to move forward into a shared future.

Shortly after the TRC's *Final Report* was released in 2015, Justice Murray Sinclair, Chief Commissioner of the TRC between 2009 and 2015, said: "Reconciliation is not an aboriginal problem—it is a Canadian problem. It involves all of us."[3] After he was appointed to the Canadian Senate in 2016, Senator Sinclair issued a further challenge to all Canadians: "Read the Truth and Reconciliation Commission's 94 Calls to Action and share one of the calls that has significance for you."[4]

In doing so, he urged us to think about how we can effect change in our own lives to make this country stronger.[5] We have been grateful for and inspired by Senator Sinclair's invitation to all Canadians to participate in reconciliation, and we have taken his challenge to heart.

We read the ninety-four Calls to Action when they were released and sensed the complexity of engaging in reconciliation in terms of the overarching issues of decolonization, land claims, structural justice, and more. Where could we even start? Yet one Call to Action resonated particularly strongly with both of us as an entry point for our own participation in this larger task. It was Call to Action 6, which calls on the Government of Canada to repeal Section 43 of the Criminal Code. This is the law that justifies the corporal punishment of children. As we read this Call to Action, we saw a possibility for shedding light on one of the many harms caused by colonization, in a way that would be informed by our own training and research platforms. Joan, a developmental psychologist, has focused on the harms of corporal punishment and the value of positive discipline throughout her thirty-year academic career. Valerie's background in child health and Christian theology has helped her to understand some of the ways that Western European interpretations of Christianity have, over centuries, been used as an ideological rationalization for violence against children, with a particularly malevolent focus on Indigenous children in Canada through church- and government-run residential schools. This project brought us together. "What would it look like," we asked, "to decolonize the discipline of children?" This was more than an academic exercise. We intended it to be an act of reconciliation.

Valerie's ancestors settled on this land over the past 400 years, coming first from England and Scotland, and more recently from South Africa. Joan's ancestors were missionaries from England who were present at the formation of the United Church of Canada, and Mennonites from Russia who came to North America to escape religious persecution and farm the land that, unbeknownst to them, had been taken from Indigenous Peoples. As we reflect on our positionality, including our family stories, we recognize that we have participated in, and benefited from, our inherited colonial-shaped world—the same world in which countless others have been marginalized and harmed.

We love our families and we love this land. Yet our own histories make us rightly uncomfortable and no longer allow us to engage with colonialism from a distance. Here we are, up close, becoming acutely aware of how deeply we are embedded in what Sarah de Leeuw, Margo Greenwood, and Nicole Lindsay have described as a relationship "in which non-Indigenous subjects, and by extension the institutions they/we inhabit, are making efforts to decolonize, to refute colonialism while still existing within and expanding it."[6] While their reflection focuses on the twenty-first-century post-secondary academic institution, we believe their work is transferable to Christian churches, which are our primary interest in this volume. Valerie has been involved in the Anglican Church of Canada for most of her adult life (and was an ordained priest for fifteen years), and Joan descends from Methodist ministers. We are aware that the deep, transformative change that decolonization requires of academic institutions and churches alike is slow and painful work. Such work is, as de Leeuw, Greenwood, and Lindsay describe it, "always shifting, floating, incomplete, unstable, and contradictory."[7] As we worked on this project, we took their words to heart: "Colonialism always was, and is right now, uncomfortable—particularly so for colonized subjects, but also for settler-colonial subjects. Unsettling colonialism, and indeed troubling good intentions, must similarly never be comfortable."[8]

This project has not been comfortable, and we think that is a good thing. Our wish is to push boundaries, begin conversations, and help bring an end to harmful and violent practices that have been taken for granted as "normal." Ultimately, our goal is to participate in shaping this country into one in which violence against children is not only not normalized, rationalized, or legal, but is unthinkable. Illuminating some of the forces that have contributed to the colonization of discipline and imagining a new way forward is one step toward this goal.

Over the past three years, many individuals have contributed to the shaping of this volume. Without their guidance, recommendations, contributions, and support, we could not have completed this project.

First, we thank the contributors who wrote the chapters that have formed this book. They include community stakeholders with remarkable lived experiences, scholars, clergy, students, and practitioners, each of whom invested tremendous time and energy into expressing their knowledge, insights, and at times deep struggles. No single person holds all of the pieces necessary to tell this story and to move this issue forward; the whole is so very much greater than the sum of its parts. We have been honoured to work with each of you, and we recognize the unique knowledge, skills, and life experiences that you have brought to this project.

We are profoundly grateful to the original twenty-eight individuals who participated so fully in the gathering that generated the *Christian Theological Statement in Support of the Truth and Reconciliation Commission's Call to Action 6*, which is elucidated in this book. Being among a group of people so diverse in their world views who came together in order to learn from each other was an unforgettable and deeply inspiring experience.

We appreciate the constant encouragement of our editors, Jill McConkey and Glenn Bergen at the University of Manitoba Press, as well as their wisdom and meaningful contributions to this work. We also thank the two anonymous reviewers, who helped us to refine our ideas and develop important content areas through their thoughtful critiques.

Less visible, but vitally important, are the many individuals who offered ideas, wisdom, and encouragement along the way.[9] We are especially grateful to Mr. Paul Carl (Aboriginal Education Coordinator) and Ms. Vanessa McCourt (Aboriginal Advisor at the Four Directions Aboriginal Student Centre), both at Queen's University in Kingston, Ontario. Mr. Carl and Ms. McCourt provided important cultural guidance and deepened our understanding of many issues. Ms. Kacey Dool was our research coordinator through this project. She supported our vision from the beginning, providing wisdom, energy, emerging cultural knowledge, and great care to help bring it to fruition. Meegwetch, Kacey!

This project was made possible through generous funding from a SSHRC Connection Grant – Connecting for Canada's 150th, and from the School of Religion at Queen's University. This book has been published with the help of a grant from the Federation for the Humanities and Social Sciences, through the Awards to Scholarly Publications Program, using funds provided by the Social Sciences and Humanities Research Council of Canada. Thank you for your commitment to and investment in reconciliation and for supporting this challenging discussion as a step along that pathway.

We particularly appreciate the support, encouragement, and patience of our families. You inspire us daily with your love, kindness, and wisdom.

In the words of Bishop Mark MacDonald, "reconciliation happens when an oppressed people act to reclaim their humanity. In this action, they move from being victims to being survivors. In becoming survivors, they create change that has deep and lasting effect; they release forces that lead to life."[10] We offer our deep respect to the survivors, for their personal courage and dedication to truth-telling.

Notes

1 We are grateful to Dawn Armstrong from the Office of Indigenous Initiatives at Queen's University who helped us to think about the purpose and importance of land acknowledgement statements, and to reflect on the role of land acknowledgement in the larger context of reconciliation. This section was developed in response to her teachings.

2 Michel Andraos et al., "Decolonial Theological Encounters: An Introduction," *Toronto Journal of Theology* 33, no. 2 (2017): 259.

3 Chloe Fedio, "TRC Report Brings Calls for Action, Not Words," CBC News, 2 June 2015, http://www. cbc.ca/news/politics/truth-and-reconciliation-report-brings-calls-for-action-not-words-1. 3096863. Cited by Jeffrey S. Denis and Kerry A. Bailey in "'You Can't Have Reconciliation without Justice': How Non-Indigenous Participants in Canada's Truth and Reconciliation Process Understand Their Roles and Goals," in *The Limits of Settler Colonial Reconciliation*, ed. Sarah Maddison, Tom Clark, and Ravi de Costa (Singapore: Springer, 2016), 137–58.

4 Senator Murray Sinclair, "My Challenge," at *Indian Horse* (film), official website, accessed 28 August 2019, https://next150.indianhorse.ca/challenges/94-calls-to-action.

5 Sinclair, "My Challenge."

6 Sarah de Leeuw, Margo Greenwood, and Nicole Lindsay, "Troubling Good Intentions," *Settler Colonial Studies* 3, no. 3–4 (2013): 385.

7 de Leeuw, Greenwood, and Lindsay, "Troubling Good Intentions," 390.

8 de Leeuw, Greenwood, and Lindsay, "Troubling Good Intentions," 391.

9 Midway through her work on this project, Valerie moved from Queen's University to Brock University, where new friends and colleagues continued to inform her ideas about and participation in reconciliation. She is particularly grateful to her mentor, Brock's Vice Provost, Indigenous Engagement, Amos Key Jr., and her colleagues at Aboriginal Student Services, Sandra Wong, Arlene Bannister, and Cindy Biancaniello. Their wisdom, encouragement, and friendship have shaped her ideas in important ways.

10 Mark MacDonald, "A Prophetic Call to Churches in Canada," keynote address delivered at Queen's Theological College, Kingston, ON, 20 October 2017.

Created for "A Christian Theological Statement in Support of the Truth and Reconciliation Commission's Call to Action 6" (see page 11), this illustration evokes the homes of First Nations and Inuit families, which are connected to represent our overlapping experiences and the universal need for safe, strong homes for our families. Smoke rises in the form of the infinity symbol of the Métis Nation. In Indigenous teachings, burning sage carries prayers to the Creator; in biblical teachings, the burning of incense is a vital part of ceremonial activities and prayer. The smoke is leaving the teepee where prayers are made, healing takes place, understanding develops, and cultural relationships can be restored. The smoke is going up toward God, the creator of people and the world. The homes are encircled by the Medicine Wheel, composed of four colours symbolizing the four stages of life—infancy, childhood, adulthood and old age. The cross, which spans from east to west and north to south, is connected to the circle and placed within the circle to represent the vision of reconciliation between Indigenous Peoples and the church. Beside the cross, the small Medicine Wheel represents the wholeness of the child.

—Ken Letander

INTRODUCTION

VALERIE E. MICHAELSON
AND JOAN E. DURRANT

The flourishing of children should be perceived as a core biblical and theological value. Yet over the past 150 years in Canada, the record of Christian churches in relation to protecting the well-being of children has been gravely marred by their involvement in the residential schools. A common theme of former students' experiences in these schools was the infliction of corporal punishment in response to their perceived misconduct, which included speaking their own languages, resisting sexual abuse, and running away to their homes.[1] The Truth and Reconciliation Commission (TRC) has brought to light the complicit role of churches in the profound damage this treatment has wrought in the lives of Indigenous children, families, and communities. The abuses against Indigenous children that were rampant during the residential school era were "nothing less than crimes against humanity."[2]

In 2015, the TRC issued ninety-four Calls to Action,[3] providing a starting place for reconciliation. The sixth of these calls upon the Government of Canada to remove the law that allows corporal punishment of children, which is Section 43 of Canada's Criminal Code. Based on British common law allowing corporal punishment "to correct what is evil in the child,"[4] the text of Section 43 justifies the use of corporal punishment by parents and those standing in the place of parents. It has been used to defend the assault of children in homes and schools for more than a century and allowed those operating the residential schools to inflict violence on children with impunity.

For decades, many have called for the repeal of Section 43, including more than 630 Canadian organizations representing the health, child protection, immigration, and education sectors.[5] Since 1989, seventeen private member's bills have been introduced in the Senate or House of Commons, calling for amendment or repeal of Section 43. One of these bills (S-206) was introduced by Senator Céline Hervieux-Payette in 2013.[6] Following her retirement in April 2016, Senator Murray Sinclair, who served as Chief Commissioner of the Truth and Reconciliation Commission of Canada between 2009 and 2015, assumed sponsorship of the bill. In March 2017, he led off a renewed debate with a speech to the Canadian Senate. In that speech, Sinclair cited numerous documents, including the United Nations' *Convention on the Rights of the Child* (1989),[7] the *World Report on Violence against Children* (2006),[8] and the TRC's *Calls to Action* (2016),[9] all of which call for an end to the legal justification of corporal punishment of children. He recounted stories of colossal damage inflicted on Indigenous children in the residential school system. Acknowledging the harm that corporal punishment does to all children, Senator Sinclair stated: "We agree that children need to be protected from strangers. Why do we think, therefore, that they do not need to be protected from their own parents or teachers or guardians or from foster parents or social workers or jail guards? The fact is that they do. It is up to us, as grandfathers and grandmothers, as aunties and uncles and as the guardians of wisdom in this society, to do this by amending this law."[10] Yet Bill S-206 was not passed.[11] To date, fifty-nine states (plus Scotland and Wales, which are constituent countries of the United Kingdom) have banned the corporal punishment of children, and thirty more have clearly and publicly committed to doing so.[12] Canada has done neither. In Canada, the law still permits parents to use corporal punishment as a means of correcting their children's behaviour.

The TRC's Call to Action 6 is addressed specifically to the Canadian government; certainly, the government holds responsibility for this law and its impact on the lives of children in Canada. Nevertheless, Christian churches also have some responsibility for moving this Call to Action forward. This is because over centuries, normative Western European interpretations of Christian texts were used to justify and propagate violence toward Indigenous children in the church- and government-run residential schools. These texts continue to be used to rationalize and normalize corporal punishment against children today. Call to Action 6 makes visible a complex and multi-dimensional problem: it is about child violence and the health of children; it is about religion; and it is about the ongoing process toward decolonization and reconciliation. In this volume, we call upon both contributors and readers to examine corporal punishment through multiple lenses: reconciliation, child well-being, and Christian theologies. Bringing these three strands of dialogue together, we aim to forge a path forward for Christian churches to participate in reconciliation by confronting the colonial theologies that continue to enable oppressions, and by so doing, contribute to a society in which all children can flourish.

We began this journey in October 2017. Supported by funding from the Social Sciences and Humanities Research Council and the School of Religion at Queen's University, we hosted a two-day forum at Queen's, which is located on traditional Anishinaabe and Haudenosaunee territory. Queen's University has a dark history with regard to colonization. Indeed, it has formally honoured two major architects of the residential school system: Duncan Campbell Scott (with an honorary degree in 1939) and Sir John A. Macdonald (with both an honorary degree in 1863 and a building that currently houses the university's Faculty of Law). Given the university's roots as a theological college, it is likely that some educators and clergy who worked in the residential schools were graduates of Queen's and had been trained in its Theological Hall. A university-wide task force has released a report acknowledging the university's historical participation in the colonial tradition that continues to cause great damage to First Nations, Inuit, and Métis Peoples.[13] To connect the forum to this troubling past, we hosted a public lecture called "The Road to Reconciliation" at the university's Theological Hall, in recognition that we cannot move forward in reconciliation until we are willing to look at the deeply troubling truths of our colonial past.

During the two-day forum, a group of twenty-eight key stakeholders came together to discuss Call to Action 6. Led by Anglican Indigenous Bishop Mark MacDonald, the group included Indigenous leaders, students, and community members; public health researchers, educators, and social workers; and Christian theologians and church leaders. Participants came from denominational commitments as diverse as Anglican, Disciples of Christ, Free Methodist, United Church, and Presbyterian. We were brought together by our mutual desire to participate in the process of reconciliation. Our purpose was to generate a Christian theological response to the TRC's sixth Call to Action.

Beyond academic presentations, our two-day process involved reflections on scripture and opportunities for prayer. The result was the *Christian Theological Statement in Support of the Truth and Reconciliation Commission's Call to Action 6*, which is presented at the beginning of this volume. This *Theological Statement* was generated through a process that involved every forum participant, respected every participant's input, and was finalized through consensus. Among other recommendations, the statement calls upon Christian churches "to petition our government to ensure the full protection of children, including the repeal of Section 43 of the Criminal Code of Canada." We created a website to host the statement, where it can be endorsed by individuals, organizations, and churches (www.churchesforchildren.net). To date, it has been endorsed by theologians, clergy, church members, the Presbytery of Ottawa in the Presbyterian Church of Canada, and the Primate of the Anglican Church of Canada.

This volume includes chapters written by the forum presenters and several additional authors, creating a rich blend of first-hand experiences of Indigeneity and colonialism, Indigenous knowledge systems, ecclesiological leadership, and academic expertise.[14] In **Part 1**, we set out the context for Call to Action 6. Chapter 1 presents Mark MacDonald's prophetic call to churches in Canada. He writes: "The opportunity before us is the creation of a society in which children are protected and can flourish. The forces set in motion by the courage of the survivors are a prophetic call to all of us to become that society. They demand the churches, awakened from their corruption by colonialism, to speak prophetically to the repeal of Section 43." Every author was invited to reflect on this foundational piece as they considered their own contribution to this book. Chapters 2 and 3 examine a strong body of evidence related to Call to Action 6. Joan Durrant summarizes thirty years of research evidence documenting the risks and harms of corporal punishment (Chapter 2), and Bernadette Saunders presents research findings on children's perspectives on corporal punishment, which helps us to understand how it leads to its long-term outcomes (Chapter 3). Valerie Michaelson (Chapter 4) ties the preceding chapters together by addressing the interrelated systems of power that underlie theological justifications for corporal punishment of children. She also draws attention to the racist Doctrine of Discovery, which has been widely recognized as the "driving force behind some of the church's worst abuses of Indigenous peoples."[15]

The discipline of theology makes a critical contribution to this book. **Part 2** presents an in-depth exploration of Christian theologies, each of our four contributors offering new ways of thinking about "previously taken for granted categories and frameworks, which in their dominant expressions were deeply Eurocentric."[16] Peter Robinson (Chapter 5) explores the complex relationship between the gospel and culture, and the problems that emerge when the gospel is conflated with cultural values and priorities. Whenever we discuss our work on Christian theologies and corporal punishment, the question we are asked most often is, "What do you say about Proverbs?" Interpretations of the book of Proverbs, and particularly chapter 13 verse 24, which reads "Those who spare the rod hate their children, but those who love them are diligent to discipline them," have been so central to justifying corporal punishment that we have devoted two chapters to their consideration. William Webb (Chapter 6) sets what he calls the "spanking proverbs" in the larger context of the Old Testament and calls for a reading and application of the Bible that recognizes the "already redemptive" movement of the biblical texts about corporal punishment as they are read in context. Taking a different hermeneutical approach, William Morrow (Chapter 7) draws from the very method by which biblical wisdom is generated to call into question biblical justification of the corporal punishment of children based on the book of Proverbs. In the final contribution to this section, Marcia Bunge (Chapter 8) illustrates the power of more vibrant theological understandings of children to inform the corporal punishment debate and empower churches to promote child well-being in families, congregations, and public life. Together, these four chapters not only provide a rich theological lens through which to view biblical passages about corporal punishment but also offer ways of thinking about children theologically and biblically that have the potential to transform and deepen all church practices related to children's well-being. Each of these authors contributes to an "unmasking"[17] of the colonial theologies that use Christian doctrine and biblical texts to justify violence and argues for an end to punitive violence against children.

In **Part 3**, the book turns to parenting, positive approaches to discipline, and spiritual practices. Martin Brokenleg (Chapter 9) describes the traditional parenting of the Lakȟóta First Nation and its focus on building strength, adaptability, and resilience in children and youth. Shirley Tagalik (Chapter 10) explores an Inuit approach to socialization, which is based on connection and relationship. The rich content and deep connections that both authors make between Lakȟóta and Inuit cultural values and their own Christian faith present a sombre reminder of what was lost through the colonial destruction of traditional Indigenous parenting. Yet these chapters also cast a vision of another way, one that is rooted deeply in Indigenous ways of knowing and being in the world. Marcia Bunge (Chapter 11) offers a fresh and robust interpretation of the biblical notion of discipline. Drawing primarily on New Testament scriptures, she argues that it is positive discipline, not pain and suffering, that leads to authentic discipleship and human flourishing. As a Cree/Métis woman who was raised with corporal punishment, Charlene Hallett (Chapter 12) shares her transformative journey to becoming a parent who is committed to raising her own children without it. Ashley Stewart-Tufescu builds on that story by describing the approach that supported Charlene's transformation—Positive Discipline in Everyday Parenting—which can provide a framework for discipline in our homes, churches, and communities. This section concludes with Amy Crawford and Andrew Sheldon drawing from Christianity's rich spiritual tradition to provide more tools that can be used to nurture children in positive, life-giving ways (Chapter 13).

In **Part 4**, we chart a practical way forward toward reconciliation that is grounded in theology, personal experience, ecclesiology, and church leadership. Kacey Dool (Chapter 14) weaves together her academic involvement in this project with her emergent discovery of her own Métis heritage and the disruption caused to her own family life by Canada's assimilation policies. A global perspective is provided by Chris Dodd (Chapter 15), who surveys the ways that religious communities around the world are addressing corporal punishment and encouraging law reform, and provides concrete resources for faith-based initiatives in Canada. John Young (Chapter 16) offers a rationale for preaching on Call to Action 6 and includes a sermon as an example of ways that church leaders can address this topic with their congregations. Michael Thompson (Chapter 17) challenges us to reflect on how churches in Canada participate in using power to dominate others, and points to the teachings of Jesus that describe another way. Clarence Hale (Chapter 18) shares his personal story of the racism and violence that he experienced in the 1960s and their impact on his life and relationships. He reflects on the relationship between his discovery of his own once-hidden Lakȟóta heritage and his deep Christian faith, and how he found the strength to break the cycle of violence in his family. Riscylla Shaw (Chapter 19) brings the book to a close with the recognition that reflecting on the pain that we have inflicted on our children is not an easy task for any of us. She calls on each of us, with the help of our Creator, to "wrestle with the inheritance we have received." Shaw issues a prophetic call to churches in Canada not only to speak strongly in support of Section 43's repeal but also to create a shared future in which true reconciliation can occur.

At the time of this writing, five full years have passed since the TRC's Calls to Action were released. The commitment of Canadian churches to reconciliation will be measured not by apologies but by the ways in which they respond to these calls. This book focuses specifically on their role in moving just one of these calls forward. But it is a crucial one. Section 43 of the Criminal Code symbolizes and enacts how we—the government, the churches, and the Canadian people—have historically thought about children and the place that they occupy in our society. Call to Action 6 challenges us to examine the assumptions, beliefs, and theologies that have played such a destructive role, and to consider what it means to provide full legal protection to children in Canada. Establishing right relationships between all peoples—including children—is not secondary to reconciliation; it is central.

This book is written for all Canadians, not just for those who self-identify with the Christian faith. But because of the role of churches in providing leadership to the residential schools, there is a particular *responsibility* and *opportunity* for those who do so identify. The TRC has given us a starting point for moving forward in reconciliation. Now is the time for action and for tangible response; through the TRC's Calls to Action, we are invited to "live out the various apologies we have made."[18] The opportunity before us is to change course, participating with our Creator to create a pattern of living in which children not only are protected from all forms of violence but are encouraged to flourish as whole human beings. Working for the repeal of Section 43 is more than a legal and moral responsibility; it is a sacred task.

Notes

1 Truth and Reconciliation Commission of Canada, *Canada's Residential Schools: The History, Part 1: Origins from 1939*, vol. 1 of *The Final Report of the Truth and Reconciliation Commission of Canada* (Kingston, ON: McGill-Queen's University Press, 2015).

2 Fred Hiltz, Mark MacDonald, and Michael Thompson, "There Was Nothing Good: An Open Letter to Canadian Senator Lynn Beyak," Anglican Church of Canada, 30 March 2017, https://www.anglican.ca/news/nothing-good-open-letter-canadian-senator-lynn-beyak/30018179/.

3 Truth and Reconciliation Commission of Canada, *The Truth and Reconciliation Commission of Canada: Calls to Action* (Winnipeg: Truth and Reconciliation Commission of Canada, 2015).

4 Michael Freeman, "Children Are Unbeatable," *Children and Society* 13, no. 2 (1999): 130–41.

5 Joan Durrant, Ron Ensom, and Coalition on Physical Punishment of Children and Youth, *Joint Statement on Physical Punishment of Children and Youth* (Ottawa: Coalition on Physical Punishment of Children and Youth, 2004), accessed 28 August 2019, available through http://www.cheo.on.ca/en/physicalpunishment.

6 Canada, Parliament, Senate, "Bill S-206: An Act to Amend the Criminal Code (protection of children against standard child-rearing violence)," accessed 28 August 2019, https://www.parl.ca/LEGISINFO/BillDetails.aspx?billId=6273086&Language=E&Mode=1.

7 UN General Assembly, *Convention on the Rights of the Child*, 20 November 1989, United Nations, Treaty Series, vol. 1577, 3, accessed 19 October 2018, http://www.refworld.org/docid/3ae6b38f0.html.

8 Paulo Sérgio Pinheiro, *World Report on Violence against Children*, General Segment United Nations Human Rights Council, Palais des Nations, Geneva, 22 June 2006.

9 Truth and Reconciliation Commission of Canada, *The Truth and Reconciliation Commission of Canada: Calls to Action*.

10 The Honourable Murray Sinclair, in Canada, Parliament, Senate, "Criminal Code: Bill to Amend—Second reading—Debate Continued," *Debates of the Senate*, Senate of Canada, 1st Session, 42nd Parliament, vol. 150, no. 102 (7 March 2017): 2499.

11 Bill S-207 passed second reading in the Senate, but died on the order paper when the 2019 federal election was called.

12 "Progress," Global Initiative to End All Corporal Punishment of Children, accessed 10 February 2020, https://endcorporalpunishment.org/countdown/.

13 Queen's University Truth and Reconciliation Commission Task Force, *Yakwanastahentéha Aankenjigemi Extending the Rafters: Truth and Reconciliation Commission Task Force Final Report* (Kingston, ON: Queen's University, 2016).

14 Readers will notice slight inconsistencies in capitalization throughout, notably around the words church/Church and scripture/Scripture. As editors, we deliberately sought theological contributions from a wide range of places in churches and beyond. We have left each author's capitalization on words such as c/Church and s/Scripture, as we recognize that there are theological implications to the choices that each author has made.

15 Bishop Mark MacDonald, quoted by André Forget in "Church's Knowledge of Doctrine of Discovery 'Woefully Inadequate,'" *Anglican Journal*, 28 August 2015, https://www.anglicanjournal.com/articles/church-s-knowledge-of-doctrine-of-discovery-woefully-inadequate/. For more on the damage incurred through the Doctrine of Discovery, see WCC Executive Committee, "Statement on the Doctrine of Discovery and Its Enduring Impact on Indigenous Peoples," World Council of Churches, 17 February 2012, accessed 17 October 2018, https://www.oikoumene.org/en/resources/documents/executive-committee/2012-02/statement-on-the-doctrine-of-discovery-and-its-enduring-impact-on-indigenous-peoples.

16 Michel Andraos, Lee F. Cormie, Néstor Medina, and Becca Whitla, "Decolonial Theological Encounters: An Introduction," *Toronto Journal of Theology* 33, no. 2 (2017): 259–60, 259.

17 Michel Andraos, "Doing Theology after the TRC," *Toronto Journal of Theology* 32, no. 3 (2017): 295.

18 David MacDonald, "A Call to the Churches: You Shall Be Called the Repairer of the Breach," in *From Truth to Reconciliation: Transforming the Legacy of Residential Schools*, prepared for the Aboriginal Health Foundation by Marlene Brant Castellano, Linda Archibald, and Mike DeGagne (Ottawa: Aboriginal Healing Foundation, 2008), 344, accessed 28 August 2019, http://www.ahf.ca/downloads/truth-to-reconciliation.pdf.

A Christian Theological Statement in Support of the Truth and Reconciliation Commission's Call to Action 6

Call to Action 6 of the Truth and Reconciliation Commission (TRC) on Indian Residential Schools calls for the repeal of Section 43 of the Criminal Code of Canada.

Section 43 provides a legal defence for the use of physical punishment by parents (and people standing in the place of parents) to correct a child's behaviour.

We acknowledge the legacy of damage caused to First Nations, Inuit, and Métis children by residential schools. The resilience and courage of the residential school survivors has awakened us to our moral failure. This compels us to imagine a new and hopeful future, supporting the healthy development of children and their families for all peoples in Canada.

Research and lived experience have revealed the destructive effects of physical punishment on the mental, physical, and spiritual health of children. Physical punishment also weakens the parent-child and other family relationships. It is time for Canada to provide children with protection from violence equal to that enshrined in the law for adults.

A full reading of scripture in light of the revelation of Jesus Christ, who embraced and welcomed children, is incompatible with physical punishment. Scripture constantly invites the people of God to imagine a better future. We affirm the following biblical principles: children are sacred gifts from God; fully human and deserving of dignity and respect;

blessed with gifts, wisdom, and strengths that enrich the common good; vulnerable persons deserving nurture, protection, and justice; and individuals with growing moral and spiritual capacities.

While parenting can be challenging, children deserve respectful discipline and mentoring, so they know their identity as beloved children of God.

In response to Call to Action 6, churches and faith-based groups have a duty to call for the repeal of Section 43 as a vital step towards reconciliation, and a more just and peaceful society.

Recommendations

Based on these principles and the final report of the TRC:

1. We call upon Christian churches to petition our government to ensure the full protection of children, including the repeal of Section 43 of the Criminal Code of Canada.
2. We call upon Christian churches to recognize the deep societal wounds that remain as a result of colonialism, and to actively address the ongoing disproportionate physical, spiritual, and emotional harm experienced by Indigenous children and youth.
3. We call upon Christian churches to increase awareness in our communities of the impact of violence, including physical punishment, in homes, families, institutions, and communities.
4. We call upon Christian churches to endorse the *Joint Statement on Physical Punishment of Children and Youth*. http://www.cheo.on.ca/en/physicalpunishment.
5. We call upon all leaders and educators in Christian communities to be active in the protection of children.
6. We call upon all Christians to work together in continuing to develop healthy, effective, and non-violent approaches to discipline in raising children and youth.

Original Signatories

The Right Reverend Mark MacDonald, National Indigenous Anglican Bishop, Anglican Church of Canada

The Venerable Dr. Michael Thompson, General Secretary, Anglican Church of Canada

The Right Reverend Riscylla Walsh Shaw, Suffragan Bishop and Ambassador of Reconciliation, Diocese of Toronto, Anglican Church of Canada

The Reverend Dr. John H. Young, Executive Minister – Theological Leadership, The United Church of Canada

The Reverend Dr. William Morrow, Professor of Hebrew and Hebrew Scriptures, School of Religion, Queen's University, Kingston, Ontario

Dr. Marcia Bunge, Professor of Religion and Bernhardson Distinguished Chair of Lutheran Studies, Gustavus Adolphus College, St. Peter, Minnesota

The Reverend Dr. Valerie Michaelson, Post Doctoral Fellow, School of Religion and Department of Public Health Sciences, Queen's University, Kingston, Ontario

Dr. William Pickett, Professor and Head, Department of Public Health Sciences, Queen's University, Kingston, Ontario

The Reverend Dr. Peter Robinson, Professor, Wycliffe College, Toronto, Ontario

The Reverend Dr. Jean Stairs, Minister of Christian Education, Outreach and Family Pastoral Care, Edith Rankin Memorial United Church, Kingston, Ontario

The Reverend Lynne Gardiner, Minister, Delta Toledo Pastoral Charge, The United Church of Canada

Sue Lyon, Elder, Next (Free Methodist) Church, Kingston, Ontario

Meaghan Armstrong, Queen's University, Kingston, Ontario

Hannah Ascough, MA Candidate in Global Development Studies, Queen's University, Kingston, Ontario

Nancy Bell, MA, RSW, MCSW, Winnipeg, Manitoba

Kacey Dool, MA Candidate in Religious Studies, Queen's University, Kingston, Ontario

Ron Ensom, RSW, Member of the Anglican Church of Canada, Ottawa, Ontario

Clarence Hale, Verger, St. James' Anglican Church, Kingston, Ontario

Hannah Michaelson, Loyalist Collegiate Vocational Institute Secondary School, Kingston, Ontario

Rita Machnik, Tyndale Seminary Student, Church School Director, St. Andrew's Presbyterian Church, Aurora, Ontario

Emma Pipes, Candidate for Ministry, United Church of Canada Storrington Pastoral Charge and Four Rivers Presbytery, Kingston, Ontario

Ashley Stewart-Tufescu, MSc, PhD Candidate in Applied Health Sciences, RSW, University of Manitoba, Winnipeg, Manitoba

PART 1: SETTING THE STAGE

Residential Schools, Canadian Churches, and Corporal Punishment

1

A Prophetic Call to Churches in Canada

MARK MACDONALD

When Navajo people describe the sun, they talk about the sun bearer. The sun bearer is pictured as a young man who carries a turquoise disk on his shoulder, and the turquoise disk is lit with grandmother fire. The teaching that comes with this story is that in order to be successful in life, you must carry high—as high as possible in your life—the teaching of your Elders, and specifically the teaching of your grandmothers.

I would like to begin by honouring the Indigenous Elders who have given to me my basic understanding of the things we examine here in this book. The Elders' affirmation of the sacred and divine character of children is primary to this work. It is my prayer that their prophetic hope and love for children will guide us in our confrontation with past and present evils, as well as inspire and direct our future for the good.

It is my honour and task to set this volume within the larger trajectory of Canada's truth and reconciliation movement. To trace the forces that have been animated by the work of Canada's Truth and Reconciliation Commission is to outline a significant path for healing in our hearts and in our society. It is my prayer and my hope that this volume will contribute to the larger healing now offered to Canada.

The Residential Schools

Before we can set a course for healing, we must look at the meaning of the residential school system. A massive systemic evil in themselves, the residential schools were a part of the broader systemic evil that is called colonialism. For our purpose in this narrative it is more than important to recognize that the churches were an animating partner in both the broader system of colonialism and the evil of the residential schools. The churches were an essential part of the colonial system, often providing the ideological pretext and an ongoing defence for colonialism and the schools. They not only participated in the functioning of colonial institutions, but as with the residential schools, they were an integral part of their supporting framework.

It is difficult to comprehend and explain the churches' participation in the massive evil of colonialism, much less to fully admit and acknowledge the dynamics of our role in it. In the residential schools, our immediate concern here, the churches acted in direct contradiction to some of their most central and essential values and beliefs. We must never forget that children were the primary victims of this system. Despite the present-day widespread agreement that the schools were wrong, our institutional capacity to explain such behaviour remains limited, and our acknowledgement of its meaning is blunted.

Because of the way in which personal autonomy has captivated modern thought, we tend to view evil as a matter of individual personal choice. A widespread evil is attributed to a great number of individual bad choices. But this is not completely helpful in explaining institutional and systemic evil. In the case of the residential schools, for instance, we might look for the villains and perpetrators, but although they are certainly present in this story, the collapse of morality involved goes far beyond the behaviours of a few, or even many. The quest to identify individual actors in an evil system, while very important, often fails to reveal the depth and breadth of systemic evil and the institutional corruption that results from it. The evil is a part of the structure of the system; it is in the very framework that allows the system to exist. The legality and governing structure of the system holds the evil, as we see in the case at hand. The evil is perpetuated by the system and only dependent upon the moral slumber of its participants and perpetrators.

The story of the residential schools is, therefore, both the story of an overriding of individual choice and the complicity of an entire institutional community. That there were many well-intentioned individuals in the schools is without doubt. The truth remains that all participated in a system of great evil.

Because our analysis of systemic evil tends to be stunted, our remedies are often meagre. After an appropriate apology, we change policy and procedures. As critical as that is, it may not be sufficient to redress the evil involved. This is only an initial step in the direction of full-hearted repentance and reconciliation.

Christian scripture helps us with a more sophisticated understanding of systemic evil by way of its description of the Principalities and Powers:[1] what today we would call the ideologies, idols, and images that are the source and strength of systemic evil. The Principalities and Powers, in their promotion of their own supremacy and in their proud rebellion against God, result in the individual and communal corruption that is the enemy of life. They become the very opposite of God's way in creation. By their name, they describe the way evil can animate and inhabit an entire society and culture, its law, structures of governance, and culture.

The way of life that we find in Jesus is in fundamental conflict with the Principalities and Powers, and so with systemic evil. The Apostle Paul, for instance, sees the critical engagement with these forces as a central part of the Christian life and a necessary prelude to the world that God has promised in Christ. The freedom from these forces and their pervasive grip on societies are a part of the liberty offered in Christ. In contrast to this, the surrender of the churches to the Principalities and Powers in the evil of colonialism is a measure of our distance, and perhaps our severe alienation, from our ideal. What is revealed in the story of the residential schools is a deep moral wound that continues to threaten Indigenous children and children in general in Canada.

It is within a more comprehensive understanding of systemic evil, in keeping with what I have described above, that the churches begin their reconstruction and repair. It is critical that we understand something of the forces in which we have participated and those from which we must be freed to live into our values and our ideal. Some awareness of where we have failed in this regard is a necessary companion to our moving forward in truth and reconciliation, and with it, in the reconstruction of the moral capacity of churches and society.

It is significant both to our understanding of systemic evil and to our particular concerns in this volume to remember that this evil was directed toward children. This reveals something of the character and morality of the systemic evil involved, and it reveals a deep vulnerability of Indigenous children in a colonial system. That Indigenous children are still disproportionately vulnerable to poverty and violence is an indication of the continuing grip of this systemic evil. At the same time, the fact that the legal framework of the abuse is still intact reveals that there is a vulnerability of children in general that needs to be addressed.

Reconciliation

Roman Catholic theologian Robert Schreiter has studied truth and reconciliation events all around the world.[2] He makes the critical observation that reconciliation never happens because an oppressor has decided to be good. Reflecting on Schreiter's writings, I have come to understand that reconciliation happens when an oppressed people act to reclaim their humanity. In this action, they move from being victims to being survivors. In becoming survivors, they create change that has deep and lasting effect; they release forces that lead to life.

As we can see in the case of the residential school survivors, the reclaiming of humanity sets in motion many different forces that are legal, personal, and societal. The survivors' legal actions, for instance, led to the establishment of the Truth and Reconciliation Commission and its process. The survivors' personal courage and dedication to the truth have ensured that the story of the residential schools will be told and no longer hidden. Though their reclaiming of humanity has deeply personal consequences for individual survivors, we witness that the larger society is also challenged with an opportunity for healing and growth. This is particularly true for the churches.

For those who have been involved with the oppression, the truth and reconciliation process offers an opportunity for the repair of the humanity defaced by participation in systemic evil. In short, repentance can lead to institutional and societal renewal. For the churches, repentance can mean the rediscovery of the grace and truth that gave birth to the Christian movement. If it is to be real and effective, this rediscovery is woven together by a vigilant humility. The perpetual institutional recognition that we have the capacity for great evil must lead to a constant watchfulness in the protection of the vulnerable.

Truth and reconciliation is, therefore, more than an attempt to deal with the past. It is fundamentally concerned with the future. It is concerned with a vision and definition of what a reconstructed society looks like. Though it is about adopting policies and protocols that resist the evils of the past, it is also about the positive shape of a society where humanity has been repaired.

The truth and reconciliation process has released forces of systemic good in our churches and in the larger society. Through this process, we can trace a trajectory of healing in our midst. The specifics of the Calls to Action provide a framework, a path, and a measure of the way that the trajectory of healing is being received in society and in the churches. Specifically for our work, we point to Call to Action 6 of the Truth and Reconciliation's ninety-four Calls to Action: "We call upon the Government of Canada to repeal Section 43 of the Criminal Code of Canada."[3]

It is very simple; very short.

Section 43 has offered the legal justification for using "reasonable force" in correcting the behaviour of children. Its repeal would remove the defence that parents and other caregivers might use in the abuse of children. The continuing presence of Section 43 reveals a weakness in our society in the protection of children. It is, in its failure to protect children from abuse, a statement of the devaluation of the humanity of children in the structure of our society. As long as it remains, Section 43 leaves intact some of the basic legal conditions that contributed to the operation of the residential schools. It is the living and dangerous remnant of a particularly distressing aspect of the horror of the schools: the physical abuse of children.

We can see that the repeal of Section 43 is an essential part of a basic and minimal commitment to a new society. It is, however, only the first step toward that new society. In order to dismantle the oppression and step into a new way of life, the repeal of Section 43 causes us to imagine more. We are called upon to imagine the way we want all children to be treated. We are called to live into a new way of being a society: one that receives and cherishes the full humanity of all its members, especially children.

So, this is our task. We are to weave together the repeal of Section 43 with a robust understanding of our need to protect the vulnerable. Interwoven with this is a heightened awareness of the ongoing vulnerability of Indigenous children in a society that is only beginning to detect the corruption of life that is the result of a still-present colonialism. This is an important element. For many Canadians, colonialism speaks of the past. For Indigenous people, colonialism is an ongoing and present reality, and understanding this is essential to understanding the task of responding fully to the ninety-four Calls to Action. Still more, there must be—with the repeal of Section 43—a positive statement of our understanding of the importance and value of all children and the need for our society to provide the care, nurture, and protection that their human dignity demands.

The forces of healing that flow from truth and reconciliation reveal to us the sacredness of children. This is a foundational affirmation of Indigenous life and culture. Revealed with this is the sacred trust that is the care of children. This is one of the most basic aspects of any human society. It is and always will be a fundamental measure of a society's strength, well-being, and wholeness. The opportunity before us is the creation of a society in which children are protected and can flourish. The forces set in motion by the courage of the survivors are a prophetic call to all of us to become that society. The survivors demand that the churches, awakened from their corruption by colonialism, speak prophetically to the repeal of Section 43.

Notes

1 Notably, the Principalities and Powers are described throughout Christian scriptures in Paul's letter to the church in Ephesus: "For we wrestle not against flesh and blood, but against principalities, against powers, against the rulers of the darkness of this world, against spiritual wickedness in high places" (Ephesians 6:12, King James Version).

2 Schreiter elucidates his thinking about reconciliation in many works; see Robert J. Schreiter, *Ministry of Reconciliation: Spirituality and Strategies* (Ossining, NY: Orbis Books, 2015); and Schreiter, *Reconciliation: Mission and Ministry in a Changing Social Order* (Ossining, NY: Orbis Books, 2015).

3 Truth and Reconciliation Commission of Canada, *The Truth and Reconciliation Commission of Canada: Calls to Action* (Winnipeg: Truth and Reconciliation Commission of Canada, 2015), 1.

2

"I WAS SPANKED AND I'M OK"
Examining Thirty Years of Research Evidence on Corporal Punishment

JOAN E. DURRANT

I am the very fortunate daughter of two loving parents. My father was the son of a Methodist missionary; my mother was the descendant of Mennonite refugees. Both were devoted to ensuring that my childhood was safe and secure, that I was loved unconditionally, and that I saw as much of the world as possible. Both were teachers, so every summer was ours to enjoy as a family. From the time I was a preschooler, the end of June meant that we would pack our little trailer and head out onto the open highway, not returning home until the end of August. We crossed the continent many times, travelling many thousands of miles. Those summers filled my heart and mind with happy memories of adventure, exploration, new friends, and most of all the love of my parents.

Little did my parents know that every mile we travelled on those grand adventures was placing me at risk. As my father drove his 1960 Ford Starliner across the Prairies, through the mountains, and along coastal shores, I was lying in the back seat completely unrestrained by a booster seat or, as I grew, a seat belt. On hot days, my legs could be seen dangling out of the windows. To entertain other drivers, I would turn myself upside down and put my feet in the back window or kneel on the seat and wave to passersby. This scene is unimaginable to parents of young children today.

Were my parents neglectful? Absolutely not. Did they not care about my safety? Nothing mattered more to them. So why did they allow me to travel unrestrained on the highways of North America? Because it was legal and normative to do so at that time. Parents around the world were unknowingly placing their children at risk simply because they did not have the information they needed to be aware of that risk. When I was a child, infant and toddler car seats did not exist, and all cars were sold without seat belts—but I am "OK." Like many children of that era, I was uninjured and unharmed despite the many hours we all spent unrestrained in the back seats of our parents' cars—or in front seats on our parents' laps.

What happened? Why do laws now mandate that car manufacturers install seat belts and airbags in every car sold? Why do today's parents ensure that their children are securely placed in car seats? After all, my friends and I are just fine.

What happened is that systematic research was undertaken through the decades, allowing us to see what was happening on a larger scale. The first major study—of more than 28,000 collisions—was conducted in Sweden in the 1960s.[1] It found that seat belts reduced the risk of injuries to drivers and occupants by 48 to 63 percent and virtually eliminated fatalities.[2] Subsequent studies conducted through the 1960s and '70s in the United States and the United Kingdom revealed similar findings—seat belts substantially reduced the risk of injury, ejection from vehicles, head injuries, and fatalities. The consistency of these findings led to the introduction of laws mandating the use of seat belts in cars—laws that rapidly spread throughout the world. Canada's first law was introduced in Ontario in 1976, even though many drivers and occupants who did not wear seat belts were "OK." These laws were enacted on a foundation of research demonstrating that travelling in a car without a seat belt increased the *risk* of injury and fatality—a finding so consistent that it was indisputable. Ongoing research found that children were at the greatest risk and needed even greater protection than seat belts could provide. Laws were then introduced requiring children to be restrained in seats specifically designed for their age and weight to minimize their risk of injury in a collision.

Public education campaigns accompanied these legal changes to raise public awareness of the risk. In 1989, the Canadian Council of Ministers Responsible for Transportation and Highway Safety set a target of achieving 95 percent use of seat belts and child restraints by the end of 1995.[3] Child car seat clinics were held to help parents learn how to keep their children safe; public service announcements were delivered on radio and television; information was distributed to schools, hospitals, and public health offices; posters were displayed; and "buckle-up challenges" were implemented. As a result, the culture shifted rapidly, demonstrated by the public condemnation of Britney Spears driving with her infant son on her lap in 2006.[4] Today, very few of us would say, "I survived without a seat belt, so my child will too."

At this time in history, we have access to more than 100 studies on corporal punishment. Like the studies on seat belts, they show consistently that corporal punishment places children at risk—and not one study has shown corporal punishment to have positive long-term impacts. Among social scientists, there is no longer a debate. The findings are unequivocal: corporal punishment does not promote the healthy long-term outcomes that most parents hope to nurture, and it places children's developmental health at risk. In this chapter, I will summarize the research on three developmental outcomes—prosocial behaviour, non-violent conflict resolution, and positive mental health. In each case, I will describe what is known about how development occurs in each of these three domains, followed by a summary of how each is affected by corporal punishment.

Prosocial Behaviour

One attribute that many parents want to nurture in their children is prosocial behaviour—those acts that benefit others, such as helping, sharing, giving, cooperating, and comforting. When intrinsically motivated, these behaviours reflect empathy, altruism, conscience, and compassion for others. Not only are these desired behaviours; they are key indicators of healthy child development that predict successful adolescent development.[5]

How is prosocial development fostered? The foundation of prosocial reasoning is found in the security of attachment between the child and at least one caregiver. A cornerstone of secure attachment is caregivers' sensitivity and warmth during the child's first year. Infants who are securely attached to their caregivers have learned to trust them and come to rely on them for support. When children are securely attached, they engage with their caregivers more, which expands children's opportunities and receptiveness to learning—and expands caregivers' opportunities to transmit values to those children.[6]

By the time children are about two years old, they begin to show rudimentary prosocial behaviours. Their concern for others becomes visible in their facial expressions, their voices, and sometimes in their behaviours. Prosocial behaviour continues to emerge gradually over subsequent years, as children's abstract thinking and recognition of emotional states grow through experience and interaction with those around them. During early childhood, consistent attachment security remains critical to prosocial development, which is fostered when parents talk about emotions, help children to identify and understand their emotions, show empathy toward their children, and recognize their children's kind acts.[7] Levels of empathy are greater among children whose caregivers accept their emotions, comfort them when they are distressed, and talk about emotions with them.[8] In other words, "children's capacities to behave positively in the social world emerge from positive experiences in close relationships within the family."[9] Research has consistently shown that cooperation and mutual responsiveness between caregivers and children are critical to early moral development.[10]

As children grow, and inevitably act in ways that hurt others, effective parents use those opportunities to draw attention to the impact of the child's action on the other person. In psychological terms, this is known as "induction"—giving an explanation that helps children understand the effects of their behaviour on others. Such reasoning fosters children's growing abilities to take the perspectives of others and to feel empathic concern for them.[11] Induction promotes internalization of values because it facilitates the child's "deep processing" of the parent's message.

What is the impact of corporal punishment on prosocial development? Parental responses that arouse stress, anxiety, or fear interfere with internalization because the child's capacity to process the parent's message becomes impaired. The child's attention is instinctively drawn to dealing with the perceived threat rather than to processing the parent's message or focusing on the feelings of another person. Punitive, threatening, or painful parental responses also undermine attachment, which is critical to moral learning. Infants who are not securely attached to their parents tend to avoid them or respond to them with anger, resisting the message the parent is trying to convey. If this pattern continues, attachment becomes eroded, the child's learning is impeded, and moral development becomes replaced by hostility and resentment. Even among children who are characteristically "fearless," a positive, cooperative parental approach is more likely to foster the development of a strong conscience than a coercive, punitive approach. Secure attachment, therefore, appears to contribute to the child's "preparedness for socialization."[12] Empirical studies have confirmed this: in families where mothers are punitive, children show lower levels of prosocial behaviour.[13]

In terms of corporal punishment specifically, there is no research showing that it has a positive impact on prosocial development. In fact, the opposite is the case. In 2002, Elizabeth Gershoff published a comprehensive meta-analysis of the research on corporal punishment. She identified fifteen studies examining the relationship between corporal punishment and children's internalization of moral values, which was measured as long-term compliance, feelings of guilt following a transgression, and/or the tendency to make reparations after harming others. Thirteen of these fifteen studies found that physical punishment predicted *weaker* moral internalization. She concluded that corporal punishment "can impel children to avoid misbehaviours in order to avoid future punishment but it cannot on its own teach children the responsibility to behave independently in morally and socially acceptable ways."[14] Subsequent studies have found similar results. Corporal punishment by mothers and fathers has been shown to have a direct negative effect on prosocial behaviour of four- to six-year-olds.[15] Parental corporal punishment also predicts weaker prosocial attitudes among pre- and early adolescents.[16]

In light of the strong association between parent-child attachment and moral/prosocial development found in Gershoff's meta-analysis, it is significant that out of thirteen studies examining the relationship between physical punishment and the quality of the parent-child relationship, all thirteen found that physical punishment predicted *poorer* relationships.[17] Gershoff speculates that children who learn that their parents will hurt them may become fearful and resentful of them. Such feelings would be expected to erode trust and attachment over time. This speculation is supported by Saunders' research (Chapter 3), which finds that children tend to experience corporal punishment as humiliating, intimidating, frightening, and damaging. The children in her study speak of feeling powerless, vulnerable, helpless, unjustly treated; of wanting to avoid their parents, hide, and run away. In this emotional state, children's capacities to learn are impaired and parents' opportunities to teach the child important values are lost.

In 2016, Gershoff and Grogan-Kaylor published a second meta-analysis that included studies published since 2002. In that analysis, they included studies specifically of the act commonly known as spanking, excluding other forms of corporal punishment. Of the eight studies examining the relationship between spanking and moral internalization, seven found that spanking predicts *weaker* moral internalization; of the five studies examining the relationship between spanking and the quality of the parent-child relationship, all of them found that spanking predicts *poorer* relationships.[18] The evidence is consistent that physical punishment promotes neither strong parent-child relationships nor strong internalization of moral values.

Non-Violent Conflict Resolution

Another attribute that most parents hope to cultivate in their children is the ability to respond to conflict with others without aggression or violence. This ability requires us to read others' emotions and use that information to guide our actions, inhibiting aggressive impulses and regulating our anger. Social scientists refer to these abilities as "emotional intelligence" or "emotional competence."[19]

How is non-violent conflict resolution fostered? Like prosocial behaviour, emotional competence has its roots in the parent-child relationship. It flourishes in environments where parents accept and respect their children's emotional responses, help them identify and label their emotions, and help them connect emotions to their own and others' behaviour.[20] Emotional competence depends on the ability to recognize, identify, monitor, and regulate one's emotions rather than denying, suppressing, or controlling them. These abilities grow out of a secure parent-child attachment in which children feel safe expressing their emotions and parents respond sensitively and supportively.[21] When parents respond respectfully to their children's anger and frustration, they provide models of how to respond to another person's expression of negative emotions and how to regulate one's own feelings in the face of those emotions.[22] Moreover, these parents are wiring their children's brains by helping them link the emotions that are instinctively aroused in the limbic system to the reasoning and regulatory functions of the frontal lobe.

It is this connection between the "emotional" and "thinking" brains that is critical to children's capacity to regulate their behavioural responses to anger and frustration. When we feel threatened, we instinctively respond to protect ourselves—the "fight, flight, or freeze" response. We may strike out, run away, or become paralyzed by fear. Striking out is what we call "aggression." We often see this response in young children, who may hit or bite others in response to conflict. Over time, this instinctive response to threat can become heightened or reduced, depending on how adults respond to it. If adults respond by helping children understand what they are feeling, why they are having those feelings, how they can calm themselves, and how they can regulate their impulses, they are helping those children to build the neural pathways needed to respond to conflict without aggression. Decades ago, neuroscientist Donald Hebb helped us understand that "neurons that fire together wire together."[23] In other words, when parents help their children connect their emotions to their growing reasoning capacities, neural pathways are formed that will become increasingly strong if they are repeatedly activated. At the same time, these parents are strengthening their emotional bonds with their children.

What is the impact of corporal punishment on the development of non-violent conflict resolution? When children are physically punished, they are placed into a situation where they are unable to express their emotions. They are stripped of their voice and their power to express it. Rather than opening a conversation about emotions that could lead to learning and understanding, corporal punishment ends the conversation, discouraging and suppressing the child's emotional expression. In this situation, the child has lost an important opportunity to learn about emotional states and the link between emotions and behaviour; the parent has lost an important opportunity to model how to listen to another person, understand another's perspective, and resolve conflict without force or coercion. The child's knowledge has not increased, nor have the child's skills been fostered. What the child has learned is how to impose one's will upon another person, which undermines their learning of non-violent conflict resolution.

It is not surprising, then, that every study conducted on the relationship between corporal punishment and aggression has found that corporal punishment predicts *higher* levels of aggression among children and youth. That aggression may be physical, verbal, or relational; instrumental (intentional and planned) or reactive (impulsive); direct or subtle; directed toward siblings, parents, peers, or dating partners; or carried out in person, through social groups, or on social media. Its common denominator is the infliction of physical, emotional, and/or social harm on another person in response to real, perceived, or anticipated conflict. In her first meta-analysis, Gershoff identified twenty-seven studies of corporal punishment and child aggression, together involving more than 12,000 children.[24] Without exception, these studies found that corporal punishment *increased* the likelihood of children's aggressive behaviour. In this same meta-analysis, corporal punishment was found to increase the likelihood of delinquent and anti-social behaviour among children and youth (twelve out of twelve studies). Perhaps most significantly, these associations were found to continue through life. Corporal punishment in childhood predicted higher levels of aggression (four out of four studies), criminal and anti-social behaviour (three out of four studies), and abuse of one's child or spouse (five out of five studies) in adulthood.[25]

Gershoff and Grogan-Kaylor's later meta-analysis, which focused solely on the act known as spanking as the measure of corporal punishment, identified seven studies of child aggression, nine studies of child anti-social behaviour, three studies of low self-regulation, and fourteen studies of child externalizing behaviour problems.[26] All but two of these thirty-three studies found that spanking *increased* the likelihood of these negative child outcomes. Again, these relationships between spanking and negative outcomes were found to continue into adulthood. Spanking in childhood consistently predicted anti-social behaviour in adulthood in three out of three studies.[27]

It could, of course, be argued that it is more aggressive children who elicit more corporal punishment from their parents. In other words, the cause-and-effect relationship might go from child behaviour to corporal punishment rather than the other way around. Researchers have addressed this question using longitudinal study designs, enabling them to follow a group of children over years. These studies have found that corporal punishment *increases* children's aggression over time and has an increasingly powerful effect on anti-social behaviour as children get older.[28] It has been suggested that the stress experienced by children who are being hurt by their parents accumulates as the punishment continues over time, leading to changes in the child's stress-regulation system.[29] Whether the impact of corporal punishment on aggression is due to modelling, neural wiring, or both, the evidence is clear and consistent that corporal punishment decreases the likelihood that children will acquire competence in non-violent conflict resolution.

Positive Mental Health

Most parents hope that their children will be happy in their adult lives and able to cope with the many challenges they will face along their pathway without developing anxiety, depression, or thoughts of suicide. Positive mental health is an overall feeling of satisfaction with life, the capacity to enhance our enjoyment of life, and a belief that we can deal with challenges as they appear. When we face adversity, we can continue moving forward if we believe that we have agency—the ability, power, and efficacy to overcome obstacles and take new directions in life. Some central concepts in mental health research are coping and resilience. "Coping" is the capacity to manage the stress of adversity, obstacles, and potential failure. "Resilience" is the capacity to *move through and surmount* adversity, processing its pain and going forward into life.

How is positive mental health fostered? Children's capacities for coping and resilience develop within interpersonal relationships. One of the critical components is the belief that one can have an impact, get a response, and effect change. This belief begins to form in infancy, when parents respond to their babies' cries and meet their babies' physical and emotional needs. When parents are consistently responsive to, and respectful of, their infants' signalling, babies begin to learn that they can have an effect on their environment. This learning is the beginning of a sense of efficacy, self-confidence, and self-worth. As babies become toddlers, they come to learn that their goals may differ from their parents' goals. The resulting frustration can be overwhelming, resulting in tantrums and other intense responses. When parents respond sensitively, helping their toddlers learn and practise self-regulation within a secure and trusting relationship, young children come to learn that they can tolerate and even master frustration, and solve problems. Over time, they learn that they have capacities to cope and that they have agency.

As children get older, they are increasingly engaged in relationships with new adults and peers. If they have learned to cope with frustration non-aggressively, gained some understanding of others' emotions, and developed expectations that others will support them, they are more likely to interact skillfully.[30] These new social experiences affirm for these children that they are competent and that social relationships are pleasurable. They also learn that they can engage with stress successfully.

What is the impact of corporal punishment on mental health? Within a parent-child relationship, the prerogative to strike is solely the parent's; the child's role is to submit to the punishment. Thus the experience of corporal punishment is inherently one of loss of agency. The more often this experience is repeated, the more powerless the child feels. Eventually, this can lead to "learned helplessness," a state in which the child comes to believe that he or she has no control over outcomes. This belief can manifest itself in anxiety, depression, addictions, and other difficulties indicative of compromised mental health.

Gershoff examined the link between corporal punishment and mental health, measured in terms of depression, sense of purpose in life, self-esteem, alcoholism, and/or suicidal tendency.[31] Out of twelve studies examining this link, all found that corporal punishment predicts *poorer* mental health in childhood. Moreover, corporal punishment in childhood predicts poorer mental health in adulthood (eight out of eight studies). In the meta-analysis by Gershoff and Grogan-Kaylor, the form of corporal punishment called spanking consistently predicted poorer mental health (ten out of ten studies), lower self-esteem (two out of three studies), and more substance abuse (three out of three studies) in childhood—as well as poorer mental health (eight out of eight studies) and more substance abuse (three out of four studies) in adulthood.[32]

This link was confirmed in a large study of more than 8,000 adults.[33] Spanking increased the likelihood of suicide attempts, moderate to heavy drinking, and use of street drugs—over and above the effects of physical and emotional abuse. The authors of this study concluded that rather than a constructive parental tool, even spanking should be considered an adverse childhood experience.

Conclusion

The research is clear and consistent: at best, corporal punishment has no positive impact on children's development; at worst, it impairs their capacities for empathy, non-violent conflict resolution, and resilience. In Chapter 3, Bernadette Saunders explores the mechanisms that explain the links between corporal punishment and negative child outcomes—mechanisms that are located within the child's cognitive and emotional responses to being hurt by those they need to trust. Just as we eventually recognized the risk of putting children into cars unrestrained, we are now finally recognizing the risk that corporal punishment poses to children's healthy development. We have all the evidence we need to stop hitting our children. But we know that such a change takes more than evidence. It requires an examination of the cultural norms that perpetuate this behaviour even in the face of overwhelming evidence documenting its harms.

Those norms are at least partially rooted in shallow and narrow interpretations of biblical scriptures. In subsequent chapters of this book, theologians look at these scriptures through fresh lenses, providing a long-needed path to amplifying decolonial Christian voices on this important public health issue. As a social scientist, I am encouraged and inspired by the commitment of growing numbers of clergy and church members to confronting the theological messages that have put children at risk for centuries. The theological vision that is presented in this volume offers a way forward that puts children at the centre of sensitive, loving, empathic families and communities where they can trust adults to keep them safe from harm. It offers them the gift of discipline that promotes their healthy physical, psychological, and spiritual development.

Notes

1 Road Safety Observatory, *Seat Belts* (United Kingdom: Road Safety Observatory, 2013), accessed 30 September 2018, http://www.roadsafetyobservatory.com/Summary/vehicles/seat-belts.

2 N.E. Bohlin, "A Statistical Analysis of 28,000 Accident Cases with Emphasis on Occupant Restraint Value," *Society of Automobile Engineers (SAE) Transactions* 76, Section 4, Papers 670805–670984 (1968): 2981–94.

3 Canadian Council of Motor Transport Administrators, *National Occupant Restraint Program 2010: Annual Monitoring Report 2008* (Ottawa: CCMTA, 2010), accessed 30 September 2018, http://www.ccmta.ca/images/publications/pdf/norp_report08.pdf.

4 "Mineta Calls Britney 'Irresponsible,'" CBS News, 13 February 2006, accessed 24 October 2018, https://www.cbsnews.com/news/mineta-calls-britney-irresponsible/.

5 R.M. Lerner et al., "Positive Youth Development: Thriving as a Basis of Personhood and Civil Society," *New Directions for Youth Development* 95 (2002): 11–34.

6 G. Kochanska, "Children's Temperament, Mothers' Discipline, and Security of Attachment: Multiple Pathways to Emerging Internalization," *Child Development* 66 (1995): 597–615.

7 G.W. Holden, *Parenting: A Dynamic Perspective* (Thousand Oaks, CA: Sage, 2015).

8 Z.E. Taylor et al., "The Relations of Ego-Resiliency and Emotional Socialization to the Development of Empathy and Prosocial Behavior across Early Childhood," *Emotion* 13 (2013): 822–31.

9 C. Pastorelli et al., "Positive Parenting and Children's Prosocial Behavior in Eight Countries," *Journal of Child Psychology and Psychiatry* 57 (2016): 825.

10 G. Kochanska and N. Aksan, "Children's Conscience and Self-Regulation," *Journal of Personality* 74, no. 6 (1995): 1587–1617; J. Dunn, "Moral Development in Early Childhood and Social Interaction in the Family," in *Handbook of Moral Development*, ed. M. Killen and J.G. Smetana (Mahwah, NJ: Erlbaum, 2006): 331–50.

11 G. Carlo et al., "The Roles of Parental Inductions, Moral Emotions, and Moral Cognitions in Prosocial Tendencies among Mexican American and European American Early Adolescents," *Journal of Early Adolescence* 31 (2011): 757–81; T.O. Afifi et al., "Spanking and Adult Mental Health Impairment: The Case for the Designation of Spanking as an Adverse Childhood Experience," *Child Abuse and Neglect* 71 (2017): 24–31.

12 G. Kochanska and R.A. Thompson, "The Emergence and Development of Conscience in Toddlerhood and Early Childhood," in *Parenting and Children's Internalization of Values*, ed. J.E. Grusec and L. Kuczynski (New York: Wiley, 1997), 53–77.

13 Michelle R. Gryczkowski, "An Examination of Potential Moderators in the Relations between Mothers' and Fathers' Parenting Practices and Children's Behavior" (PhD diss., University of Southern Mississipi, 2011); E. Romano et al., "Multilevel Correlates of Childhood Physical Aggression and Prosocial Behavior," *Journal of Abnormal Child Psychology* 33, no. 5 (2005): 565–78.

14 Elizabeth Thompson Gershoff, "Corporal Punishment by Parents and Associated Child Behaviours and Experiences: A Meta-Analytic and Theoretical Review," *Psychological Bulletin* 128, no. 4 (2002): 555.

15 E. Regev, N. Gueron-Sela, and N. Atzaba-Poria, "The Adjustment of Ethnic Minority and Majority Children Living in Israel: Does Parental Use of Corporal Punishment Act as a Mediator?," *Infant and Child Development* 21 (2012): 34–51.

16 S.A. Ohene et al., "Parental Expectations, Physical Punishment, and Violence among Adolescents Who Score Positive on a Psychosocial Screening Test in Primary Care," *Pediatrics* 117 (2006): 441–47.

17 Gershoff, "Corporal Punishment by Parents."

18 E.T. Gershoff and A. Grogan-Kaylor, "Spanking and Child Outcomes: Old Controversies and New Meta-Analyses," *Journal of Family Psychology* 30, no. 4 (2016): 453–69.

19 J.D. Mayer and P. Salovey, "What Is Emotional Intelligence?," in *Emotional Development and Emotional Intelligence: Educational Implications*, ed. J.D. Mayer and P. Salovey (New York: Basic Books, 1997), 3–31.

20 R.A. Fabes et al., "Parental Coping with Children's Negative Emotions: Relations with Children's Emotional and Social Responding," *Child Development* 72, no. 9 (2001): 907–20.

21 N. Eisenberg, A. Cumberland, and T.L. Spinrad, "Parental Socialization of Emotion," *Psychological Inquiry* 9 (1998): 241–73; L.F. Katz, A.C. Maliken, and N.M. Stettler, "Parental Meta-Emotion Philosophy: A Review of Research and Theoretical Framework," *Child Development Perspectives* 6 (2012): 417–22.

22 M. Davidov and J.E. Grusec, "Untangling the Links of Parental Responsiveness to Distress and Warmth to Child Outcomes," *Child Development* 77 (2006): 44–58; Eisenberg, Cumberland, and Spinrad, "Parental Socialization of Emotion"; Fabes et al., "Parental Coping with Children's Negative Emotions."

23 D. Hebb, *The Organization of Behavior: A Neuropsychological Theory* (New York: Wiley, 1949).

24 Gershoff, "Corporal Punishment by Parents."

25 Gershoff.

26 Gershoff and Grogan-Kaylor, "Spanking and Child Outcomes."

27 Gershoff and Grogan-Kaylor.

28 M.K. Mulvaney and C.J. Mebert, "Parental Corporal Punishment Predicts Behavior Problems in Early Childhood," *Journal of Family Psychology* 21, no. 3 (2007): 389–97; M.A. Straus, D.B. Sugarman, and J. Giles-Sims, "Spanking by Parents and Subsequent Antisocial Behavior of Children," *Archives of Pediatrics and Adolescent Medicine* 151, no. 8 (1997): 761–67; A. Grogan-Kaylor, "Corporal Punishment and the Growth Trajectory of Children's Antisocial Behavior," *Child Maltreatment* 10, no. 3 (2005): 283–92.

29 Mulvaney and Mebert.

30 S.A. Denham et al., "Preschool Emotional Competence: Pathway to Social Competence?," *Child Development* 74 (2003): 238–56; W.W. Hartup, "Peer Relations in Early and Middle Childhood," in *Handbook of Social Development: A Lifespan Perspective*, ed. V.B. Van Hasselt and M. Hersen (New York: Plenum Press, 1992), 257–81.

31 Gershoff, "Corporal Punishment by Parents."

32 Gershoff and Grogan-Kaylor, "Spanking and Child Outcomes."

33 T.O. Afifi et al., "Spanking and Adult Mental Health Impairment."

3

CORPORAL PUNISHMENT
The Child's Experience

BERNADETTE J. SAUNDERS

The powerlessness and vulnerability of children is poignantly apparent in the spoken and written recollections of adults and, more recently, children who have been subjected to violence in its many forms. Children's human rights to dignity, physical integrity, and protection from harm have too frequently been denied by the very adults—parents, teachers, and staff of children's institutions—whom communities and their government representatives have recognized as responsible for children's care, protection, and optimal development. Children are characteristically vulnerable and dependent upon adults, especially when they are physically small and their temporal life experience is short. Children's vulnerability to violence is amplified in societies in which children are regarded and treated as lesser beings and considered subservient to, even owned by, parents and other adults *in loco parentis*. In contexts where children's obedience may be enforced through normalized and legally sanctioned corporal punishment—variously referred to as "lawful correction," "reasonable physical chastisement," and "justifiable assault"—pain, fear, and humiliation may be a common and unquestioned childhood experience.

The silencing of children's voices, characterized by the adage "children should be seen but not heard," has historically served both to put children in their place as subservient to, and too often endangered by, adults' whims and demands, and to deny children a respected voice on matters that affect them. In more recent times, the United Nations *Convention on the Rights of the Child* has prompted some positive changes in attitudes toward children and has enhanced recognition of their human rights.[1] Article 12(1), in particular, has led to an increasing number of opportunities for children to be directly consulted about various issues and to enlighten us about their experiences and perspectives.[2] In Australia, insights into children's experiences of, and reflections upon, corporal punishment and other forms of violence in childhood have been gained through adults' retrospective accounts given at several commissions of inquiry[3] and through qualitative research that has consulted children themselves. While Australia's most recent commission of inquiry was being conducted, Tim Moore directly consulted children about their views in relation to institutional safety.[4] Significantly, he concluded that "children's interpersonal, generational, organizational and structural powerlessness, rather than just their physical vulnerability . . . influence their experiences and perceptions of safety."[5] One young person observed that adults "stand over you and make you feel really small. They want to remind you that you are weak, and you have to do exactly what they say. There is nothing you can do because you are a kid and you can't fight back. That's why kids are unsafe because they can't stand up and protect themselves."[6] Similarly, in Jan Mason and Jan Falloon's research, young people perceived "abuse as the use of power to control children . . . through physical actions, emotional constraints and boundary-setting which devalues and excludes younger people . . . children are abused by adults as a consequence of their positioning in the generational order."[7]

This chapter provides a glimpse into the experiences of some Australian children whose childhoods unfolded either at a time when both parents and teachers could lawfully resort to corporal punishment to enforce children's compliance, or more recently, when this right—or rather privilege—has been reserved almost exclusively for parents. Among the former group of children are Australia's Indigenous children who were stolen from their parents between 1910 and 1970 and often institutionalized in boarding schools under the supervision of adults, commonly religious professionals, responsible for both their indoctrination into their Christian faith and their assimilation into the "superior" white community. "Civilize and Christianize" typified assimilationist discourse.[8] Many of these children's experiences can only be described as abhorrent and the motivations behind their treatment shamefully misguided and hypocritical. Attempts to justify the removal of Indigenous children from their families as "acting in their best interests" have been repudiated, as it now seems clear that children were stolen in an effort to destroy the Aboriginal culture.[9] In evidence at the Australian Human Rights and Equal Opportunity Commission (HREOC) inquiry, an Indigenous woman who was removed to Cootamunda Girls Home in the 1940s described her experience of seeing "girls naked, strapped to chairs and whipped. We've all been . . . locked in dark rooms. I had a problem of fainting . . . and I got belted every time I fainted, and this is belted, not just on the hands or nothing. I've seen my sister dragged by the hair . . . and belted because she's trying to protect me . . . How could this be for my own good? Please tell me."[10] The following excerpt, from the Australians Together website,[11] succinctly describes the assimilation attempts that took place:

> Children taken from their parents were taught to reject their Indigenous heritage and forced to adopt white culture. Their names were often changed, and they were forbidden to speak their traditional languages . . . many were placed in institutions where abuse and neglect were common.
>
> Assimilation policies focused on children, who were considered more adaptable to white society than Indigenous adults. "Half-caste" children (a term now considered derogatory for people of Aboriginal and white parentage), were particularly vulnerable to removal, because authorities thought these children could be assimilated more easily into the white community due to their lighter skin colour.
>
> Assimilation, including child removal policies, failed . . . primarily because white society refused to accept Indigenous people as equals.[12]

Although each individual's childhood is unique, the positioning of children in a society at a particular point in history impacts the experiences of all children living at that time. Particular groups of children, such as Australia's Stolen Generation, may have uniformly been subjected to the harshest forms of cruel and denigrating corporal punishment when placed in the hands of white adults whose responses to children were motivated by both racist and oppressive religious doctrines. Though some

Australians look to Canada as being further ahead in terms of efforts to achieve justice for survivors,[13] the policies and practices of both countries did comparable damage in the "maltreatment, abuse and neglect" that was suffered by many of the children who were removed from their homes and communities.[14] Thus, in the paragraphs to follow, the narratives and recollections of corporal punishment in some Australian childhoods, across a spectrum of time and circumstances, serve to provide insights into the likely impact of corporal punishment on the children who attended the residential schools in Canada. These voices also add weight to calls for the abolition of corporal punishment of all children, and greater recognition and redress of the "deep societal wounds" and "physical, spiritual and emotional harm" that Indigenous children and young people around the world have experienced during periods of colonialism.[15]

The Stolen Generation: Indigenous Adults' Recollections of Their Childhoods in Institutions

Australia shares with Canada a history of colonization in which "the political, military and economic might of the Europeans" disempowered and demoralized each country's Aboriginal people.[16] Integral to this process was the forced removal of children from their Indigenous communities, with the intent of denying them further contact with their families, forcibly extinguishing their cultural heritage and, at best, mercilessly "training" them for subservient future roles such as "farm hands and domestic servants" within a predominantly racist white culture.[17] These policies of forced removal from family and culture, and the often detestable treatment of Indigenous children in European "care," have contributed to lasting intergenerational trauma and socio-economic disadvantage. Indigenous people today characteristically experience very poor health, limited education, and impoverished living conditions, leading to disproportionate and increasing numbers of Indigenous children coming to the attention of child protective services and continuing to be removed from their families and placed in out-of-home care.[18]

Referring to many Indigenous adults' testimonies about their childhood experiences, Buti notes that these institutionalized children might have received some education in the "3Rs"—basic reading, writing, and arithmetic—in addition to religious teaching, but most of the time children were engaged in work that "merely provided for their own survival" within contexts of persistent harsh punishment and other abuse.[19] An

Indigenous woman who was removed from her family in 1948 when she was five years old recalled in evidence to the HREOC (1997) inquiry that "dormitory life was like living in hell. It was not a life. The only thing that sort of come out of it was how to work, how to be clean, you know and hygiene. That sort of thing. But we got a lot of bashings."[20]

The many children who tried to escape from these institutions were usually tracked down and punished. An Indigenous woman reported "bad memories of . . . Roelands Mission [and] being subjected to physical punishment every time she ran away," and an Indigenous man "was about 11 years old, [when he] and his brother ran away in the middle of the night back to Mount Barker. The authorities caught [them] and returned them to Marribank Mission where they were flogged with a hose and a stock whip." Another Indigenous woman remembered running "away from the Mission once but she got caught and two nuns returned her to New Norcia Mission, to the biggest flogging she got in her life."[21]

The following recollections of Indigenous people further enhance awareness of the children's experiences.[22] Children lived in fear. They were denied nurturing relationships that would enable the development of a positive sense of self. One Indigenous adult recalled that "the nuns at New Norcia used to beat us every day for the simplest of mistakes; even for clearing our throats. I lived in fear of the next hiding which I knew would come at any time. Most of the time we didn't know what we'd done wrong. The nuns who were in charge of us were always telling us we were wicked, evil, dirty savages" (5). Children were punished for behaviours beyond their control, such as "nocturnal *enuresis,*" and humiliated in front of other children, reinforcing all of the children's powerlessness, vulnerability, and low status. An Indigenous adult recalled sleeping "in dormitories with about 20 girls in each of them. If we wet the bed you were flogged, and your nose was rubbed into the wet sheet" (4). Another remembered that "at the Norseman Mission . . . my penis [was wired] to receive electric shocks when I wet the bed. . . . Another punishment was [being] put into the pig pen naked for hours at a time. I was terrified of the pigs attacking me . . . [and was belted] with strips of conveyer belts" (4). Indigenous adults recalled that numerous methods and instruments of punishment were used, often resulting in severe and painful physical injuries and emotional suffering that endured into their adult lives. An Indigenous woman recalled receiving "a number of floggings with a double horse strap as a form of punishment for back chatting the nuns, not completing some schoolwork or talking whilst in the queue waiting for meals. [She] has a scar on her right cheek as a result of a beating with a strap . . . [She] believes that she was robbed of a happy childhood. . . . She has nightmares about the punishments she received at the New Norcia mission" (93–94). An Indigenous man described Wandering Mission as a place where "life was very strict . . . I had a few good hidings for [swearing]. Really bad hiding with a stick . . . all over . . . I seen a lot of kids get hidings. I had my mouth washed out with sand, soap and nearly drowned. They held my head under water for swearing. . . . One time I was pretty well flogged . . . when I was six or eight . . . For any little thing we had some sort of punishment. Belting, stay at night in the cold for a couple of hours . . . And sometimes . . . they don't give you nothing to eat" (165).

Non-Indigenous Adults' Recollections of Corporal Punishment

While corporal punishment was an omnipresent experience in the lives of the Stolen Generation, it was far from absent in the lives of non-Indigenous children. In my research, forty adults—parents, grandparents, and professionals who worked with children and families—shared their recollections of corporal punishment in childhood, at home and in schools.[23] They reflected upon childhoods lived during a time when the legitimacy of corporal punishment in childhood was less questioned than it is currently in Australia. From their memories, several themes emerged.

Parents' Ownership, and Parents' and Teachers' Power over Children

As children, adults remembered thinking that parents and other adults *in loco parentis* were their superiors with immense control over them. One adult observed that "if you made [your parents] angry enough . . . they had this power that you had no control over" (69); another remembered "hitting us . . . happened so often . . . it was just normal [it] hurt and I was scared . . . You are so powerless. Even if you've observed [other children being physically punished] you become a victim and you're silenced" (69).

It Was Frightening and Upsetting

As well as being corporally punished themselves, children with siblings lived with the sight and sound of their brothers' and sisters' punishment. Adults reflected upon times as children at home and at school when they felt fearful, vulnerable, distressed, and powerless to intervene to stop the physical punishment of siblings, friends, or other children. Moreover, though expressing their concern and providing comfort to other children was what children empathetically wanted to do, they frequently felt restrained. Exposure to a sibling's pain and distress could be very frightening and upsetting. One adult remembered her dad giving her "younger brother the strap, and . . . I got really distraught . . . saying . . . 'Stop it, stop it'" (69). Another remembered the instruments used to hit her siblings: "hand, stick, hairbrush . . . Sometimes I would cry if I would see them being hit . . . I'd be distressed . . . It often made me really angry at my parents, it made me very upset, I felt very powerless" (73). Another adult vividly described her mother "chasing [her brother, and when finding] this plastic racquet on the ground whacked him [and] left imprints . . . I just felt devastated for him . . . It upset me . . . I didn't like watching him being hit [and] jump or cower" (73). Adults recalled their "helplessness" when siblings were experiencing physical and emotional pain from corporal punishment: "I didn't feel like I could do anything, but also . . . the guilt that . . . I didn't intervene . . . I can remember . . . my dad taking his belt off and strapping [my brother] several times across his back" (75), and another adult remembered fighting to try to protect her "naughty" brother: "I used to lie [to] protect [him]. I hated it when he was hurt . . . I'd get in the middle [and] be pulled out of the way and he'd get the smack anyway" (75). Another described "hearing [her brother] screaming. The rest of us would be in absolute fear . . . that we were going to get it . . . Our fear was also in sympathy for him and our helplessness; we couldn't help him . . . He was made to sit alone . . . sobbing . . . He had all these marks and his face would be tear-stained. . . . We [were] wanting to . . . tell him how sad and sorry we were but . . . we were scared" (73).

Some adults recalled that when seeing other children's pain, they experienced an awful sense of relief that "it wasn't me" this time. One adult said that she often thought about her dad "hitting [her brothers] when they wouldn't go to sleep . . . maybe ten or fifteen times each . . . I felt . . . sick in the stomach . . . thinking, 'Thank God it was them and not me this time'" (74). Another uneasily admitted, "I was glad it wasn't me . . . I remember my youngest sister getting a thrashing . . . the noise she made, 'Dad, Dad, don't, don't!'. . . more noise than the boys did . . . We didn't bellow [but] he would keep on going until he made you cry" (74). And another recalled thinking about the precariousness of childhood: "'They're getting a smack and I'm not [and] my mother's got a bad temper' . . . I remember being scared. There would be a feeling of fear . . . It underlines your vulnerability. You thought, 'This only happens to kids, I'm a kid, we really are vulnerable'" (74).

Adults also recalled "living in fear" of corporal punishment at school, where it regularly occurred. To intimidate schoolchildren, implements of punishment were hung on walls or strategically placed where children would see them. Some children cried when physically punished, but others tried to appear unemotional, as crying "would be giving too much." Many children regularly felt the pain of teacher-inflicted welts and cuts. If they were fortunate enough to avoid corporal punishment at school, seeing the marks and even injuries to other children's limbs would regularly traumatize and undermine all of the children. Adults vividly recalled feeling pain and humiliation at school. One talked about "the ruler across the hand. [It] hurt, and it was humiliating . . . There was a whole process to it . . . sitting outside the principal's office so you were clearly visible. [The] sense of powerlessness [and the] fear . . . that got you to . . . conform" (76). Another remembered children who had not learned the times table standing "in front of the class and . . . whack, whack, whack, whack, whack, whack, whack" (76). Adults relived the embarrassment, struggling not to cry and seeing the merits of cunningness and protective caution. One adult specifically remembered spilling ink: "[T]he teacher went ballistic, 'Outside!' and . . . with a cane whacked me three or four times across the backs of the legs. I couldn't sit down afterwards . . . I can remember getting whacks on the knuckles. . . . If you did something in class, 'Step outside . . . ,' and you'd get whacked . . . In the playground, 'Come here, bend over,' and whack. I felt . . . extreme discomfort . . . very, very pained . . . It was often embarrassing or humiliating . . . in front of a group, often with little explanation . . . Crying . . . was always awkward . . . It would make you more cunning . . . You lived in fear" (76). Another adult recoiled at the memory of "being dragged up to the board to do a sum, and not being able to do it and . . . getting my hair pulled, getting shoved, pulled around by the hair . . . I was in shock emotionally . . . It made me more cautious . . . probably restricted my learning . . . I was so anxious to do the right thing and get it right." Another described "the queue for the black strap . . . the stinging . . . being told if you didn't hold still, that you'd get worse. . . . I don't think I ever cried at school . . . 'cause . . . that gave them far too much" (76).

At school, one adult recalled being "regularly struck . . . horribly with various implements, but . . . never . . . around the head with a hand. . . . Others . . . got injuries from it. . . . I was standing next to a kid [who] turned to me and spoke . . . and unbeknown to us the master was walking behind, and he just thumped this kid to the side of the head so hard he crashed into me. . . . I thought I was next. . . . This . . . kid was just crying; the whole side of his face was all red. . . . Your overwhelming sense is, 'Thank God it's not me'" (77).

It Might Be Me Next

As children, adults recalled feeling vulnerable and afraid because they knew that parents and teachers could, and did, physically punish children—so they might be next. One adult recalled her brother "getting the strap. [You feel] more upset in some ways when it's happening to someone else. . . . I was frightened . . . at home because you are thinking, 'Oh my God it might be me next'" (73). Another similarly recalled her brother "getting a slap to the back of the legs. I can remember him getting the clip around the ear, and I can picture Dad fighting him to the ground and hitting him uncontrollably. . . . [It was] frightening . . . I don't know that I was able to draw a distinction between [my brother] and myself so I feared that that could . . . happen to me" (74).

At school, fear and anxiety because "it might be me next" was also a part of childhood for many. One adult remembered "some of the boys getting the cuts. . . . He gave them six of the best . . . It was a lesson to everybody . . . Six whacks of the strap . . . Three on [each] hand . . . [They] held their hands afterward, one or two might have cried. . . . I was frightened. It made my blood run cold" (77). Another recalled "the big ruler . . . and someone not doing their work or answering back . . . then being told to come out the front . . . [to] bend over and the teacher whacks . . . saying, 'This is what happens.' Kids would cry, would really get upset" (77). Others recalled children "standing at the front of the classroom, and [teachers would] use a yardstick . . . you could see marks on [children's] hands. . . . I was scared stiff . . . you knew there was a cane waiting for you if you did the wrong thing" (77); and always being "frightened . . . because you'd seen . . . other children get the strap."

Wanting to Escape from the Violence

Adults recalled wanting to escape from seeing other children corporally punished: "I would physically remove myself . . . while it was happening" (74). Another adult thought she must have closed her eyes: "I'd be distressed . . . my sister . . . she was really insolent and would stand up to [my father] and I remember her getting . . . no I don't actually remember because I think I shut my eyes. . . . I remember the noise and her crying and I remember the whack noises. . . . I remember . . . his anger, having this power [struggle]" (74). One adult whose friend "used to get belted . . . would always run home scared [from her friend's house]. I was a real wuss. . . . I just couldn't handle [it] . . . I used to hide [my friend] under my bed . . . and mum would find out . . . and [phone] her mum, and then [my friend] would get a belting" (74).

Children's Views of Corporal Punishment

In my research, I also interviewed children aged eight to seventeen living in Australia.[24] Like Indigenous and non-Indigenous adults, children expressed their discomfort, concern, and sense of powerlessness when confronted with other children's—especially siblings' and friends'—distress when they were hurt by or threatened with corporal punishment. A child, aged twelve, was puzzled when he watched a little girl "just playing around in [a shop] and then she just walked out the doors [and] the mother . . . hit her hard. . . . Then she just picked her up and was hugging her" (91). Another child, aged nine, talked about his brother drawing "on a wall . . . We got into a lot of trouble and got smacked." His brother "cried and [was] angry" (91). A child, aged twelve, "was sad" when his sister "got smacked across her head. She was arguing" (91). Children in another twelve-year-old's family "get a Harley [very thick leather] belt . . . and that hurts." A child, aged eight, described an incident in which her "best friend and her little brother started having a fight and [their mum] smacked them [and] sent [my friend] to her room. . . . She started crying . . . I couldn't go in . . . I felt sorry for her" (91). The physical punishment of a four-year-old cousin led a child of ten to feel immobilized, and "a bit worried . . . I was gonna you know kind of I dunno . . . I felt sorry for her" (91). Children described how corporal punishment "intimidates them and hurts them. They get really emotionally scarred" (ten-years-old) (155). A twelve-year-old child felt physically vulnerable when she observed her father hurting her brother: "[He] accidentally scratched my dad's car and [dad] picked him up off his bike and dragged him along . . . with one arm . . . Dad was just over angry . . . his new car being precious . . . I [was] scared that he might go off and do something to me" (91).

Some children talked about other children considering running away after corporal punishment. A nine-year-old observed that "after [children are] 'smacked' if it doesn't hurt too much they sort of walk off . . . sad and want to like run away from home . . . to be on their own, but if it hurts they usually go in their room . . . and . . . think . . . 'What am I gonna do to stop this from happening?'" (91). Another child, aged eleven, said, "[S]ometimes kids just like run away . . . they don't like face their fears and stuff and I don't think that [parents] should just smack because nothing is as precious as your children's feelings" (91).

Children's Perceptions of Their Rights, Position in Society, and Sense of Self

When we listen to children talk about their experiences of corporal punishment and hear how it makes them feel about themselves and others, we are especially compelled to recognize its adverse impact. Children's accounts are closest to the experience. We can sense and understand their eroded sense of self, their intense feelings of powerlessness and vulnerability, their physical and emotional pain, their lowered perceptions of the adults they want to respect and from whom they seek guidance and support, and their sometimes unchallenged acceptance of the message that violence is an acceptable means of resolving conflict and controlling others—even people you love.[25]

Themes emerged from the children's contributions to my research that particularly highlighted their perceptions of their rights and position in societies and contexts that normalize corporal punishment in childhood. Especially apparent was children's poor self-esteem. Some expressed a belief that their parents owned them, and they could therefore treat them however they liked: "Parents have a right to smack you . . . 'cause you are their kids" (eleven-year-old). (138). A nine-year-old child similarly observed a child's heightened vulnerability in the privacy of the home, because when adults make "physical contact with someone, like punching 'em, it's against the law . . . they could go to jail, they could be charged with assault. . . . And that's exact same for smacking. But . . . if you're a kid, and it's in the house, it's okay because they're your kids. . . . If you are a kid, it doesn't really matter. . . . You barely have any say" (138). Children's insights drew attention to their vulnerability and helplessness. An eight-year-old child was aware that "[a]dults have more power . . . They can get really mad and swear . . . and stuff . . . Children can't do anything like that because they don't have enough power. We have to do what they say. Adults can . . . hurt them" (135). Expressing a similar emotion, a thirteen-year-old described "the control . . . over you. . . . There is . . . helplessness . . . with being a child. . . . I don't think it's appropriate for [my parents] to physically punish me any more . . . 'cause I think I am becoming a bit of a person, not a child anymore" (134). Her comments suggest a perception that the child is not a person, and that children, as less than people, could expect to be physically punished.

Children are well aware of their subordinate place in relation to adults. Corporal punishment is reserved only for children. A ten-year-old child observed, "[I]t's what keeps us apart, adults are more important than children" (136), and the thirteen-year-old who claimed to now being "a bit of a person" expressed her sense of unjust containment: "Adults have basically more power. They have a greater say. . . . It really frustrates me when . . . I will have an opinion, but I can't do much with it" (137). Children express an intensified sense of inequality and double standards when adults physically punish them and, given the opportunity, eloquently voice their discontent. An eight-year-old child was very clear that "[y]ou shouldn't smack people. You shouldn't smack children, 'cause it's hurting them. Treat others like you treat yourself" (223). Another child had no doubts that respect should be reciprocal: "Your parents . . . wouldn't want you to smack them . . . it's like that saying 'respect your elders'. . . [They] should respect their children . . . not just smack them . . . sure they'll be good, but is that what you wanna be doing with your kid, intimidate them . . . so they're good . . . hit them . . . an' yell at them? [They feel] frightened"(157).

Children urged us to respect children and to act responsibly. "Children are our future, so they have got to be important. . . . Parents think hitting children is sort of their right . . . I guess parents have gotta learn to respect children" (thirteen-year-old) (222). Twelve-year-old children commented that "because children are small and . . . can't fight back, [adults] shouldn't take advantage of them. [Children] have rights too . . . adults are . . . there to teach their children, and if they do it the right way [it] can be some of the happiest times of your life, but if treated badly it can wreck . . . your life" (228); and "this is not the way to discipline, by hitting a child. Why?

Think about it for a minute, any hitting, you can see a bruise, but you can't see how it mentally affects someone and they'll carry that right through their childhood, right through their adulthood" (231).

Children's comments demonstrate that there is much that we can learn when we value children as people, engage them in conversation, and grant them the dignity they deserve. As an eight-year-old asserted, "Adults do not 'have to smack because you can choose!'" (233).

Conclusion

Children are important people whose position in society is unique and special. In the words of Nelson Mandela, former president of South Africa, "we owe our children, the most vulnerable citizens in our society, a life free of violence and fear," and "there can be no keener revelation of a society's soul than the way in which it treats its children."[26] How we regard and treat children will shape the adults they will become and will therefore influence the nature of societies in the future. Neil Postman succinctly recognized this when he wrote, "Children are the living messages we send to a time we will not see."[27]

Too often we deny children dignity and respect, and their lived experiences may fall below—sometimes well below—acceptable or humane standards. This is evident in the extreme when we listen to the recollections of Indigenous adults who, as children, were stolen from their parents and often severely abused in attempts to cruelly assimilate them into a foreign culture. Yet common themes of sadness, pain, fear, powerlessness, and impediments to optimal human well-being and development run through all of the above accounts of childhood in contexts that allowed the corporal punishment of children.

Manifesting their low status and subjugation is children's persistent exposure to and experience of violence—particularly corporal punishment, because it is legitimated and normalized by the adults around them. Until all adults are willing to empathize with children, to acknowledge children's perspectives, and to uphold children's human rights to dignity and respect, many children will be denied the opportunity to "help adults see things in a different way" (sixteen-year-old) (222).

Notes

1 UN General Assembly, *Convention on the Rights of the Child*, 20 November 1989, United Nations, Treaty Series, vol. 1577, 3, accessed 19 October 2018, http://www.refworld.org/docid/3ae6b38f0.html.

2 Article 12(1) of the *Convention on the Rights of the Child* says, "States Parties shall assure to the child who is capable of forming his or her own views the right to express those views freely in all matters affecting the child, the views of the child being given due weight in accordance with the age and maturity of the child."

3 Eight reports have emanated from six major government inquiries: the Human Rights and Equal Opportunity Commissions' Inquiry (1995–97); the Queensland Forde inquiry (1998–99); two Australian Senate Committee inquiries, one on Child Migrants (2000–2001), and another on Forgotten Australians in residential care (2000–4) and those in foster care (2000–5); the Mullighan inquiries into sexual abuse in South Australia and on the Aboriginal Anangu Pitjantjatjara Yankunytjatjara (APY) lands (2006–8); and the Royal Commission into Institutional Responses to Child Sexual Abuse (2013–17).

4 Tim P. Moore, "Children and Young People's Views on Institutional Safety: It's Not Just Because We're Little," *Child Abuse and Neglect* 74 (December 2017): 73–85, https://doi.org/10.1016/j.chiabu.2017.08.026.

5 Moore, 74.

6 Moore, 76.

7 Jan Mason and Jan Falloon, "Some Sydney Children Define Abuse: Implications for Agency in Childhood," in *Conceptualizing Child-Adult Relations*, ed. Leena Alanen and Berry Mayall (London: Routledge Falmer, 2001), 111.

8 Linda Briskman, "Beyond Apologies: The Stolen Generations and the Churches," *Children Australia* 26, no. 3 (2001): 4.

9 Madeline H. Engel, Norma Kolko Phillips, and Frances A. DellaCava, "Indigenous Children's Rights: A Sociological Perspective on Boarding Schools and Transracial Adoption," *International Journal of Children's Rights* 20 (2012): 296.

10 Human Rights and Equal Opportunity Commission, *Bringing Them Home* (Sydney: Commonwealth of Australia, 1997).

11 Australians Together is a not-for-profit organization "that believes better outcomes for Indigenous Australians begin with a change in our attitudes. . . . By listening to the voices of Indigenous Australians, [this organization helps] non-Indigenous people learn the true story of our shared history, understand how it's still having an impact today and imagine new ways to live together more respectfully." Philanthropists fund this organization in the hope of seeing positive change in Australia. See Australians Together, "About Us," Australians Together, accessed 20 May 2018, https://www.australianstogether.org.au/about-us/.

12 Australians Together, "The Stolen Generations: The Forcible Removal of Indigenous Children from Their Families," Australians Together, accessed 20 May 2018, https://www.australianstogether.org.au/discover/australian-history/stolen-generations.

13 Initiatives of Change Australia, "Reflecting on the National Apology to Australia's Stolen Generation," Initiatives of Change Australia, accessed 9 January 2019, https://au.iofc.org/reflecting-national-apology-australia's-stolen-generations.

14 Antonio Buti, "The Removal of Indigenous Children From Their Families: U.S. and Australia Compared," *University of Western Sydney Law Review* 8 (2004): 152.

15 See *A Christian Theological Statement in Support of the Truth and Reconciliation Commission of Canada's Call to Action 6*, beginning of this volume.

16 Antonio Buti, "The Removal of Aboriginal Children: Canada and Australia Compared." *University of Western Sydney Law Review* 6 (2002): 25.

17 Buti, "The Removal of Indigenous Children," 133.

18 Susan Baidawi, Philip Mendes, and Bernadette Saunders, "Indigenous Young People Leaving Out of Home Care in Victoria: A Literature Review," *Indigenous Law Bulletin* 8, no. 7 (July/August 2013): 24–27; Linda Briskman, *Social Work with Indigenous Communities* (Sydney: Federation Press, 2014); S. Gray, *The Northern Territory Intervention: An Evaluation* (Melbourne: Castan Centre for Human Rights Law, 2015); Australian Institute of Health and Welfare, *Child Protection Australia 2014–15* (Canberra: Australian Institute of Health and Welfare, 2016), accessed 20 May 2018, http://www.aihw.gov.au/publication-detail/?id=60129554728.

19 Buti, "The Removal of Aboriginal Children," 28.

20 Human Rights and Equal Opportunity Commission, *Bringing Them Home.*

21 Aboriginal Legal Service of Western Australia, *Telling Our Story: A Report by the Aboriginal Legal Service of Western Australia on the Removal of Aboriginal Children from their Families in Western Australia* (Western Australia: Aboriginal Legal Service of Western Australia, 1995), 100, 217; 225.

22 Page numbers following quotes in the remainder of this paragraph refer to Aboriginal Legal Service of Western Australia, *Telling Our Story.*

23 Page numbers following adults' and children's quotes in the remainder of this chapter refer to their appearance in Bernadette J. Saunders and Chris Goddard, *Physical Punishment in Childhood: The Rights of the Child* (Chichester: John Wiley and Sons, 2010). The quotes are also drawn from Bernadette J. Saunders, "'Because There's a Better Way Than Hurting Someone': An Exploratory Study of the Nature, Effects and Persistence of 'Physical Punishment' in Childhood" (PhD diss., Monash University, 2005), upon which the book was based; therefore, some quotes in this chapter are more detailed than in Saunders and Goddard.

24 Saunders and Goddard, *Physical Punishment*; Saunders, "Because There's a Better Way."

25 Bernadette J. Saunders, ""Ending the Physical Punishment of Children by Parents in the English-Speaking World: The Impact of Language, Tradition and Law," *International Journal of Children's Rights* 21, no. 2 (2013): 278–304; Bernadette J. Saunders, "Ending Corporal Punishment in Childhood: Advancing Children's Rights to Dignity and Respectful Treatment," in *Law and Society: Reflections on Children, Family, Culture and Philosophy*, ed. Alison Diduck, Noam Peleg, and Helen Reece (Leiden: Brill Nijhoff, 2015), 243–71.

26 Launch of the Nelson Mandela Children's Fund, Mahlamba Ndlopfu, Pretoria South Africa, 8 May 1995, accessed 21 October 2015, https://www.sahistory.org.za/archive/speech-president-nelson-mandela-launch-nelson-mandela-childrens-fund-mahlambandlopfu-pretori.

27 Neil Postman, *The Disappearance of Childhood* (New York: Delacorte Press, 1982), xi.

4

LIES THAT HAVE SHAPED US

Racism, Violence, and Ageism in Canadian Churches

VALERIE E. MICHAELSON

Violence affects the majority of children around the world.[1] At some point in their childhood, most Canadian children will suffer some form of violence and experience its effects. Those who observe or experience violence learn how power is gained by intimidation and how control is gained through fear.[2] Experiences of violence in childhood track strongly into the adult years, where violence often diversifies into more sophisticated forms of aggression and tends to be transferred to the next generation of children.[3]

One might hope that church involvement would serve as a protective factor or buffer against experiences of violence during childhood; however, research findings indicate that this is not always the case.[4] Reports of sexual violence and abuse experienced by children at the hands of clergy and other faith leaders seem to have no end,[5] and the incessant cover-ups of such events reflect an institutional betrayal of children that is reprehensible.[6] While our focus in this volume is on violence in the form of corporal punishment, attitudes and beliefs about corporal punishment are not held in a void. In practical reality, the socio-cultural norms and theologies that have provided the fertile ground for condoning corporal punishment are fundamentally related to the attitudes and beliefs that overlook, tolerate, or rationalize other kinds of harm as well.

The purpose of this chapter is to consider corporal punishment and other forms of violence against children in light of three distinct but interrelated systems of power as they relate to a variety of beliefs and practices that have undergirded the colonial theological narrative of domination and control. The first is *racism* and involves the ways that Christian texts and theologies have been used to dehumanize and marginalize Indigenous Peoples. The second system is *ageism* and relates to the power imbalance that historically children have experienced very simply because they are not yet adults, particularly in relation to assumptions and norms around obedience. The third system is *religion* itself. Specifically, I discuss ways that religious framing has been used to justify and rationalize violence in the name of God and for some perceived greater good.

In the case of the residential schools, First Nations, Inuit, and Métis children were sitting at the intersection of interlocking systems of power related to race and age. The willingness of many church leaders to overlook, or even rationalize, acts of violence against them through religious messaging further contributed to their vulnerability. As Crenshaw's theory of intersectionality suggests, each interlocking system of power—in this case racism, ageism, and religious attitudes toward violence—overlapped to create numerous layers of injustice, oppression, and abuse.[7] It was the perfect storm.

The Lies That Have Shaped Us

Racism

In the Canadian context, the ways that non-white populations were "historically represented . . . as racially inferior"[8] was a noxious form of colonial violence. Numerous arguments have been used to justify the racist roots and practices of colonization,[9] but it is the Western European Doctrine of Discovery that has been widely recognized as the impetus for some of the church's worst abuses of Indigenous Peoples—not only in Canada but around the world.[10] Rooted in the papal bull "Inter Caetera," which was issued by Pope Alexander VI in 1493, the Doctrine of Discovery promotes the idea that Christians enjoy a moral and legal right to dominate Indigenous Peoples and to invade and seize any lands populated by non-Christians. One of the main ways that this doctrine was justified was through the Great Commission, the last recorded directive of Jesus to his followers, that is found at the end of Matthew's gospel: "All authority in heaven and on earth has been given to me. Therefore go and make disciples of all nations, baptizing them in the name of the Father and of the Son and of the Holy Spirit, and teaching them to obey everything I have commanded you. And surely I am with you always, to the very end of the age."[11] As long as people were being converted, according to this thinking, they "were being colonized for their own benefit, either in this world or the next."[12] The Doctrine of Discovery fed the view that the Indigenous people "were so savage and so primitive that [their children] would be better off being schooled and separated from their families."[13] This in turn supported the racist pattern of domination and control that was used in the residential schools (and is still being used against many Indigenous Peoples today, not only in Canada but around the world). The wide acceptance of this kind of thinking made it remarkably easy for Europeans to justify the domination of Indigenous children through corporal punishment and other means in order to establish authority and control.

Ageism and Obedience

Despite advances over the past century, including the nearly universal ratification of the United Nations *Convention on the Rights of the Child* (which Canada ratified in 1991), children are still marginalized in adult-centred societies and experience unequal power relationships with the adults who primarily control their lives.[14] In church contexts, one way this has been lived out is through notions of authority and obedience. While a wide range of interpretations exist, biblical passages such as Exodus 20:12 (honour your father and mother),[15] Ephesians 6:1–2 (children obey your parents), and 1 Timothy 3:4–5 (overseers must manage their families well and require obedience from their children) are often used to determine a normative hierarchy of family relationships. With this hierarchy comes the God-given right and responsibility to punish children: in order to ensure that they learn obedience.

Though this issue is complex, two main arguments are often cited as to why obedience is so imperative. The first relates to the belief that children are born inherently sinful, with a proclivity to rebellion from birth. Without discipline, it is argued, "children will experience a lifetime of frustration . . . [because they] lack the capacity to subordinate their own wilfulness and accept the requirements of duly-constituted leaders."[16] The second reason this hierarchy is important, however, is often perceived to be far more serious: to avoid eternal separation from God by submitting one's own will to God and accepting divine grace. Without learning to submit to parents or others in authority, the argument goes, children will not learn to submit to God.[17] While many theologians have proposed more complex and nuanced theologies related to obedience and authority that to an extent shape contemporary ideas and practices,[18] this kind of thinking about the relationship between obedience and sin has informed at least some of the accepted social and cultural norms related to the "discipline" of children in churches today.

Certainly, this kind of fearful theological argument was used to rationalize the harsh punishment of Indigenous children in the residential schools, where it was overwhelmingly justified as "for their own good."[19] Illustratively, Celia Haig-Brown recounts the story told by a girl who attended the Kamloops residential school in the 1930s. This child describes being marched down to the chapel where students would spend over an hour "every blessed morning. And there they interrogated us on what it was all about being an Indian. . . . [the priest] would just get so carried away; he was punching at that old altar rail . . . to hammer into our heads that we were not to think or act or speak like an Indian. And that we would go to hell and burn for eternity if we did not listen to their way of teaching."[20] Recounting her experience at the Kalamak residential school, another student describes how this same kind of theological messaging was used to "scare students into submission:"

> That night, just before she turned the lights off, Sister Maura taught us how to pray on our knees with our hands folded. Then she told us about devils. She said they were waiting with chains under our beds to drag us into the fires of hell if we got up and left our beds during the night. When she turned the lights off I was scared to move, even to breathe. I knew those devils would come and get me if I made a sound. I kept really still. . . . Someone was crying. A long time later, I was still afraid to get up and use the bathroom. In the morning my bed was wet and Sister Superior strapped me. I had to wear a sign . . . saying, I was a dirty wetbed.[21]

In both of these examples—and the Truth and Reconciliation (TRC) report provides countless other like examples—the children were essentially frightened into obedience to the ways of thinking, believing, and behaving that were imposed by those in charge of them. In effect, the distorted logic of this approach to obedience is not far removed from the destructive and arrogant logic of the Doctrine of Discovery: learning submission to the authoritarian structures that were in place was central to children gaining success (and safety), not only in this life but also in the life to come.

Violence

The third issue that demands attention is the way that religious messaging has been used to justify violence. There are many variations in how this is done, but one helpful framework is what Walter Wink has described as "the myth of redemptive violence."[22] This is a widely accepted narrative that fuels a tendency to justify violence as a necessary—even noble—part of the Christian life, and integral to bringing about God's plan. Very simply, the premise behind this myth is that "good ends justify violent means."[23] The Christian faith is built in part on stories that embody this myth. For example, the story of David and Goliath (1 Samuel 17) describes the widely celebrated victory of a future king over the enemies of God's people through the strategic use of a weapon and force. The punishment of Pharaoh by God (Exodus 7–11) depicts the sequential physical and psychological punishments enacted on an Egyptian ruler in response to his enslaving of the Israeli people. At best, such stories are used to convey how good ultimately prevails in our world. But the means by which that is achieved—fighting, aggression, and the use of weapons—is rarely considered in their interpretation.

Wink does not specifically include the use of corporal punishment in his list of situations related to redemptive violence (though the list does include issues as diverse as gender inequality, domestic violence, economic injustice, and other forms of child maltreatment). However, many scholars have built on his work, recognizing the utility of the myth of redemptive violence for understanding why corporal punishment has been so readily accepted as a means to achieving some greater good.[24] As Jane Hall Fitz-Gibbon has argued, this myth insists on the viability of "good violence";[25] not only is violence useful, it is necessary, and often the only thing that will teach our children the lessons they need to live godly lives. The myth of redemptive violence protects any moral "higher ground" a perpetrator might claim, and once again we hear the same tired refrain: "It's for your own good."

Sitting at the Intersection of Race, Age, and Religion

In isolation, each of the narratives I have described related to race-, age- and religiously-justified violence provides a distinct recipe for those in power to obtain domination and control over those who are deemed less powerful. But they also share a common thread. They have been used repeatedly to argue that power and control over another, even to the point of violence, can be justified for a greater good. This "greater good" may even be considered as the ultimate act of saving a soul.

Together, these theological positions contributed to the "ideological pretext" (see MacDonald, Chapter 1) that provided an ongoing rationalization, and even defence of, colonialism broadly, and more specifically for the harsh punishment of Indigenous children in the residential schools. As we have learned through the deeply troubling TRC report, the cumulative effects of these multiple forms of oppression continue to produce painful physical, emotional, material, and cultural consequences that span generations.

When violence like this occurs against children, it is tempting to shake our heads not only in dismay but in bewilderment. We ask, "How could such a thing have happened?" But it is critical that we do not stop with this superficial response, because problems that are not fully understood cannot be adequately confronted and addressed. As William Morrow argues, we "have everything to gain and nothing to lose by demystifying violence." He continues: "To leave violence without explanation is to mystify it and grant it a numinous power that it does not deserve."[26] As urgent as the repeal of Section 43 of the Criminal Code of Canada is, unless the underlying values, attitudes, and beliefs that allow one person to justify having power and control over another person are understood and confronted, the violence will find ways to rematerialize in other forms.

Unmasking the colonial theologies that have been—and continue to be—used to justify violence and other forms of oppression is essential to the task of decolonization.[27] Thus far in this chapter, I have identified some of these theologies under the categories of racism, ageism, and religious justifications for violence, and argued that these are lies that have shaped Canadian churches for far too long.[28] This process of unmasking these theologies not only helps us understand the past, it strengthens our ability to identify more fully where these same narratives continue to guide policy and practice, and fuel continued harm today so that they can be addressed in the strongest possible way.

Where Are We Today?

There are glimpses that some church bodies are moving in healing and constructive directions. The first apology for playing a role in the residential schools came from the United Church of Canada in 1986. It states: "We tried to make you be like us and in so doing we helped to destroy the vision that made you what you were. As a result you, and we, are poorer and the image of the Creator in us is twisted, blurred, and we are not what we are meant by God to be."[29] In 1998, then moderator Bill Phipps offered a more focused apology to former students of United Church residential schools, their families and their communities: "To those individuals who were physically, sexually, and mentally abused as students of the Residential Schools in which the United Church of Canada was involved, I offer you our most sincere apology. You did nothing wrong. You were and are the victims of evil acts that cannot under any circumstances be justified or excused."[30] Though they were slower to respond, the Anglican Church (1993), the Presbyterian Church of Canada (1994), and the Missionary Oblates of Mary Immaculate (2001) have all issued formal apologies for their roles in the residential schools. The delivery of a papal apology was number 58 of the TRC Calls to Action. Yet up to the time of this writing, the request for Pope Francis, head of the Catholic Church, to apologize to residential school survivors and their families for the role of Roman Catholic churches in the abuses that were suffered by children in the residential schools in which they were involved has been declined.[31]

Beyond apologies, other reconciliation initiatives continue to emerge. For example, the Doctrine of Discovery has been repudiated (as called for in Call to Action 49) by many Christian churches in Canada.[32] In 2016, the United Church of Canada began a Dialogue on Reconciliation with the Uniting Church in Australia, with the purpose of exploring their shared—yet distinct—histories of colonization and journeys toward self-determination and reconciliation.[33] And in 2019, the United Church launched a national initiative calling on church members to write to senators in support of Bill C-262, an act to ensure that the laws of Canada are in harmony with the United Nations Declaration on the Rights of Indigenous Peoples (UNDRIP).[34] In 2016, the Anglican Church of Canada established a Council of Elders and Youth to monitor how the Anglican Church would honour its commitment to adopt the principles of UNDRIP as a framework for reconciliation.[35] That council (now called Vision Keepers) continues to this day as a permanent forum. Another important step forward was taken in July 2019, with the establishment of a fully self-determining Indigenous church within the Anglican Church of Canada. More ecumenically, KAIROS, an organization that unites Canadian churches and other religious bodies to advocate for social change, has made decolonization and reconciliation initiatives clear priorities. Their popular Blanket Exercise has become a powerful tool for helping people to understand the harms caused by colonization, the significance of the TRC and the complexity and importance of reconciliation. Created in 1997, the Blanket Exercise is being used across Canada and around the world.[36]

We Have a Long Way to Go

These are hopeful stories, and there are many more stories of reconciliation initiatives that are happening across the country. However, there remains a very long way to go. Call to Action 6 provides a crucial rallying call to Christian leaders in Canada. Yet even after Section 43 of the Criminal Code is repealed, unless the *underlying narratives* that enable the rationalization of abuse against children are addressed, children will still be vulnerable to other manifestations of these same narrow theological frames that justify the power and control of one group over another. For churches in Canada, one of the key tasks of reconciliation is to confront the ways that *these very colonial systems* that have shaped this country continue to enable various oppressions. This includes the threats that these systems pose to the ways of life, identities, well-being, and very existence of Indigenous peoples.

Post TRC, it is shameful that racism, ageism, and colonial religious messaging *continue* to shape systems of power that oppress Indigneous children. As Bishop MacDonald writes: "For significant parts of Canadian society . . . outright prejudice against Indigenous people is no longer accepted in polite conversation and behaviour. But, the systemic nature of racism is revealed in that long after direct statements of prejudice are rejected, bias and fear of 'the other' are still embedded in all the various structures and institutions of our society—including the institution of the church."[37] If we are to move forward in the true spirit and action of reconciliation, these racist narratives and their fruit must be disrupted and replaced. Further, until the underlying structural dynamics of power and advantage that leave Indigenous children vulnerable to inequitable disparities in education, health, and infrastructure are addressed, these children are still vulnerable to the systemic and structural forms of violence that exist in Canada today. Church communities in Canada can play an important role in demanding that these problems be addressed at all levels in society. A critical contribution to reconciliation entails fighting for a system in which all First Nations, Inuit, and Métis children have equitable access to culturally appropriate resources and equitable opportunities to thrive. Until that happens, apologies mean little.

The Persistent Rationalization of Violence

The repeal of Section 43, while urgent in itself, would not solve the broader problem of the justification—or tacit acceptance—of violence in Canadian churches. Violence in the church is not a relic of the past. Illustratively, a recent (2016) national study of Canadian young people found that religious involvement was consistently associated with *higher* reported levels of both perpetrating violence and experiencing victimization than among those who were not religiously involved.[38] This finding is startling. The patterns that these data reveal point to an uncomfortable reality: there is a persistent and systemic problem related to violence among church-connected young people. This should compel leaders and participants in Canadian churches to ask hard questions about violence toward Indigenous children—and toward all children—that is justified or even encouraged by religious messaging. We need to ask uncomfortable questions about the communal social norms that condone violence as an acceptable way to resolve conflicts, regulate behaviours, and determine how individuals and groups should interact with and treat one another. And we need to ask whether the very systems that have protected, ignored, or condoned violence in the past, such as were revealed through the TRC, still endure in Canadian churches. These lies about violence being for some greater good have shaped church cultures for far too long.

The Opportunity before Us

In Chapter 1 of this volume, Bishop MacDonald issues a clear and compelling call to the church. He writes, "The forces set in motion by the courage of the [residential school] survivors . . . demand the churches, awakened from their corruption by colonialism, to speak prophetically to the repeal of Section 43." The repeal of Section 43 will be a tangible symbol of our willingness to take up the challenge of creating a society in which all children are protected. Creating a childhood that is free from violence is a first step toward what is our moral imperative and must be our fundamental goal: a world that is free from all inequities and oppressions, in which all children have the opportunity to reach their full potential and to thrive.

What does it mean to set up conditions in which children truly flourish? Even as people grumble about dwindling Sunday schools, outside their own walls churches generally have not been either strong or consistent public advocates for children. The opportunity before us is to become champions for children and courageous, committed allies: to raise outrage, for example, that one in five Canadian children live in poverty,[39] and that Indigenous children have less access to education and experience poorer health outcomes than any other population of children in Canada.[40] The opportunity before us is to invest time and resources into developing and implementing healthy, effective, non-violent, and theologically rich approaches to raising children and youth. Repealing Section 43 is both a highly symbolic and substantive piece of a coherent strategy that reconstructs society in the best interests of all children.

Throughout Canada, including in the church, there is consensus that the physical abuse of children is unacceptable. But despite the overwhelming evidence of the risks that corporal punishment poses to the health and development of children, barriers to changing social and cultural norms around it often remain rooted in tired and narrow interpretations of biblical texts.[41] For the most part church leaders have been silent on the issue, even if corporal punishment is not something that they personally support. It is my hope that the theological vision presented throughout this book will open up new horizons for thinking and acting, prompting Christian leaders to take up wholeheartedly and unequivocally the call to care for all children. Reflecting on our own history and present state with humility opens up the possibility of participating in the creation of a shared future in which all children are protected from violence and have equitable opportunities to flourish on this land.

Notes

1 Desmond Runyan et al., "Child Abuse and Neglect by Parents and Other Caregivers," in *A World Report on Violence and Health*, ed. Etienne Krug et al., 57–81 (Geneva: World Health Organization, 2002).

2 PREVNet, "Bullying: What We Know and What We Can Do," PREVNet: Promoting Relationships and Eliminating Violence Network, last modified 2015, http://www.prevnet.ca/bullying/facts-and-solutions.

3 PREVNet, "Bullying."

4 Valerie Michaelson et al., "Violence, Adolescence, and Canadian Religious Communities," *Journal of Interpersonal Violence* (May 2018): 1–25; Truth and Reconciliation Commission of Canada, *The Truth and Reconciliation Commission of Canada: Calls to Action* (Winnipeg: Truth and Reconciliation Commission of Canada, 2015), 1, accessed 18 October 2018, http://www.trc.ca/websites/trcinstitution/File/2015/Findings/Calls_to_Action_English2.pdf.

5 Tracy J. Trothen, *Shattering the Illusion: Child Sexual Abuse and Canadian Religious Institutions* (Waterloo, ON: Wilfrid Laurier University Press, 2012).

6 Carly Parnitzke Smith and Jennifer J. Freyd, "Institutional Betrayal," *American Psychologist* 69, no. 6 (2014): 575–87.

7 Kimberle Crenshaw, "Mapping the Margins: Intersectionality, Identity Politics, and Violence against Women of Color," *Stanford Law Review* 43, no. 6 (1991): 1241–99, https://doi.org/10.2307/1229039. Crenshaw originally articulated her theory of intersectionality as a way of illustrating the experiences of discrimination and oppression of African American women. I use it here to describe the experiences of Indigenous children because Crenshaw's work is a useful way of understanding the interlocking systems of power that work together to marginalize and discriminate.

8 Carrie Bourassa, Kim McKay-McNabb, and Mary Hampton, "Racism, Sexism and Colonialism: The Impact on the Health of Aboriginal Women in Canada," *Canadian Woman Studies* 24, no. 1 (2004): 2.

9 Truth and Reconciliation Commission of Canada, *Honouring the Truth, Reconciling for the Future: Summary of the Final Report of the Truth and Reconciliation Commission* (Winnipeg: Truth and Reconciliation Commission of Canada, 2015), 1.

10 Bishop Mark MacDonald, quoted by André Forget in "Church's Knowledge of Doctrine of Discovery 'Woefully Inadequate,'" *Anglican Journal*, 28 August 2015, https://www.anglicanjournal.com/articles/church-s-knowledge-of-doctrine-of-discovery-woefully-inadequate/. For more on the damage incurred through the Doctrine of Discovery, see WCC Executive Committee, "Statement on the Doctrine of Discovery and Its Enduring Impact on Indigenous Peoples," World Council of Churches, 17 February 2012, accessed 17 October 2018, https://www.oikoumene.org/en/resources/documents/executive-committee/2012-02/statement-on-the-doctrine-of-discovery-and-its-enduring-impact-on-indigenous-peoples.

11 Matthew 28:18b–20, New Revised Standard Version (NRSV).

12 Truth and Reconciliation Commission of Canada, *Honouring the Truth, Reconciling for the Future*, 49.

13 Bishop Mark MacDonald, in Forget, "Church's Knowledge of Doctrine of Discovery."

14 Priscilla Alderson and Christopher Goodey, "Research with Disabled Children: How Useful Is Child-Centred Ethics?," *Children and Society* 10 (1996): 106; Samantha Punch, "Research with Children: The Same or Different from Research with Adults?,"

Childhood 9, no. 2 (2002): 321–41; Elspeth Webb, "Discrimination against Children," *Archives of Disease in Childhood* 89, no. 9 (2004): 804–8.

15 While this call to "honour your father and mother" (from Exodus 20) is often used to establish parental authority over young children, many biblical scholars argue that its original purpose was to admonish adult children to care for frail and elderly parents. Rather than rein in unruly children, its original purpose was to ensure care for the elderly. See Thomas G. Long, "The First Commandment with a Promise: Recent American Preaching on 'Honor Your Father and Your Mother,'" *Journal of Law and Religion* 31, no. 2 (2016): 169–82, https://doi.org/10.1017/jlr.2016.14.

16 C.G. Ellison and M. Bradshaw, "Religious Beliefs, Sociopolitical Ideology, and Attitudes toward Corporal Punishment," *Journal of Family Issues* 30, no. 3 (2009): 324.

17 Ellison and Bradshaw, 324.

18 Illustratively, see Walter Brueggemann, *Truth-Telling as Subversive Obedience* (Eugene, OR: Cascade Books, 2011).

19 The phrase "for their own good" is used by J.S. Milloy to describe how, when senior officials from the Department of Indian Affairs became aware of cases of outright abuse of children by the staff, "they routinely failed to come to the rescue of children for whom they were the "legal guardian" and who they had, supposedly for their own good and for the good of their communities, removed from their real parents." J.S. Milloy, "Suffer the Little Children": The Aboriginal Residential School System 1830–1992," submitted to the Royal Commission on Aboriginal Peoples, May 1996, 199.

20 Celia Haig-Brown, *Resistance and Renewal: Surviving the Indian Residential School* (Vancouver: Arsenal Pulp Press, 1988), chap. 3, "School Life."

21 Dan Eshet, *Stolen Lives: The Indigenous Peoples of Canada and the Indian Residential Schools* (Facing History and Ourselves, 2015), 53–54, accessed 15 September 2019, https://www.facinghistory.org/sites/default/files/publications/Stolen_Lives_1.pdf. Originally cited in Shirley Sterling, *My Name Is Seepeetza* (Toronto: Groundwood, 2008), 19.

22 Walter Wink, *Engaging the Powers: Discernment and Resistance in a World of Domination* (Minneapolis: Augsburg Fortress Press), 1992.

23 Theodore L. Dorpat, *Crimes of Punishment: America's Culture of Violence* (New York: Algora Publishing, 2007), 161.

24 Dorpat, *Crimes of Punishment*; Jane Hall Fitz-Gibbon, *Corporal Punishment, Religion, and United States Public Schools* (Ithaca, NY: Palgrave Macmillan, 2017).

25 Fitz-Gibbon, 86.

26 William S. Morrow, "Violence and Religion in the Christian Tradition," in *Teaching Religion and Violence*, ed. Brian K. Pennington (Oxford University Press, 2012), 111.

27 Michel Andraos, "Doing Theology after the TRC," *Toronto Journal of Theology* 32, no. 3 (2017): 295.

28 Others have drawn attention to additional theological themes that also merit focused critique. See Andraos, "Doing Theology after the TRC"; Michel Andraos, Lee F. Cormie, Néstor Medina, and Becca Whitla, "Decolonial Theological Encounters: An Introduction," *Toronto Journal of Theology* 33, no. 2 (2017): 259.

29 United Church of Canada, "The Apologies," United Church of Canada, accessed 15 September 2019, https://www.united-church.ca/sites/default/files/resources/apologies-response-crest.pdf.

30 United Church of Canada, "The Apologies."

31 Mia Rabson, "Pope Won't Personally Apologize for Catholic Church's Role in Residential Schools," *Globe and Mail*, 27 March 2018, accessed 15 September 2019, https://www.theglobeandmail.com/canada/article-pope-wont-personally-apologize-for-catholic-churchs-role-in/.

32 The TRC's Call to Action 49 is a direct charge for the church bodies who have not yet repudiated the Doctrine of Discovery to do so. See Truth and Reconciliation Commission of Canada, *The Truth and Reconciliation Commission of Canada: Calls to Action*, 5.

33 United Church of Canada, "United Church Reconciliation Journey to Australia," United Church of Canada, accessed 28 August 2019, https://www.united-church.ca/news/united-church-reconciliation-journey-australia. These kinds of international initiatives are important, because while the legacy of the residential schools in Canada is unique, the widespread colonial mission to "civilize and Christianize" children and families by imposing European understandings of punishment as discipline was animated around the world. Reconciliation journeys not only in Australia but in New Zealand and South Africa, for example, are also cause for cautious optimism. See Marlene Brant Castellano, Linda Archibald, and Mike DeGagné, conclusion to *From Truth to Reconciliation: Transforming the Legacy of Residential Schools*, Aboriginal Healing Foundation Research Series (Ottawa: Aboriginal Healing Foundation, 2008), 403–10, accessed 28 August 2019, http://www.ahf.ca/downloads/truth-to-reconciliation.pdf.

34 United Church of Canada, "Church Leaders: Make C-262 Unanimous," United Church of Canada, accessed 28 August 2019, https://www.united-church.ca/news/church-leaders-make-c-262-vote-unanimous; UN General Assembly, *United Nations Declaration on the Rights of Indigenous Peoples : resolution / adopted by the General Assembly*, 2 October 2007, A/RES/61/295, accessed 21 January 2020, https://www.refworld.org/docid/471355a82.html.

35 Matt Gardner, "Vision Keepers: Primate's Council of Indigenous Elders and Youth Holds First Meeting," Anglican Church of Canada, accessed 28 August 2019, https://www.anglican.ca/news/vision-keepers-primates-council-indigenous-elders-youth-holds-first-meeting/30019491/.

36 See KAIROS, "History of the Blanket Exercise," KAIROS Canada 2019, accessed 27 September 2019, https://www.kairosblanketexercise.org/about/#history.

37 Mark MacDonald, "Spiritual Struggle, Systemic Evil," *Anglican Journal*, 26 February 2018, https://www.anglicanjournal.com/articles/spiritual-struggle-systemic-evil/.

38 Michaelson et al., "Violence, Adolescence, and Canadian Religious Communities."

39 Canada Without Poverty, "Just the Facts," Canada Without Poverty, accessed 11 April 2018, http://www.cwp-csp.ca/poverty/just-the-facts/.

40 Assembly of First Nations Environmental Stewardship Unit, *The Health of First Nations Children and the Environment: Discussion Paper* (Ottawa: Assembly of First Nations), last modified March 2008, accessed 18 October 2018, https://www.afn.ca/uploads/files/rp-discussion_paper_re_childrens_health_and_the_environment.pdf.

41 Mark Penninga, "Spanking Does Have a Place in Canada," *Reformed Perspective: A Magazine for the Christian Family*, 10 February 2017, http://reformedperspective.ca/its-still-legal-to-use-physical-discipline-and-it-should-remain-so/.

PART 2: EXAMINING SACRED TEXTS

Christian Theological Reflections on Corporal Punishment

5

ACCULTURATION, ENCULTURATION, AND SOCIAL IMAGINARIES

The Complex Relationship between the Gospel and Culture

PETER ROBINSON

> In 1922, Andrew Paull, the corresponding secretary of the Allied Tribes of British Columbia, wrote to W.E. Ditchburn, the chief inspector of Indian agencies in British Columbia, to complain that the principal of Alberni Residential School, Mr. Currie, "unmercifully whips the boys on their backs, which is objected to as well as Mr. Curry [*sic*][1] fighting and kicking the boys for the purpose of correction. It is further reported that Mr. Curry gets extremely mad at the slightest provocation, and whips or hits the boys with his fists or chokes them." Currie said he thought himself to be "patient, kind and lenient with every child who shows any attempt at obedience to the rules, but certain offences must be dealt with firmly." But, he said, Aboriginal parents never punished their children. "The result is that when the teacher does it they magnify the thing to appear that the child was being murdered."[2]

Reading this description from the Truth and Reconciliation Commission (TRC) report, we are left wondering how someone like Mr. Currie was allowed to have any role of authority in the residential schools. His "discipline" of the children is abusive and his self-justification is shocking, all the more so since he had been given a singular position of authority in their lives. Why was his offensive bullying not dealt with immediately and severely? The sobering and corresponding question for the Church is this: how is it possible that the Church could have, in any way, been complicit in this type of behaviour?

Acculturation and the Gospel

The missionary movement of the Western Church has often been criticized for its colonial tendencies. These included the attempt to convert people to European culture by imposing European standards, values, and practices, and the often explicit attempt to convert people to a westernized form of Christianity.[3] In the preceding chapter, the damage done by the Doctrine of Discovery and similar theologies was recognized. In this chapter, I consider the lack of discernment regarding the complex relationship between the gospel and a given cultural situation, another element that fed these colonialist tendencies; in other words, the failure to acknowledge the ways in which culture inevitably shapes people's understanding of the Christian faith and of the gospel.[4]

This lack of discernment as to which priorities, concerns, and commitments truly reflect the gospel, and which are more reflective of cultural norms (and may indeed have been in conflict with, if not antithetical to, the gospel) is an example of *acculturation*. Acculturation occurs when particular expressions of the Christian faith (usually within a dominant culture) are imposed on another culture with little or no discernment as to the ways in which the understanding of the gospel that is being imposed has been shaped by cultural norms. When this occurs—and to some degree this is part of every encounter between the gospel and culture—this acculturated gospel is no longer *the gospel*.

The "Social Imaginary"

There is no ideal or pure understanding of the gospel or the Bible.[5] Rather, faith is always situated within particular cultural situations and it cannot be otherwise, for understanding or knowing the gospel occurs in the context of what Charles Taylor calls the "social imaginary." Taylor describes the "social imaginary" as "the way ordinary people 'imagine' their social surroundings. This is often not expressed in theoretical terms; it is carried in images, stories, legends, etc."[6] Insofar as the gospel finds its centre in the person of Jesus Christ, it is itself particularized in a specific, historical, and local, cultural situation. The gospel always is located, and continues to be rooted, in particular social imaginaries.

Our social imaginary shapes what we understand and how we perceive people and situations through what we have experienced, practised, witnessed, and heard. This *practical* or common-sense knowing is not based solely on a set of facts or principles but is a more embodied knowing in which an often unspoken but shared understanding shapes and is shaped by our values, perceptions, and practices. This practical knowing not only shapes what we perceive to be true or of value, it also shapes the way we read, listen to, or apprehend different sources of input. This inevitably includes how we read the Bible and engage with any tradition of interpretation.

Enculturation of the Gospel

When the gospel is communicated in a new situation, it cannot simply be translated from one language to another but must take root over time in the new situation in a manner that is coherent with the practices and values of that situation if it is to remain *the gospel.* To have coherence and integrity, the gospel must become rooted within particular cultures and be expressed in ways that resonate with those cultures, even while it will in some ways critique the culture within which it is embedded, just as Jesus critiqued his own culture.[7] *Enculturation* occurs when the gospel becomes embedded within a particular setting through a dialogue between gospel and culture. Through this process, the gospel finds expression in the language and patterns of life of a particular situation and people, reflecting and enlivening the culture in constructive and beneficial ways.[8]

Conflating the Gospel with European Culture

In the colonization of North America, *acculturation* rather than *enculturation* was the rule. The identification of the Christian faith with European culture was so integral to the self-understanding of European settlers in Canada that in many cases there was a corresponding failure to make any differentiation between European culture and the Christian faith; for many European settlers in Canada, to be European was to be Christian. The distinctives of the gospel became conflated with European cultural norms.[9] In the residential schools, it was often assumed that converting (conforming) First Nations, Inuit, and Métis children to European culture was identical with introducing them to the Christian faith.

Thoughtful, attentive, and appropriate engagement with another culture enables people to listen to and learn from each other. This not only leads to greater appreciation of the other but helps one to see oneself and one's own cultural idiosyncrasies more clearly. At its best, for missionaries this would involve coming to understand the gospel itself more clearly through intentional engagement with people of another culture.[10] Both this kind of appreciation for other cultures and the recognition of one's own biases as shaped by one's cultural context are vital in allowing for enculturation rather than acculturation. Unfortunately, the assumption that European culture was *the* Christian culture meant that acculturation, not enculturation, was the rule once Europeans began to settle in Canada in significant numbers.

The Residential Schools and Cultural Assimilation

Residential schools were set up as protected enclaves of European culture, with the express intention of amalgamating First Nations, Inuit, and Métis children into that culture. In many cases, the residential schools were not primarily about educating Indigenous children for their own sake but were intended to assimilate them to European culture or to form them in that context by eliminating all aspects of their own culture. The assumption that Indigenous Peoples were inferior and that it was to their benefit to convert them to European practices paved the way for this cultural assimilation. The TRC report on residential school history captures this view: "Indians, in terms of civilization, are children, having human minds just emerging from barbarism."[11] The racist notion that the cultures of Indigenous Peoples were inferior to European culture contributed to the belief that conversion—not only to Christianity but to European-style societies—was for their own good.

The whole basis on which residential schools were established provided an environment within which abuse was inevitable. Given the basic motivations driving the establishment of residential schools, the uprooting of the children from their homes and families, the denigration of their culture, and the attempted imposition of European culture, there was a disorientation and dis-ease that fostered a conflictual, unhealthy dynamic in the schools. In turn, strict or harsh discipline was normalized by some leaders of the residential schools, in part because of their underlying operating premise that Indigenous children required assimilation. The lack of adequate resources, both human and financial,[12] is also evident in the presence of individuals such as Mr. Currie who were put in charge of these institutions, and who exercised discipline in violent ways and allowed others to do so as well.[13] When challenged, they would often defend their practices or endeavour to cover up or diminish what had occurred. The working assumptions informing the residential schools provided an ideal climate in which even extreme forms of corporal punishment could be inflicted with impunity.

Systemic Failure

The TRC has established that the individuals who abused their positions of authority in residential schools bear some responsibility, but the government and Church leadership that failed to call these individuals to account and to address the abuse carry a much larger responsibility. As Bishop Mark MacDonald (Chapter 1) has noted, this is not simply a case of rogue individuals but of systemic evil. Societal structures, including the structure and functioning of both the government and churches, enabled the gross abuses that characterized residential schools. This is not to diminish individual responsibility but to acknowledge the complexity of the situation so that the root issues might be addressed. Identifying these abuses with particular dysfunctional individuals only serves to distance us from these situations and sustains a corresponding failure to acknowledge and address what precipitated the abuses.

The fact that there was no will to stop the infliction of corporal punishment confirms the existence of a "common-sense" assumption that corporal punishment was an appropriate practice in raising children. Corporal punishment was a culturally accepted practice in the raising and formation of children in European culture, including in the public school system in Canada.[14] It is sobering that within the public school system, guidelines were considered necessary to ensure that corporal punishment was used "appropriately": "The 1891 Ontario *Education Act* instructed teachers not to exceed measures that would be taken by a 'kind, firm, and judicious parent.' Teachers who went beyond these boundaries could be charged with assault under the Criminal Code."[15] Yet within the residential schools, there was little space or incentive for setting "appropriate guidelines" for discipline, and little or no accountability for those leaders who hurt children. This was in spite of the fact that some individuals within the system recognized what was happening. As we learn in the TRC report, even though "it would appear that senior Indian Affairs officials such as Scott, Semmens, and McLean viewed corporal punishment as being self-defeating and unnecessary, no one was prepared to ban it."[16] The result was a failure to constrain individuals who acted aggressively, were abusive, were strict disciplinarians, or simply did not know how to address disciplinary issues constructively.[17]

At first there were no guidelines whatsoever on corporal punishment in the residential schools, and when they were finally put into place in 1953 they were often ignored.[18] This was, of course, before the emergence of the very strong body of evidence demonstrating that guidelines were not enough (see Chapters 2 and 3). *All* corporal punishment should have been replaced with positive approaches to discipline that did not put children's health at risk for adverse health outcomes and that were more effective and constructive (Chapters 11 and 12).

Cultural Assimilation and Corporal Punishment

Cultural differences further confused the legitimation of corporal punishment in that European cultural assumptions were perceived to be superior to those of Indigenous Peoples. Instead of valuing cultural differences, those assumptions provided further grounds for cultural assimilation. The assumption that there was an appropriate place for corporal punishment was not part of most Indigenous cultures. As a result, for many First Nations parents, for example, any form of corporal punishment would be considered excessive since it was not a part of their social imaginary or cultural background.[19] In Chapter 9, Brother Martin Brokenleg writes further about this view from the perspective of his Lakȟóta heritage.

Underlying and sustaining the practices in the residential schools was the assumption that the Bible legitimized and even *required* the use of corporal punishment in the formation of children. Passages such as Proverbs 13:24, 22:15, and 29:15 were regularly referenced to this end,[20] and "corporal punishment was a biblically authorized way of keeping order and of bringing children to the righteous path."[21] What was not recognized or acknowledged was the hermeneutical or interpretative principles that informed the use of biblical passages to justify corporal punishment. (This is addressed by William Webb and William Morrow in Chapters 6 and 7, respectively.) Nor was there any willingness to call into question the hermeneutical principles in the face of different cultural practices and understandings.

Conflating the Gospel with Cultural Values and Priorities

The legitimation of corporal punishment based on biblical interpretation brings us back to the fundamental issue of the acculturation of the gospel within Western European culture. Biblical scholar N.T. Wright, in *The New Testament and the People of God*, suggests that all readers or interpreters of the Bible begin reading it from within a particular framework, a particular social imaginary, and find it difficult to allow for alternative readings of the text: "Interpreters typically see the interpretations of others as hopelessly subjective and their own as objectively true; they are antirealists about beliefs they disagree with and naïve realists about their own beliefs."[22] Inevitably, it becomes much more difficult to discern which beliefs or practices, including hermeneutics or principles of interpretation, are coherent with the gospel and which are more deeply rooted in accepted cultural norms when, within a particular cultural setting, the gospel becomes conflated with cultural values and priorities—particularly those that are assumed to be superior.

The belief that we can be neutral, independent thinkers who see or perceive situations in an unbiased manner is an illusion and is itself an aspect of modern Western culture's social imaginary. Moreover, this belief is exacerbated in a context where we are not forced to recognize or acknowledge different perspectives or different understandings than our own.[23] This was certainly the case in Canada during the time of the residential schools. In reality, the fact that European settlers believed that their culture was superior to Indigenous culture allowed them to ignore or diminish the very different approach of Indigenous Peoples to raising children, and to avoid questioning the hermeneutics that shaped their own interpretation of biblical texts in the legitimation of corporal punishment.

Conclusion

It would be misleading to isolate the issue of corporal punishment, and particularly its legitimation through a tradition of interpretation of select biblical texts, as the sole form of violence in the residential schools. At the same time, a biblical justification for corporal punishment was clearly an essential contributor to the terrible abuses that occurred. A clearer understanding of the complex relationship between gospel and culture is not only a first step in identifying problematic patterns in the interpretation of biblical texts, it also invites more humility in our interpretation. Realizing our inability to recognize the distortions of our own social imaginaries forces us to recognize how we must learn from those who are different than we are. An appreciation of social imaginaries different from our own and a recognition of the necessity of hearing alternative perspectives in the interpretation of biblical texts are essential to a deepening understanding of the gospel itself. They also are essential in the enculturation or embedding of the gospel within particular cultural situations. In the meantime, a recognition of the limitations that arise from the inevitable subjectivity inherent in our own interpretations combined with clarity regarding the tremendous risks of corporal punishment should lead us to oppose the practice in our society at large.

Notes

1 As directly quoted from the Truth and Reconciliation Commission of Canada, *Canada's Residential Schools: The History, Part 1: Origins to 1939*, vol. 1 of *The Final Report of the Truth and Reconciliation Commission of Canada* (Kingston, ON: McGill-Queen's University Press, 2015), the principal of Alberni Residential School was Mr. Currie. However, in his letter, Mr. Andrew Paull uses the misnomer Mr. Curry. As such, the inconsistency of the spelling of Mr. Currie's name remains in order to respect the integrity of Mr. Paull's letter, and to preserve the manner by which the TRC has retained the content of documents in their original form. For further examples of the spelling of Principal Currie's name, historically recorded as such, see United Church of Canada Archives, "Alberni Indian Residential School," Residential Schools Archives Project: Children Remembered, accessed 6 July 2018, http://thechildrenremembered.ca/school-locations/alberni/#ftn22; United Church of Canada British Columbia Conference Archives, "Fonds-Alberni Indian Residential School," MemoryBC, last modified 28 January 2015, https://www.memorybc.ca/alberni-indian-residential-school-fonds.

2 Truth and Reconciliation Commission of Canada, *Canada's Residential Schools: The History, Part 1*, 524.

3 See Vinay Samuel and Chris Sugden, *Mission as Transformation* (Oxford: Regnum, 1999).

4 By the gospel I mean the story of God's engagement through creation, redemption, and fulfillment as it is made complete in the person and work of Jesus Christ.

5 Lesslie Newbigin develops this idea further as he writes, "The idea that one can or should at any time separate out by some process of distillation a pure gospel unadulterated by any cultural accretions is an illusion," in *Foolishness to the Greeks: The Gospel and Western Culture* (Grand Rapids, MI: Eerdmans, 1980), 4.

6 Charles Taylor, *A Secular Age* (Cambridge, MA: Belknap, 2007), 171–72.

7 "The gospel is about the word made flesh. Every statement of the gospel in words is conditioned by the culture of which those words are a part, and every style of life that claims to embody the truth of the gospel is a culturally conditioned style of life. There can never be a culture-free gospel. Yet, the gospel, which is from the beginning to the end embodied in culturally conditioned forms, calls into question all cultures including the one in which it was originally embodied." Newbigin, *Foolishness to the Greeks*, 4.

8 "The Reverend Henry Venn oversaw the Church Missionary Society for much of the 19th century. Venn's long-term goal was the establishment, not of separate branches of the Church of England, but of national churches throughout the world. He believed if the missionaries respected the habits of the people they converted, the churches they established would come to be seen as part of the way of life of each community, rather than as the Europeans' church." Truth and Reconciliation Commission of Canada, *Canada's Residential Schools: The History, Part 1*, 31.

9 "Under colonialism, the European missionary enterprise was of a piece with Europe's military, political, commercial, and cultural expansion overseas." Lesslie Newbigin, *The Open Secret: An Introduction to the Theology of Mission*, rev. ed. (Grand Rapids, MI: Eerdmans, 1995), 5.

10 Lesslie Newbigin speaks of what happens when missionaries truly engage with other peoples: "The missionary and through him the church he represents, can become aware of the element of syncretism in his own Christianity, of the extent to which his culture has been allowed to determine the nature of the gospel he preaches, instead of being brought under judgment by that gospel. If this happens, great possibilities for mutual correction open up." Newbigin, *Foolishness to the Greeks*, 9.

11 Truth and Reconciliation Commission of Canada, *Canada's Residential Schools: The History, Part 1*, 554.

12 As we learn from the TRC's report, "the schools responded to such predictable resistance with a regime of harsh discipline. In the context of residential schools, discipline refers not simply to punishment of wrongdoers, but also to the maintenance of order and obedience. Given that the schools were understaffed and poorly equipped, they sought to control student behaviour through strict regimentation." Truth and Reconciliation Commission of Canada, *Canada's Residential Schools: The History, Part 1*, 517–18. Here we further read: "A system as poorly funded and supervised as Canada's residential school system for Aboriginal children was bound to lead to tragedy" (366).

13 "The failure to develop, implement, and monitor effective discipline sent an unspoken message that there were no real limits on what could be done to Aboriginal children within the walls of a residential school." Truth and Reconciliation Commission of Canada, *Canada's Residential Schools: The History, Part 2: 1939–2000*, vol. 1 of *The Final Report of the Truth and Reconciliation Commission of Canada* (Kingston, ON: McGill-Queen's University Press, 2015), 398.

14 In 1933 the strap was administered to 1,500 Toronto school students. Truth and Reconciliation Commission of Canada, *Canada's Residential Schools: The History, Part 1*, 520.

15 Truth and Reconciliation Commission of Canada, 520.

16 Truth and Reconciliation Commission of Canada, 540.

17 In the Department of Indian Affairs correspondence on corporal punishment, there are frequent references to students being "whipped" or "thrashed." It also appears that principals were left to devise their own disciplinary tools. Truth and Reconciliation Commission of Canada, 522.

18 "The establishment of a nationwide discipline policy in 1953 did not bring an end to abusive disciplinary practices. During the final thirty years of the system's history, the policies that existed were poorly enforced and often simply ignored." Truth and Reconciliation Commission of Canada, *Canada's Residential Schools: The History, Part 2*, 388.

19 Truth and Reconciliation Commission of Canada, *Canada's Residential Schools: The History, Part 1*, 524.

20 The Northern Light Gospel Mission School at Poplar Hill, funded by First Nations–controlled education councils, still legitimated the use of corporal punishment on the basis of biblical principles in 1989. See Truth and Reconciliation Commission of Canada, *Canada's Residential Schools: The History, Part 2*, 394.

21 "[Egerton] Ryerson, a leading figure in the Methodist Church, believed that opposition to corporal punishment was 'contrary to Scripture.'" Cited in Truth and Reconciliation Commission of Canada, *Canada's Residential Schools: The History, Part 1*, 520.; J.G. Hodgins and Department of Education, Ontario, *Documentary History of Education in Upper Canada (Ontario), from the Passing of the Constitutional Act, 1791 to the Close of Ryerson's Administration of the Education Department in 1876* (Toronto: Warwick Bros. and Rutter, 1900), 9.

22 Quoted in Richard Middleton, *The Liberating Image: The Imago Dei in Genesis 1* (Grand Rapids, MI: Brazos Press, 2005), 51.

23 The quest for a literal or a singular *objective* meaning of the text is itself indicative of a particular set of cultural presuppositions. It reflects what Richard Bernstein has labelled a "Cartesian anxiety" with the belief that there is one right interpretation of a given text; see Bernstein, *Beyond Objectivism and Relativism: Science, Hermeneutics and Praxis* (Philadelphia: University of Pennsylvania Press, 1983), 16–20.

6

Reading the Bible Redemptively

WILLIAM J. WEBB

This chapter looks at how we interpret biblical texts.[1] Its central thesis is simple: *we need to read and apply the corporal punishment texts redemptively.* I wish to address Christian and Jewish parents who advocate the practice of corporal punishment with children based upon their understanding that to do so reflects obedience to biblical teaching. In other words, if you are someone who wants to retain spanking children because corporal punishment is taught in Scripture, then this chapter is for you. Hopefully it will nudge you toward the idea that it is okay to replace spanking with effective non-corporal disciplinary methods and experience God's blessing upon your parenting practices.

This essay reflects the hermeneutical or interpretive journey that my wife (Marilyn) and I (Bill) travelled in the midst of raising three children in our home.[2] As a couple, we needed to rethink the way we read Scripture in tandem with changing the child-discipline patterns that had been handed down to us from our parents. The move to non-corporal (no spanking) parenting practices meant that we consciously had to think about the role of Scripture in our lives and what exactly it meant to be "biblical" in the way that we disciplined our children.

Scripture Often Reflects an Incremental (not Ultimate) Ethic

As a starting point, Christians must come to grips with the fact that many biblical texts reflect an incremental (not an ultimate) ethic. Just because we find something—an instruction, command, or teaching—in the Bible does not mean that those words, at least in their concrete expression, reflect a best-possible ethic. The biblical instruction may well have moved redemptively in some measure relative to the ancient world within which it was expressed. But that redemptive movement is often incremental and not fully realized in the original-audience context.

What this means is that Christians today cannot automatically appeal to "the Bible says it" for including spanking within their parenting practices. In fact, as one explores the subject of corporal beatings (rod and whip) and corporal mutilation (the axe or heavy knife) in the Bible, it becomes evident that its teachings about the use of the rod and whip are well situated within—and very much accommodated to—an ancient, agrarian society. The biblical corporal punishment instructions reflect an ethic that moves redemptively within its day but not in any fully realized sense. If I may invoke a sports metaphor, biblical teaching in its concrete instructions often moves the ethical scrimmage markers downfield (ten, twenty, or thirty yards) but not all the way to the goal line. Our job as Christians in *applying* Scripture is to extend the trajectory of its redemptive spirit and, if you will, carry the ball further.

We should not be surprised to find an incremental ethic within Scripture. Jesus challenged his own disciples on this matter when they made the (wrong) "all is good" assumption about Moses's teaching concerning divorce. While one could argue that biblical teaching on divorce (Deuteronomy 21:14, 24:1–4) was redemptive in limited or incremental ways within its ancient world context, that does not mean that it was even close to an ultimate ethic. Jesus clearly teaches us that the hardness of human hearts (and, by inference, probably a lot of other factors) impeded the extent of redemptive movement within biblical instructions.

Yet the divorce texts do not stand alone. Numerous other examples of biblical teaching on a wide array of topics (slavery, polygamy, levirate marriage, rape, gender [in]equality, sacrifice, treatment of female war captives, total-kill war rhetoric, prayers for the smashing of enemy babies, collective family punishments for the crime of one person, mutilation laws, capital punishment, etc.) reflect extensive cultural accommodation. Put theologically, God reluctantly departs from a best-possible ethic to work with where people are in this fallen, messed-up world. Scripture often makes gradual redemptive moves. If so, it is the redemptive spirit reflected in the incremental movement of Scripture (not the concrete aspect of its instructions) that carries us to an ultimate ethic.

Seven Ways Contemporary Pro-Spankers Do Not Obey Biblical Teaching

In rethinking our convictions about "spanking being biblical," my wife and I were further helped along by exploring the gap—a Grand Canyon–sized gap—between what contemporary parents practise and what the Bible really teaches. Pro-spankers with their ethical reasoning locked into the concrete-specific teaching of Scripture should ponder their massive departure from what the Bible truly teaches on the subject:

	Concrete-specific teaching of the Bible	**"Two-smacks-max" spanking ethic**[3]
Age limitations	no age limits; corporal punishment used even in teen years[4]	primarily preschool age; no spanking teens
Number of lashes	graduated increase to forty strokes at most (reasonable inference from Scripture)[5]	one or two smacks at most
Bodily location	back[6]	buttocks (or hand)
Bruising and welts	acceptable; seen as a virtue[7]	unacceptable; abusive
Instrument	rod (or whip)[8]	open palm (broader displacement of impact; less physical damage)
Frequency and type of offences	frequently used; defiant and non-defiant actions[9]	infrequently used; as a last resort and only defiant acts
Emotive disposition	rod expresses parental love and anger (reasonable inference within Scripture)[10]	spank only in love; no anger permitted

If pro-spanking advocates take a hard look at how their spanking practices line up with what the Bible teaches in its concrete-specific instructions, they will realize (perhaps to their surprise) that a huge fissure exists. That gap invalidates any claim that "they are being biblical" in their parenting approaches through "two-smacks-max" spanking of preschoolers, and so on. Once this realization dawned upon Marilyn and me, we began rethinking what exactly it meant to be "biblical" in our appropriation or application of the spanking proverbs today, along with other corporal punishment texts. Surely, it did *not* mean living out an exact duplicate of the left-hand column in the chart above.

We began to see that our understanding of biblical authority was wrongly tied to the concrete-specific, culturally locked, and ethically problematic elements of the biblical instructions. Our own journey required a far stronger grounding in biblical authority. That led us to embrace a more deeply rooted meaning in the biblical text through two avenues: *functional* meaning and *redemptive-movement* meaning. After a discussion of adult/child overlap, those are my next two points.

Overlapping Adult/Child Domains

When discussing the Bible's rod and whip texts, some advocates of "two-smacks-max" spanking practices wish to keep the *adult* corporal punishment texts completely removed from the *child* corporal punishment texts.[11] After all, the genre, setting, ages, infractions, and severity of beatings would surely have been different. Contemporary pro-spankers appeal to these differences to minimize the impact of any ethical implications derived from (1) how we apply adult-beatings texts in our contemporary world for (2) how we apply the child-beating texts today. If they can keep the two domains—adult and child—clinically separated, then they can limit the ethical discussion of "biblical beatings" of children to only a handful of spanking proverbs read in isolation from the broader subject of corporal punishment in the Bible. Peering through this ill-constructed narrow window, these readers satisfy themselves by imagining that the Bible is describing some ancient form of one-or-two-smacks practice when it speaks of child beatings. But this adult/child dislocation creates an artificial understanding of what happened in the ancient world. While granting certain differences between adult beatings and child beatings, the evidence strongly favours seeing an overlap (not clinical separation) between the two domains and using that overlap for ethical insight. We can recreate the workings of the ancient world by asking several questions.

First, where exactly were adult beatings [of free persons] administered in Israel? Answer: in the open as public beatings, typically at the city gates where judicial cases were decided. The text of Deuteronomy 25:1–3 assumes such a public setting:

> When people have a dispute, they are to take it to court and the judges will decide the case, acquitting the innocent and condemning the guilty. If the guilty person deserves to be beaten, the judge shall make them lie down and have them *flogged in his presence* with the number of lashes the crime deserves, but the judge must not impose more than forty lashes. If the guilty party is flogged more than that, your fellow Israelite will be *degraded in your eyes*. (emphasis mine)

In the Israelite community an adult was flogged immediately after the judge pronounced the verdict and the number of lashes to be meted out. This public display of flogging happened typically at the city gates in front of the judge and before the eyes of others witnessing the case. There was no private structure (such as a little house nearby) where the judge would go with the convicted person to perform a private beating. No; adult beatings took place in front of the judge and before everyone else present—from those pressing charges to others simply gathered to watch. The expression "degraded in your [the community's] eyes" implies a visual and openly public context. Those gathered at the city gates could confirm for others not present that the number of lashes was proportionate to the crime but did not exceed forty, and that justice was served. Unlike the practice of beatings in the broader ancient world, the Hebrew text demonstrates a concern not to leave the person as a pulverized piece of flayed meat. But my point here is that the public aspect of adult beatings at the city gate would have permitted the whole community to visually reflect upon the city-gates scene and carry those images over to the domestic setting where both adults and children were also beaten.

Second, did Israelite masters beat their slaves? In public? And, whom did they beat—adults and children? Answer: the beating of slave adults and children (no age restrictions) at times occurred before the entire household. The biblical text assumes that Israelite masters beat their slaves.[12]

In fact, it was acceptable to beat slaves severely provided they did not die and that they could get up after a day or two. In the ancient world, such slave beatings were often intentionally carried out before the rest of the master's household as part of the broader social control of slaves. There is nothing in the biblical texts to suggest that slave beatings in Israel were a private affair. The beating of adults at the city gates (free persons) and in the home context (slaves) would have created a lasting visual connection between public beatings and the pedagogy of the proverbs that sought to teach adults (and children) about the way of wisdom. So, ponder for a moment these two public settings—at the city gates and in front of the household—for adult beatings. The entire community would have seen these adult beatings. Men, women, and perhaps older children—possibly even young ones sneaking a glimpse—would have gathered (or been forced to gather, in the case of slaves) to view beatings with the rod or whip. How in that kind of public setting can one imagine that *adult* beatings did not to some extent overlap with and have an impact on *child* beatings? Within a world of societal public beatings for teenagers and full adults—slaves and free persons—the beating of children (slave and free) was most likely viewed as an interrelated phenomenon.[13]

Third, in the ancient world were children (and adults) at times punished through bodily mutilation? Answer: Yes, adults and children were punished through bodily mutilation. Before going further, let us be clear: *The Bible nowhere advocates the punishment of children through bodily mutilation.* This departure by the biblical text from broader ancient societal norms is part of Scripture's wonderful (incremental) redemptive character relative to the surrounding culture. (More on this kind of redemptive-movement meaning below.) Nevertheless, bodily mutilations provide a larger window through which to peer into the social conventions of punishment in the ancient world—in both the domestic and criminal settings—and they once again confirm a significant adult/child overlap. In addition to parents beating their children (the rod and whip), at times they also disfigured and/or cut off certain body parts (the knife). It is important to shed our naive contemporary readings of the Bible's corporal punishment texts that clinically separate what happened with adults from what happened to children. Here are a few illustrations where ancient laws prescribed the right of parents to mutilate their children . . . and (similarly) masters to mutilate their slaves, husbands their wives, and so on:[14]

Crime	**Punishment**
adopted child says "you are not my father/mother"	cut out the child's tongue
child strikes a father	cut off child's hand
slave strikes a free person	cut off the slave's hand
hired man steals seed or fodder	cut off his hand
slave challenges authority of his master	cut off the slave's ear
slave steals goods from owner	cut off slave's nose and ears
wife steals from a neighbour	return goods and the husband cuts off his wife's ears; if no ransom, the owner cuts off her nose
wife leaves her husband and lives in another house supported by the wife of the second residence	first husband mutilates abandoning wife; second husband cuts off the ears of the supportive wife
unspecified offences of a wife	a husband has the right to whip his wife, pluck out her hair, mutilate her ears, and strike her

In the broader ancient world, punishment by the whip, the rod, *and the knife* often took place in the home setting. The criminal—and civil—offence worlds were blurred. This contextual-setting evidence surely suggests that even severe beatings for children would have been viewed as acceptable in that world. We should not succumb to modern (mis)readings of the Bible that artificially separate adult punishments from child punishments. While we can posit more limited beatings for children compared to adult beatings (that is logical), this section fleshes out what corporal punishment for children in the biblical world would have looked like. In short, child beatings according to the Hebrew Bible would have been far more severe than most Christians today would care to contemplate. The contemporary Christian teaching about parents using only one or two smacks on the child's behind with their open palm (no marks or bruises permitted; no anger permitted) is completely foreign to the ancient world context.

Functional Meaning within the Biblical Text

Christian parents need to understand biblical authority in terms of the text's *functional* (not formal or instrumental) meaning. The functional meaning could be described as the *purpose* or *goal* of Scripture's teaching about parents disciplining their children. In the case of biblical corporal punishment texts, the stated goal of beatings with the rod for *both* children and adults are (negatively) to turn children from folly, and (positively) to help them embrace wisdom.[15] What Marilyn and I had to wrestle with was whether the "beatings with a rod" (the concrete, how-to, or instrumental meaning of "hitting children") was somehow sacrosanct. Was it an ongoing, transcultural part of what God really wanted us to do? Or was its underlying functional meaning that which was truly sacred? Could the formal/instrumental meaning simply reflect Scripture being communicated within an ancient world culture? Over time, we came to see that God did *not* hold the means (hitting children with a physical object) as sacrosanct. Rather, what was sacred was the abstracted/functional meaning, namely, some form of discipline (abstracted meaning) that helped children embrace wisdom instead of folly (functional meaning).

Our journey to this "what was sacred" conclusion involved numerous pieces of a hermeneutical puzzle—more than I can mention here. But one sample piece might help illustrate the sort of interpretive, ethical, and logical reasoning that enabled us to realize we were *not at all* obligated to spank or hit our children in order to honour biblical teaching about raising children. We might call it our "cleaning the garage" story. Let's say that on a Saturday morning, I take my son Joel (fourteen years old) out to the garage, hand him a broom and say to him, "In our family we all have spring chores to do; this one is yours. Please *sweep out the garage* [handing him a broom]. After winter salt, sand, and road debris, this garage needs a good sweeping out. I will be back in two hours to check on your progress." Now, let me present two scenarios about what could happen next. *Scenario 1:* I come back to the garage and find Joel listening to music through his earbuds, sitting on a stool, and strumming the broom like a guitar. No cleaning—not one ounce—has taken place. Was Joel obedient to my instructions? The answer obviously is, "No!" Fair enough. *Scenario 2:* I come back to the garage and find Joel working away (yes, his earbuds and music engaged), but this time I am very impressed by how clean the garage looks. Almost spotless. On his own initiative Joel had gone down to our basement, carried up the ShopVac suction cleaner, and vacuumed most of the garage. And here is the point of introducing scenario 2. What father would turn to his son and yell at him, "But I told you to *sweep* out the garage!" That would be ridiculous. It would be nonsensical for a father to tie instrumentality to the issue of obedience. By way of analogy and hermeneutical insight, I suggest that it would be equally ludicrous for God, our heavenly Father, to be displeased with parents who have chosen to use non-corporal methods of discipline if those do just as good or even a better job than corporal hitting.[16]

Here is the rub. If the functional objectives of the biblical corporal punishment texts (turning children away from folly and helping them embrace wise and skillful living) can be met through using non-corporal methods, then parents who choose that path should surely be viewed as faithfully following Scripture's teaching. They are very much obedient (not disobedient) to biblical authority. The instrumentality—hitting a child with an object—is *not* sacrosanct within the biblical text. Once readers have figured that out, the closely related question is a practical one: Can parents achieve reasonably well-behaved children through using *only* non-corporal methods of discipline? The answer is, most assuredly, yes! There are some wonderful and varied "ShopVac" methods that do just as good a job, and often much better, than our old "brooms." Marilyn and I included thirty pages in *Corporal Punishment in the Bible* to describe very practical insights that work in the real world.[17] Discovering the best alternative (non-corporal) discipline methods was just as important as it was for us to learn how to read and apply Scripture in a more credible manner. This practical focus on parenting methods—ones that work well—can also be found within Chapters 9 to 13 of this multidisciplinary volume, with a specific focus on positive discipline in Chapter 12.

Redemptive-Movement Meaning within the Biblical Text

Christians must learn to embrace biblical authority in terms of its *redemptive-movement* (not static) meaning. Biblical texts were meant to be read in context. For many Christians, a great step forward starts with learning to read texts in their *literary* context—up and down the page—in relationship to the words around the text in question. Add to that the literary context of genre—what it means to read a proverb compared to reading apocalyptic material. Should these various literary contexts be embraced, lay Christians (as well as seminary-trained individuals) can make credible advances on interpreting Scripture. However, there is yet another kind of context that is equally important as literary context, and that is the text's ancient *social* context. The words of Scripture must be read and understood within the ancient social world within which they were given. In biblical studies pertaining to the Hebrew Bible, scholars talk about the social-historical context of the ancient Near East (ANE).[18]

When we read biblical corporal punishment texts within their ancient social-historical context, we hear something wonderful and exciting that we easily miss if reading them *only* within their literary context. Listening to the rod-and-whip and beating passages in the Bible requires that we know something about the ancient world in which they were given. Within *Corporal Punishment in the Bible,* I provide numerous examples of ancient world crime and punishment laws (typically involving bodily beatings and/or mutilations)[19] from Sumer, Egypt, Babylon, Assyria, and Anatolia. These regions represent the ancient social context for understanding the Hebrew Bible. In that setting, it is important to note that (1) there was *no limit* in any ANE country to the number of strokes permitted for punishing crimes; and (2) where punishments were prescribed for certain crimes, the un-capped samples ranged as high as *two hundred blows with the rod and five open wounds*. When one adds to that picture of ancient world beatings the extensive use of bodily mutilations, these often-public punishments are rightly seen as horrifying by contemporary readers. However, by way of contrast, in Deuteronomy 25:1–3, Israel's corporal punishment laws (1) imposed a clear limit—no more than forty lashes for any crime-and-punishment scenario; (2) moved the ethical scrimmage markers of the ancient world considerably downfield to one-fifth (40/200) of the highest non-capped, prescribed ANE samples; and (3) offered an explicit humanitarian emphasis in their redemptive actions by requiring that such beatings "not degrade" the person being punished in the eyes of those watching.[20]

Now one could in our contemporary world stay with the static "on the page" meaning in the Bible and argue that adults, both free persons and slaves, should be punished today with beatings. But such would be morally repugnant and hardly offer best-possible ethical practices. Alternatively, one can choose to embrace the redemptive spirit of Scripture that is so evident and present already within its ancient world context. That redemptive spirit captures a sense of an ethic on the move—an incremental ethic that represents real-world steps toward something better in the treatment of people. Good application of Scripture in our contemporary lives does not mean staying with a static understanding of biblical texts (reading texts in a way that is isolated or removed from their social world context) as if their words magically float in mid-air, devoid of any historical mooring. No—we must capture the redemptive movement of Scripture as read within its ancient historical context and think logically and ethically about where that trajectory should lead us today. One should be able to sense and "hear" that something wonderful is happening in the biblical text as it is read within the ANE environment—something that enshrines the greater dignity of human beings.[21]

If we listen to the biblical corporal punishment texts within their ancient world setting, we will not fail to hear clearly marked steps that were incrementally redemptive in that day and time. The biblical text was moving relative to its ancient world context. To invoke a well-known line from *The Lion, the Witch, and the Wardrobe*, "Aslan is on the move."[22] True, we have not fully changed seasons when it comes to biblical corporal punishment instructions. The change is not total in the sense of moving all the way from winter to summer. But the ice is starting to melt, and the warmth of spring is here. One can sense a strange and intriguing redemptive force at work.

So, what do we do with the redemptive-movement meaning that is a strikingly obvious component of the rod-and-whip beating texts of Scripture? As with other biblical texts that do not convey an ultimate or fully realized ethic, our obligation is not to stay with the concrete-specific "on the page" words of the text (remember the garage broom: it's not sacrosanct). It is our sacred task to champion Scripture's redemptive spirit. Christians in community must discuss where the redemptive-movement meaning of the biblical text should logically lead us. It is this last step that I will now address.

Logical and Ethical Trajectory in Applying the Corporal Punishment Texts

The task of biblical readers who have observed redemptive-movement meaning within the biblical corporal punishment texts is to talk about where that ethical trajectory should logically lead us today. Where does God want us to move *with* his Spirit (and *with* the corporal punishment text's redemptive spirit) in our contemporary application of these passages? Can we take the gentler (less harsh) movement meaning (already present in these ancient texts) and extend it further? Can we increase the already existing concern in the biblical corporal punishment texts for greater protection of the one punished? Can the spirit of greater dignity for the person be more fully realized? Can we take that incremental movement and, through logical and ethical reasoning, extend its trajectory?

In short, I would argue that the trajectory of the redemptive spirit that resides within the biblical beating texts should lead us not simply to gentler and kinder beatings, but to *the abolition of bodily beatings altogether*—even in the case of more limited hitting, namely, "two-smacks-max." Let us draw an analogy with the slavery texts of the Bible, which cast considerable light on what Christians should do in applying the corporal punishment texts today. When the slavery texts are read within their ANE environment, these passages provide important dimensions of redemptive and incremental movement toward a better treatment of fellow human beings. The biblical slavery passages in the context of an ancient world reflect movement toward something better—greater kindness, gentleness, dignity, and worth. It is the *logical extension* of this very redemptive spirit (already present in the ancient text in partially realized expression) that carries us to the abolition of slavery. An ultimate ethic—or stated another way, a best possible ethic—requires the freedom of all human beings.

Sometimes a particular form needs abolishing altogether, and we should replace it with something better. *It would not simply do for the church to endorse a kinder and gentler form of slavery*, in other words, making progress now and then with further steps of improvement. The greatest expression of kindness and human dignity meant the abolition of slavery completely, not simply a "nicer" form of slavery. In a similar way, a logical extension or trajectory of the redemptive spirit within the corporal punishment texts means the abolition of physical beatings (hitting or smacking) of children and bodily mutilations altogether. Softer and gentler beatings, while arguably better, do not offer the fullest expression or realization of redemptive movement. Likewise, less harsh mutilations (a finger chopped off instead of a hand)[23] are better than harsh forms, yet obviously not an ultimate ethical application of Scripture's original-setting incremental movement.

The ethics of violence used by police officers provides an excellent analogical case study. Most people are aware of various forms of violence that a police officer may reluctantly use in order to protect the public.

At times police use guns with bullets, stun guns, clubs, mace, physical grabbing, tackling a person to the ground, etc. But these procedures and the extent to which they are applied are governed by strict moral reasoning that delimits their use. In short, two main ethical guidelines (logical reasoning) direct the use of such violence: (1) *no violence* at all is permitted unless it is absolutely necessary for achieving policing goals; and (2) if violence is required, police are instructed to use the *least-violent* method(s) that will work. Should Christians ponder the first premise (no violence unless *absolutely* necessary), they will eventually realize that no violence is necessary for achieving parenting goals, so there is an ethical obligation to replace spanking—whether "two-smacks-max" or some other version—with effective non-corporal methods that are completely violence free. Once parents discover that they can discipline their children through loving and effective non-corporal means *with even better results*, a powerful case for change has been made. Once again, we should remember the "ShopVac" lesson and figure out which *components* within biblical instructions are truly sacrosanct.

Conclusion

At times, Marilyn and I describe our story of rethinking and replacing spanking as our "stumbling, bumbling parenting journey." You might say that we wandered backwards at times and awkwardly bumped our way along. Two things happened that permitted us in good conscience to change our minds and practices: (1) discovering effective non-corporal discipline strategies for raising children; and (2) rethinking what it means to live out biblical teaching. This chapter has primarily focused on the second part of that journey. It was essential for us as parents to understand that *functionality* in biblical meaning was far more important to God than instrumentality. As we grew in our ability to read the Bible *redemptively*, we became aware of our calling to live out the text's redemptive spirit and not simply remain bound to its concrete-specific meaning. This process involved wrestling through a trajectory or logical extension of the incremental, already redemptive movement seen in the biblical corporal punishment texts as they are read against the backdrop or context of their ancient world setting. At the end of the day we happily replaced spanking with methods that offered even better results.

Notes

1 Unless otherwise noted, all biblical passages that are used in this chapter are cited from the New International Version of the Bible.

2 The redemptive-movement or redemptive-trajectory perspective advocated in this chapter is more fully developed in my book, *Corporal Punishment in the Bible.* Should readers find some of the ideas helpful, that source will offer a fuller explanation and more supporting evidence. See William J. Webb, *Corporal Punishment in the Bible: A Redemptive-Movement Hermeneutic for Troubling Texts* (Downers Grove, IL: InterVarsity Press, 2011).

3 This summary of contemporary pro-spanking teaching reflects publications by Christian organizations such as Focus on the Family and their leading spokespersons (James Dobson; more recently, John Day) along with certain theologians: Andreas Köstenberger, Albert Mohler, Wayne Grudem, Paul Wegner, etc. For full bibliographic details, see Webb, *Corporal Punishment in the Bible*, 25–54.

4 The rod drives foolishness out of children (Proverbs 22:15) as well as adults (Proverbs 18:6; 19:29, 26:3; cf. 10:13); the use of the rod for beatings also encourages wisdom in children (Proverbs 29:15; cf. Sirach 30:12) and adults (Proverbs 29:19, 19:25). In other words, biblical teaching teaches the use of corporal punishment across all ages. It would be inconsistent for Christians to lobby their government to use corporal punishment on children but not for its use in society as a means of punishing adults.

5 For adults, the Bible teaches that the maximum number of strokes with a rod or lashes with a whip was forty (Deuteronomy 25:3). A reasonable inference is that for children and teenagers the number of strokes would clearly be less than forty but moving upwards, given the age of the child or teen. Placing a "two-smacks-max" cap on spanking for preschool children and then no spanking at all for teens hardly accords with the concrete-specific teaching of Scripture.

6 The bodily location is the back (Proverbs 10:13, 19:29, 26:3; cf. Isaiah 50:6) or sides (Sirach 30:12).

7 According to Proverbs 20:30, "blows that wound [bruise]" are viewed in a positive light; cf. the normative expectation of welts and wounds from beatings in Exodus 21:20–21; Sirach 23:10, 28:17; and (metaphorically) Isaiah 1:5–6.

8 Proverbs 22:15; cf. other texts already cited.

9 The Wisdom of Sirach teaches the parent not to spare the rod or whip: "He who loves his son will whip him often [frequently]" (Sirach 30:1). At another point the same wisdom text states in similar fashion that the repeatedly disobedient slaves will "never lack for bruising marks" (Sirach 23:10). Proverbs likewise encourages parents not to withhold the rod but to be diligent in its application (Proverbs 13:24).

10 God often mixes righteous anger with the use of his disciplinary rod (see Deuteronomy 8:5; Psalms 89:32; 2 Samuel 7:14; Proverbs 3:11–12 [cf. Hebrews 12:5–7] for the discipline parallel and other texts for connecting the rod and discipline to anger—Psalms 6:1, 38:1; Isaiah 10:5, 24–25, 30:30–31; Lamentations 3:1). True, we are not God. However, one can make this (reasonable) inference about an *assumed* biblical perspective by the authors on corporal punishment because the divine portrait is theological metaphor. That metaphor of beatings with the rod did not come out of thin air; it would have been derived almost certainly from Israel's societal and/or parenting practices.

11 William J. Webb, "Appendix: Response to Andreas Köstenberger," in *Corporal Punishment in the Bible*, 174–82. For other detractors, see Daniel M. Doriani, "A Response to William J. Webb," in *Four Views on Moving beyond the Bible to Theology,*

ed. Stanley N. Gundry and Gary T. Meadors (Grand Rapids, MI: Zondervan, 2009), 259; Thomas Schreiner, review of *Corporal Punishment in the Bible,* by William Webb, The Gospel Coalition, 12 September 2011, https://www.thegospelcoalition.org/reviews/corporal_punishment_in_the_bible.

12 Exodus 21:20–21; cf. 21:26–27.

13 Israel's judicial setting (not more than forty lashes) would have logically impacted the beating of adult slaves in the domestic setting. And since the household domain included beatings for both free and slave children, we must surmise that some sort of continuum existed and that these domestic punishments of both children and adults were conceptually connected.

14 For an extensive list of mutilation texts from ancient Sumer, Egypt, Babylon, Assyria, and Anatolia see Webb, *Corporal Punishment in the Bible*, 103–10.

15 Children: Proverbs 22:15, 29:15 (cf. Sirach 30:12). Adults: Proverbs 18:6, 19:25, 29, 26:3, 29:15, 19 (cf. Sirach 30:12).

16 In fact, God might well be more pleased with them for certain ethical reasons; see the discussion of how "least violence possible" impacts all ethical considerations in Webb, *Corporal Punishment in the Bible.*

17 In a closing section called "Postscript: An Unplanned Parenting Journey," we walk through some of the best (1) preventive discipline strategies, (2) corrective discipline strategies, and (3) practical resources. See Webb, *Corporal Punishment in the Bible*, 140–70. We raised three children, one with significant learning disabilities—that was our practical laboratory. But we also had the advantage of Marilyn's getting a master's degree in special education, working as a special education teacher in the Waterloo Board (ON), and in time, becoming a consultant to about twenty schools. She has spent her entire life working with children who present severe behavioural challenges. Simply put, she advocates for non-corporal methods that work well.

18 For the New Testament the social-world context is GR (Greco-Roman) and 2TJ (Second Temple Judaism).

19 Webb, *Corporal Punishment in the Bible*, 78–85 (for ANE rod and whip/beatings), and 103–9 (for ANE mutilation of bodily parts).

20 One could also reflect upon the redemptive-movement meaning found in passages curtailing the beating of slaves in Israel. Contrary to the broader ANE setting, where social control by masters at times led to beating of slaves to death or mutilating body parts (creating a public example for other slaves), Israel's laws prohibited the beatings from being life threatening, and if a beating resulted in bodily mutilation, the slave was to be set free. See Exodus 21:20–21, 26–27. On reading the slavery texts within a redemptive-movement framework, see Webb, *Corporal Punishment in the Bible*, 57–73.

21 The redemptive measures found in Israel's *domestic* punishments (family, civil, and criminal), as read within their ancient environment, mirror the incremental extensions of greater humanity and dignity in the treatment/punishing of their enemies in the *foreign* context of ancient warfare, often understood as "punishing" insubordinate nations. A survey of ancient war atrocities permits contemporary readers to see and hear the biblical war texts in fresh and redemptive ways and posit at least an intriguing logical correlation with the incremental ethic evident in the corporal punishment texts. See William J. Webb and Gordon K. Oeste, *Bloody, Brutal, and Barbaric? Wrestling with Troubling War Texts* (Downers Grove: InterVarsity Press, 2019), 263-87.

22 Clive Staples Lewis, *The Lion, the Witch and the Wardrobe* (London: Geoffrey Bless, 1950).

23 Deuteronomy 25:11–12. For a discussion of ancient world mutilation texts (part of the broader corporal punishment topic), see Webb, *Corporal Punishment in the Bible*, 97–118.

7

What Do We Do with Proverbs?

WILLIAM S. MORROW

This chapter takes as its starting point the position articulated by Joan Durrant and Bernadette Saunders (Chapters 2 and 3, respectively): modern social-scientific studies strongly suggest that corporal punishment is detrimental to healthy child development. Such information does not sit well with various constituencies in the Christian church who insist that the Bible authorizes parents to spank their children. The purpose of this essay is to make the case that scriptural teachings commending the physical punishment of children need not be pursued by contemporary Christians. Following the methods of biblical wisdom, there are grounds for supporting the sixth Call to Action of the Truth and Reconciliation Commission (TRC) and for advocating for the repeal of Section 43 of Canada's Criminal Code.

As biblical teachings that recommend the use of corporal punishment are found almost exclusively in the book of Proverbs, I begin by making some observations about the theological methods that underlie its collections of instructions. I then survey the counsels to use physical punishment found in Proverbs and how they are interpreted by modern advocates in the Christian church. The contemporary thinkers to whom I refer can be largely identified within the ambit of evangelical Protestantism. It will become clear that none of these writers actually follows the counsels of

Proverbs verbatim. Rather, they use various interpretative strategies to limit the applicability of its advice about corporal punishment.

The question that emerges is whether those same interpretative strategies can also be used to make the case that Christians should forego the corporal punishment of children altogether. I suggest that this possibility is inherent in the way in which biblical wisdom actually works. I will illustrate this claim with reference to the ways biblical thinkers qualify the wisdom tradition found in Proverbs. In addition, I will discuss a case in which a contemporary community of faith with a high regard for the authority of the Bible has departed from the plain meanings of biblical teachings as a result of fresh insights into the nature of the reality God has called into being. It will become clear that the major issue is not what the Christian scriptures may or may not say about bodily punishment of children, but the dangers of the practice itself.

Wisdom as a Method for Interpreting Reality

According to Proverbs 9:10, "the fear of the Lord (Yahweh) is the beginning of wisdom" (RSV, see also 1:7). This highly compressed statement has many implications for the search for wisdom. One of its meanings is that Yahweh was the source of the world order and therefore was not entirely bound by it.[1] In time, Israel's thinkers would come to equate the written Torah with divine wisdom;[2] however, the wisdom teachings of Proverbs do not show dependence on the Mosaic tradition.[3] On the contrary, they reflect a commitment to articulating life skills based on careful observation of the natural and social worlds.[4] In fact, the wisdom tradition of Proverbs makes no pretense to claiming an origin in divine revelation or inspiration: God is never quoted or addressed.[5]

The rationally acquired knowledge contained in Proverbs' collections of instructions and sayings was taken from disparate spheres of life, including the family and politics. Some of it was undoubtedly not native to Israel but was assimilated from other ancient Near Eastern cultures.[6] This observation is one indication that Israelite wisdom tradition was not a closed system of thought. Another indication of openness in Israel's wisdom tradition has to do with the fact the sages knew they had only partial knowledge of Yahweh and the world God had brought into being.[7] According to Proverbs, the wise person is someone who is always open to further instruction (e.g., 1:5; 9:9; 19:25).

That the wisdom of Proverbs was open to challenge or refinement can be seen in the ways some of its basic premises are qualified in the biblical canon. For example, in both Job and Ecclesiastes, crucial components of the ideology of the wise are disputed. Ecclesiastes, for example, calls into question the rationality of traditional wisdom's construction of the world order (e.g., Ecclesiastes 3:10–15).[8] Job, for its part, queries various assumptions of traditional wisdom, including the idea that distinctions between order and chaos can be rigidly maintained.[9] In both cases, these challenges are grounded in observation and experience.

As for the New Testament, Jesus said, "Every scribe who has been trained for the kingdom of heaven is like a householder who brings out of his treasure what is new and what is old" (Matthew 13:52). Evidently, the ethics of the kingdom permit one to evaluate the effectiveness of instructions in the Old Testament canon as a means for following Jesus. This is because Jesus himself is the wisdom of God incarnate.

One area of social organization Jesus queried was the wisdom tradition's prioritization of the family. For example, there is no authorization for the single life in Proverbs: it expected that its addressees were or would be married (e.g., 5:15–20). In a culture in which everyone was expected to marry, Jesus not only lived as a single person but taught that it was acceptable to remain unmarried for the sake of the kingdom of God (Matthew 19:12). Moreover, Jesus regarded discipleship as having such priority that it overrode normal filial obligations such as working for the family business (e.g., Mark 1:19–20) or ensuring a parent's proper burial (e.g., Luke 9:59–60). He also seems to have accepted the fact that discipleship had the capacity to tear ordinary family relationships apart (e.g., Luke 12:51–53; 14:26).

The wisdom of Jesus also touched on perceptions of subordinate family members, including wives and children. While some biblical traditions held a rather diffident view of the child,[10] Jesus seems to have had a very high regard for children, as Marcia Bunge (Chapters 8 and 11) points out.[11] In addition, adjustment in the morality of family relationships seems to have affected the early church. For example, the Pauline counsel in Ephesians 5:25 to husbands to love their wives as Christ loved the church suggests some kind of revision in the status of wives in Hellenistic marriages.[12]

A Brief Survey of Corporal Punishment in Proverbs

Corporal punishment is recommended in a number of passages in Proverbs, including the following:

> My son, do not despise the LORD's discipline (*mûsār*)
> or be weary of his reproof,
> for the LORD reproves him whom he loves,
> as a father the son (*bēn*) in whom he delights. (3:11–12)
>
> On the lips of him who has understanding (*nābōn*) wisdom is found, but a rod (*šēbeṭ*) is for the back of him who lacks sense (*ḥăsar lēb*). (10:13)
>
> He who spares the rod (*šēbeṭ*) hates his son (*bēn*),
> but he who loves him is diligent (*š-ḥ-r*) to discipline (*mûsār*) him. (13:24)
>
> Strike a scoffer, and the callow will gain shrewdness;
> reprove a man of understanding (*nābōn*), and he will gain knowledge. (19:25)
>
> Condemnation is ready for scoffers,
> and flogging for the backs of fools (*kĕsîlîm*). (19:29)
>
> Blows that wound cleanse away evil;
> strokes make clean the innermost parts. (20:30)
>
> Folly is bound up in the heart of a child (*naʿar*),
> but the rod (*šēbeṭ*) of discipline (*mûsār*) drives it far from him. (22:15)
>
> Do not withhold discipline (*mûsār*) from a child (*naʿar*);
> if you beat him with a rod (*šēbeṭ*), he will not die.
> If you beat him with the rod (*šēbeṭ*)
> you will save his life from Sheol. (23:13–14)
>
> A whip for the horse, a bridle for the ass,
> and a rod (*šēbeṭ*) for the back of fools (*kĕsîlîm*). (26:3)
>
> The rod (*šēbeṭ*) and reproof give wisdom,
> but a child (*naʿar*) left to himself brings shame to his mother. (29:15)

Discipline (*y-s-r*) your son (*bēn*), and he will give you rest;
he will give delight to your heart. (29:17)

By mere words a servant is not disciplined (*y-s-r*),
for though he understands, he will not give heed. (29:19)

These translations are from the Revised Standard Version (RSV). I have chosen this translation because it more clearly reflects the underlying Hebrew than some other modern translations. In a number of cases I have provided a transliteration of a key Hebrew term. In the brief commentary below, I will highlight three aspects of these scriptures: (1) the frequency of corporal punishment they recommend; (2) the sex and age of those who are to be so punished; and (3) the similarity in terms and context to other ancient Near Eastern cultures, especially Egypt.

The first thing to be noted is that the sages thought corporal punishment should be administered frequently.[13] Informative here is Proverbs 13:24. The Hebrew word behind the translation "diligently" is from the root š-*ḥ*-r. Verbs connected to this root mean to do something "wholeheartedly" and "eagerly."[14] The thought seems to be that one should discipline a child from an early age and do so persistently.[15] A similar idea occurs in the inter-testamental book of Jesus ben Sirach (Ecclesiasticus), who clearly stands in the tradition of Israelite wisdom:

He who loves his son will whip him often,
in order that he may rejoice at the way he turns out.
(Ecclesiasticus 30:1)

Proverbs' esteem for physical punishment is also implied by the word *mûsār*, which combines the sense of teaching on the one hand and beating on the other (3:11, 13:24, 22:15, 23:13).[16] Instructions to physically punish the son and the slave in 29:17 and 19 use a verb that comes from the same root as *mûsār* (*y-s-r).* Nor was beating conceived simply as punishment; it was for the purpose of asserting parental control.[17] This can be seen in sayings such as 26:3, which draws an analogy between the need to control domestic animals and the unintelligent, and the spectre of the wayward child in 29:15.

Second, it is noteworthy that all the passages above are confined to the education of young males. When singular terms are used, they are masculine in gender and reference. This is obvious in references to the son (*bēn*) in 3:12, 13:24, and 29:17. Moreover, where the RSV uses the word "child," the underlying Hebrew term is *naʿar*. In biblical Hebrew *naʿar* has both a literal and a metaphorical use. Although the word *naʿar* can refer to an adult male of any age in a subordinate position to a social superior, the references in Proverbs are to boys and young men. For example, a saying such as 19:29 must apply to the young, since they are the only ones a wise man would try to educate by the application of force.[18] The way in which the term *naʿar* is used in Proverbs makes the boys' age somewhat indeterminate.[19] However, it appears that the *naʿar* is sometimes conceived as a sexually mature teen. Note, for example, the overlap in the term *ḥăsar lēb* ("lacking sense") in 10:13 and the description of the senseless youth (*naʿar ḥăsar lēb*) as one who can be tempted by the "strange woman" (7:7).

Finally, the ideology implicated in Proverbs' commendation of beating for the education of boys has strong resonances in other ancient Near Eastern cultures. Significant here are parallels with the wisdom literature of Egypt;[20] for example,

- similar rhetoric is used to describe the "wise" and his opposite, "the fool";[21]
- both literatures place a premium on being cool-headed and circumspect in speech;[22] and
- both sets of writings use the word for "instruction" to connote both verbal reproof and physical punishment.[23]

As in Proverbs, there was a strong belief in the efficacy of corporal punishment for the education of sons, for the threat of beating occurs often in Egyptian wisdom texts concerned with education. Here are few examples:

> Spend no day in idleness or you shall be beaten, a boy's ear is upon his back, he harkens to his beater. (Papyrus Anastasi III 3,12–13)[24]
>
> Thoth has placed the stick on earth in order to teach the fool by it . . . A son does not die from being punished by his father. (Papyrus Insinger 9, 6–7)[25]
>
> You beat my back; your teaching entered my ear. (Papyrus Lansing 11,11–12)[26]
>
> I was brought up as a boy beside you, you smote my back and your teaching entered my ear. (Papyrus Anastasi IV 4, 8–15)[27]

Of course, such ideas were not confined to ancient Egypt. Similar sentiments can be found in Mesopotamian literature. Here is a citation from a collection of proverbs written in Aramaic that probably originated around the same time as the oldest collection in Proverbs (during the First Temple period). According to *The Words of Ahiqar*,

> Spare not your son from the rod,
> otherwise can you save him [from wickedness]?
> If I beat you, my son, [you will not die];
> but if I leave you alone [you will not live].
> A blow for a serving boy, a rebuke for a slave girl,
> and for all your servants, discipline![28]

Note that in this text, the child and slave more or less trade places in terms of their status in the family hierarchy. A similar observation can be made about the status of the child in Proverbs (compare 29:17 and 19).[29]

To summarize: the counsels of Proverbs recommend the frequent use of corporal punishment as a means for educating boys. In this, they closely resemble instructions in other wisdom collections of the ancient Near East.

Proverbs and Contemporary Christian Teachings Compared

The following statements are representative of arguments made by Christians who claim the Bible gives parents the right to administer corporal punishment to their children. Albert Mohler, president of Southern Baptist Theological Seminary, writes: "Of course, the Bible refers to punitive corporal punishment, not to injurious abuse. Parents should learn the method of judicial spanking, never using spanking as a demonstration of anger or wrath. As a judicial act, the spanking should be administered in a serious, private, and sober way by a parent who teaches the child that this punishment is necessary for the specific act of disobedience. Spanking is judicial in the sense that it is not the result of a parental loss of temper, nor of a parent's whim, but of moral necessity."[30] Baptist New Testament scholar Thomas Schreiner observes that "wisdom and prudence should be applied in understanding Proverbs, which means corporal punishment is not administered in the same way it is applied to law-breakers and adults. Nor is it evident that because both fools and children are flogged that the punishments would be of the same nature and to the same extent. . . . Using the same word for children and fools does not mean they are in the same category!"[31] Old Testament scholar Paul D. Wegner suggests that parenting advice in Proverbs can be systemized as follows:

> Level 1: Encourage proper behaviour . . . (Proverbs 1:8–9, 2:2–5, 3:13–15, 4:7–8)
>
> Level 2: Inform improper behaviour (Proverbs 1:10–15, 3:31–32)
>
> Level 3: Explain the negative consequences of sin (Proverbs 1:18–19, 5:3–6)
>
> Level 4: Gently exhort (Proverbs 4:1–2, 14–16)
>
> Level 5: Gently rebuke or reprove (Proverbs 3:12, 24:24–25)
>
> Level 6: Use corporal punishment that does not cause physical harm: A wise parent knows when to apply corporal, non-abusive punishment (Proverbs 13:24, 19:18, 23:13–14, 29:15)
>
> Level 7: Use corporal punishment that causes physical harm: the book of Proverbs does not suggest that parents employ this technique for discipline, but that serious sin can lead to serious punishment (Prov. 10:31; 20:30)
>
> Level 8: Punish with death: The book of Proverbs does not include this in the realm of parental discipline but in the realm of consequences meted out by government (or society's leaders)[32]

The Christian organization Focus on the Family advises parents: "Generally speaking, it's our view that corporal punishment should be applied only in cases of willful disobedience or defiance of authority—never for mere childish irresponsibility. It should never be administered harshly or impulsively. We also believe that spankings are not appropriate for children 15 to 18 months old or younger. And spanking an adolescent is almost always a serious mistake."[33]

All the writers cited above would claim the book of Proverbs as a biblical source that supports their position. However, as William J. Webb (Chapter 6) has pointed out, none of these positions fairly represents the thinking of Proverbs. For example, mainstream Christian writers on child discipline only recommend spanking with the hand. For them the stick (*šēbet*) of Proverbs is but a metaphor.[34] With respect to Mohler, Proverbs does not consider spanking as a judicial act, only to be employed in cases that warrant moral chastisement. On the contrary, it was considered a necessary and regular component in the training of boys. Schreiner's analysis makes assumptions about the status of children in the world view of Proverbs that cannot be sustained. In passages such as 10:1, 15:20, 17:21, and 19:13, it is clear that the "fool" is a young boy whose manners can be corrected.[35] Wegner's systematized conception of the stages of parental discipline has been cited approvingly by other Christian writers on the family.[36] His model suggests that Proverbs recommends several steps prior to the application of corporal punishment. However, both the wording of Proverbs and its original cultural context indicate that corporal punishment of boys was the preferred method of discipline. It was not used simply as a last resort in the administration of parental correction. The restrictions placed on the use of spanking by Focus on the Family are at odds with Proverbs. While it brands discipline of the adolescent as a "mistake," Proverbs has exactly the opposite perspective. By naming the boy as *na'ar,* Proverbs clearly intends its advice to include the physical punishment of teens.

Why is it that some contemporary Christians appeal to the teachings of Proverbs while so often qualifying its counsels on the use of corporal punishment? One way in which they have read Proverbs more moderately than it deserves is by ignoring its enmeshment with discourses on child-rearing in related ancient Near Eastern cultures. But there are other hermeneutical moves afoot as well. Christian writers such as those cited above would strenuously object to the premise that the counsels of Proverbs, as I have described them, should be woodenly applied.[37] According to the Reformed tradition, scripture interprets scripture. Following this, it is possible to discover a humanitarian ethic elsewhere in biblical literature that can control a literal appropriation of Proverbs.

Nevertheless, it is doubtful that the writers cited above are simply drawing from other biblical teachings. The idea that corporal punishment should be a last resort, with age-specific restrictions, and the advocacy of spanking with the hand and not a stick are hard-won lessons from observation that cannot be derived directly from the Bible. In applying a more measured and humane approach to the corporal punishment passages from Proverbs, these writers are engaged in interpretative strategies drawn directly from human experience. In effect, they have followed the method of biblical wisdom in allowing observations taken from their understanding of the world to qualify Proverbs' instructions on the use of corporal punishment.

To be sure, a desire to ameliorate the plain sense of Proverbs does not lead the writers cited above to relinquish the principle of corporal punishment. Some point out that there is one New Testament passage that appropriates the counsels of Proverbs in a way that appears to reinforce the conviction that physical correction of children has divine sanction. Hebrews 12 supports its argument with a citation of Proverbs 3:11–12. This passage was cited above and clearly stands in the context of a series of instructions that recommend that fathers use means of physical chastisement (*mūsār*) in raising their sons.[38]

In the context of Hebrews 12, the passage from Proverbs 3 is used as part of an argument in which those addressed by the letter are being urged to reframe their experiences of persecution. Their temptation is to abandon their Christian identity in order to avoid social oppression—a temptation which is described as a struggle against sin (v. 4). According to Hebrews 12, these persecutions are to be understood both as punishment for desiring to forego discipleship to Christ as well as a kind of schooling that produces Christian character.[39] This argument appeals to the metaphor of parental punishment found in Proverbs and it assumes that God is in control of the fate of the followers of Jesus. If God wills that they suffer persecution, this is for their own good, just as a father physically punishes his son so that the child will grow up correctly.[40]

The argument succeeds because the writer of Hebrews 12 assumes that his readers assent to the notion that parents should physically punish their children. Actually, sentiments such as those expressed by Hebrews 12 were commonly shared in the Hellenistic world.[41] In this regard, the cultural consensus of that time period shows no difference from the wisdom of child-rearing shared between Israel and the ancient Near East in the era in which the collections of Proverbs were composed.

Underlying the argument of Hebrews 12, however, are questions about justice that deserve to be further investigated. The presumption of the chapter is that when fathers punish their children it is for the sake of justice and in the spirit of righteousness. Ironically, those who are being persecuted in Hebrews 12 are subject to the actions of unrighteous, sinful agents who belong to the same category as those responsible for the crucifixion of Jesus. The fact that God permits the suffering of the church does not override the perception that what is happening to it on the human level is unjust—just as the belief that God permitted the death of Jesus does not negate the fact that he was killed by hostile sinners (Hebrews 12:3). Here I think we come to a fundamental difference in the wisdom of applying the metaphor of corporal punishment to divine action as opposed to human action. While the cross has a definite part to play in divine providence, there is a difference in how the cross applies to divine action and human agency. The crucifixion of Jesus was a sinful human action, even if it accomplished God's will in history. By the same token, the persecution of the church is a sinful action, even if it accomplishes God's will in history. This perception qualifies any blanket acceptance of the right of parents to physically punish their children. It is imperative that they not act toward them in a manner that inadvertently puts children on the cross. In this regard, Hebrews 12 does not resolve the question about the wisdom of using corporal punishment as a means of child-rearing. We are still left with the need to mediate between appropriating the counsels of Proverbs metaphorically and literally.

Seeking Wisdom in the Contemporary Debate on Corporal Punishment

Should Christians be constrained by the teachings of Proverbs with regard to the use of corporal punishment? Any response to this question has to begin with an appreciation of the origins of the instructions in Proverbs to administer physical punishment to children. These instructions reflect the cultural consensus of the ancient world. They were the product of human observation and reason by the sages of the time, and by no means were they exclusive to Israel or early Judaism. Such instructions are not immune from question; they are open to qualification because of the methodology for the acquisition of wisdom implicated in the biblical canon. Above I described the method of wisdom teaching as one that assumed that the created order was only partially known by the sages of ancient Israel. The contingent nature of Proverbs' teachings on corporal punishment is clear from the ways in which biblical wisdom is generated. There was an openness to the possibility that new knowledge about the life skills required to succeed in the created order could be acquired. This is apparent in approaches applied to traditional wisdom categories in both the Old and New Testaments.

Similar approaches can be found in church history.[42] The example I will use is the rejection of alcohol consumption in some Christian traditions. Not so long ago, Protestant evangelical churches played an important role in advocating for temperance and prohibition throughout North America.[43] Although modern evangelical Christians are divided on the question of whether one should or should not consume alcohol, contemporary advocacy for total abstinence continues in the Southern Baptist Convention, which reaffirmed its opposition to alcohol in 2006 in the following terms: "Years of research confirm biblical warnings that alcohol leads to physical, mental, and emotional damage (e.g., Proverbs 23:29–35) . . . [We] express our total opposition to the manufacturing, advertising, distributing, and consuming of alcoholic beverages. . . . We urge Southern Baptists to take an active role in supporting legislation that is intended to curb alcohol use in our communities and nation."[44]

Two observations are warranted. First, while biblical warnings are highlighted in this resolution, passages that regard alcohol usage more positively are ignored. Indeed, supporters of banning alcohol must explain them away,[45] for while there are a number of passages that warn against the abuse of alcohol, there is no blanket condemnation of alcohol in the Bible. For example, the book of Proverbs, for all its diffidence about imbibing liquor, actually recommends providing strong drink to the poor and hapless (31:6–7). Psalm 104:14–15 speaks of wine as a gift of God that "makes the heart glad." In the New Testament, Paul commends the use of alcohol for medicinal reasons (1 Timothy 5:23), and according to John 2, Jesus turned water into wine at the wedding feast in Cana.

The second point concerns the call by the Southern Baptist Convention to lobby the state to regulate rights to manufacture and sell alcohol. This is important because one argument made in favour of retaining Section 43 of the Criminal Code is that its repeal would interfere with scripturally given parental rights. Fidelity to the Christian revelation certainly authorizes the church to keep a critical eye on the operations of the state. Nevertheless, while there is no unqualified endorsement of the power of the state in the Bible, scripture clearly grants governments a place in the divine economy to oppose unrighteous conduct (Romans 13). Evidently, the Southern Baptist Convention believes the manufacture and consumption of alcohol constitute unrighteous conduct that the state ought to control. Are there grounds for Christians to conclude that the corporal punishment of children might represent unrighteous conduct as well?

These considerations suggest a model for addressing the debate over corporal punishment in the contemporary Christian church. Those who advocate corporal punishment do so because they believe it can be applied without harming the child. In other words, they are confident that it is a practice that is not, in and of itself, intrinsically dangerous to the welfare of children.[46] But what if, on the basis of close observation of the world that divine wisdom has called into being, the church comes to a different conclusion? It is at this point that the dangers of corporal punishment need to be acknowledged.[47] In Chapters 2 and 3 of this volume, Joan Durrant and Bernadette Saunders have presented a substantial body of contemporary evidence showing that corporal punishment is much more harmful to the development of children than previous generations thought.

With respect to biblical teachings on the corporal punishment of children, the church must ask itself where wisdom lies. The Southern Baptists are quite right: no modern health authority considers it a good idea that those in deep distress should "drink and forget their poverty and remember their misery no more" (Proverbs 31:7). Why should it still be a good idea to permit parents to strike their children when the results of a sustained observation of God's world show that it is detrimental to child development?

The methods of biblical wisdom provide ample reason to call into question a defence for the corporal punishment of children on the basis of the instructions of Proverbs. If certain communities continue to insist on following its advice, the real problem is not what is said in the Bible, it is that they do not believe the practice is dangerous enough to prohibit. If they did, the means for abrogating the corporal punishment passages in Proverbs are available by following the methods for acquiring wisdom sanctioned in and by the Christian scriptures.

Notes

1 Gerhard von Rad, *Wisdom in Israel* (London: SCM, 1972), 63–64.

2 See, for example, Ecclesiasticus 24.

3 von Rad, *Wisdom in Israel*, 95–96.

4 James L. Crenshaw, *Old Testament Wisdom: An Introduction*, rev. ed. (Louisville, KY: Westminster John Knox, 1998), 55.

5 Michael J. Fox, *Proverbs 1–9: A New Translation with Introduction and Commentary*, The Anchor Bible 18A (New Haven, CT: Yale University Press, 2008), 7.

6 Grant R. Osborne, *The Hermeneutical Spiral: A Comprehensive Introduction to Biblical Interpretation* (Downers Grove, IL: InterVarsity, 1991), 191.

7 von Rad, *Wisdom in Israel*, 72–73.

8 Crenshaw, *Old Testament Wisdom*, 117.

9 William S. Morrow, "Toxic Religion and the Daughters of Job," *Studies in Religion* 27, no. 3 (1998): 263–76.

10 See, for example, T.M. Lemnos, "Did the Ancient Israelites Think Children Were People?," *Bible History Daily* (blog), Biblical Archeology Society, accessed 16 March

2018, https://www.biblicalarchaeology.org/daily/biblical-topics/bible-interpretation/ancient-israel-children-personhood/.

11 Marcia J. Bunge, "Christianity's Commitments to Nurturing and Protecting Children: Biblical Foundations," *Journal of Abuse and Neglect* 38 (2014): 580–81; see also Keith J. White, "'He Placed a Little Child in the Midst': Jesus, the Kingdom and Children," in *The Child in the Bible*, ed. Marcia J. Bunge, Terence E. Fretheim, and Beverly Roberts Gaventa (Grand Rapids, MI: William B. Eerdmans, 2008), 353–74.

12 Elna Mouton, "Reimagining Ancient Household Ethos? On the Implied Rhetorical Effect of Ephesians 5:21–33," *Neotestamentica* 48, no.1 (2014): 163–85.

13 Crenshaw, *Old Testament Wisdom*, 69.

14 See D.J.A. Clines, ed., *The Dictionary of Classical Hebrew* (Sheffield: Sheffield Phoenix, 2011), 8:324–25.

15 Fox, *Proverbs 10–31*, 571.

16 Crenshaw, *Old Testament Wisdom*, 69.

17 Fox, *Proverbs 10–31*, 839.

18 Fox, 792.

19 The biblical word *na'ar* can designate children as young as infants and as old as twenty; see G.J. Botterweck, H.-J. Fabry, and H. Ringgren, eds., *The Theological Dictionary of the Old Testament* (Grand Rapids, MI: Eerdmans, 1998), 9:480–81.

20 Crenshaw, *Old Testament Wisdom*, 44.

21 Nili Shupak, *Where Can Wisdom Be Found? The Sage's Language in the Bible and in Ancient Egyptian Literature*, Orbis Biblicus et Orientalis 130 (Fribourg: Universitätsverlag; Göttingen: Vandenhoeck & Ruprecht, 1993), 348.

22 Shupak, 167.

23 Shupak, 49.

24 Cited in Shupak, 49.

25 Shupak, 49–50.

26 Cited in John T. Fitzgerald, "Proverbs 3:11–12, Hebrews 12:5–6, and the Tradition of Corporal Punishment," in *Scripture and Traditions: Essays in Early Judaism and Christianity in Honor of Carl R. Holladay*, ed. P. Gray and G.R. O'Day (Leiden: Brill, 2008), 298.

27 Fitzgerald, 298n30.

28 J.M. Lindenberger, "The Words of Ahiqar," vi, 3–5, in *The Old Testament Pseudepigrapha*, vol. 2, ed. James H. Charlesworth (Garden City, NY: Doubleday, 1985), 498. Portions in square brackets are restorations based on parallel texts.

29 William P. Brown, "To Discipline without Destruction: The Multifaceted Profile of the Child in Proverbs," in *The Child in the Bible*, ed. Marcia Bunge, Terence E. Fretheim, and Beverly Roberts Gaventa (Grand Rapids, MI: William B. Eerdmans, 2008), 66.

30 Albert Mohler, "Commentary: Should Spanking Be Banned? Parental Authority under Assault," Albert Mohler, personal website, 24 June 2004, https://albertmohler.com/2004/06/22/should-spanking-be-banned-parental-authority-under-assault/.

31 Thomas Schreiner, Review of *Corporal Punishment in the Bible*, by William J. Webb, The Gospel Coalition, 12 September 2011, https://www.thegospelcoalition.org/reviews/corporal_punishment_in_the_bible/.

32 Paul D. Wegner, "Discipline in the Book of Proverbs: 'To Spank or Not to Spank,'"

Journal of the Evangelical Theological Society 48, no. 4 (2005): 720–28.

33 Focus on the Family, "Questions about Spanking," Focus on the Family, accessed 21 October 2018, https://www.focusonthefamily.com/family-q-and-a/parenting/questions-about-spanking.

34 William J. Webb, *Corporal Punishment in the Bible: A Redemptive-Movement Hermeneutic for Troubling Texts* (Downers Grove, IL: InterVarsity Press, 2011), 25–28.

35 Shupak, *Where Can Wisdom Be Found?*, 202.

36 See, for example, Andreas J. Köstenberger, *God, Marriage, and Family: Rebuilding the Biblical Foundation* (Wheaton, IL: Crossway, 2010), 145; Andy D. Naselli, "Training Children for Their Good," *Journal of Discipleship and Family Ministry* 3, no. 2 (2013), 48–64.

37 See, for example, Köstenberger, *God, Marriage and Family*, 342–43n37; Walter Kaiser Jr., "A Response to William J. Webb," in *Four Views on Moving beyond the Bible to Theology*, ed. S.N. Gundry (Grand Rapids, MI: Zondervan, 2009), 252.

38 See, for example, Köstenberger, *God, Marriage, and Family*, 342n28; Naselli, "Training Children for Their Good," 57. The author of Hebrews 12 has used the translation of this passage contained in the Old Greek version called the Septuagint, in which the allusion to corporal punishment is even more apparent than in the Hebrew original; see Fitzgerald, "Proverbs 3:11–12," 317.

39 Ched Spellman, "The Drama of Discipline: Toward an Intertextual Profile of *Paideia* in Hebrews 12," *Journal of the Evangelical Theological Society* 59, no. 3 (2016): 487–506.

40 Fitzgerald, "Proverbs 3:11–12," 312–13; Spellman, "The Drama of Discipline," 494–95.

41 Fitzgerald, 314–16.

42 An example I will not discuss here, but which bears careful reflection, is the decision by the entire Western church to forego a literal interpretation of biblical injunctions against lending money at interest (Exodus 22:25; Leviticus 25:35–37; and Deuteronomy 23:19–20) in the sixteenth and seventeenth centuries. See, for example, Mark Valeri, "The Christianization of Usury in Early Modern Europe," *Interpretation* 65, no. 2 (2011): 142–52; Charles R. Geisst, *Beggar Thy Neighbor: A History of Usury and Debt* (Philadelphia: University of Pennsylvania, 2013), 73–90.

43 Joe L. Coker, *Liquor in the Land of the Lost Cause: Southern White Evangelicals and the Prohibition Movement* (Lexington, KY: University Press of Kentucky, 2007), 15–16.

44 Southern Baptist Convention, *On Alcohol Use in America*, Southern Baptist Convention, Greensboro, NC, 2006, accessed 19 October 2018, http://www.sbc.net/resolutions/1156.

45 See, for example, Richard Land and Barrett Duke, "The Christian and Alcohol," *Criswell Theological Review* 5, no. 2 (2008): 33.

46 Of the writers cited in this paper, see, for example, Köstenberger, *God, Marriage and the Family*, 144; Naselli, "Training Children for Their Good," 56–57; Wegner, "Discipline in the Book of Proverbs," 729–31.

47 See, for example, Joan E. Durrant, Ron Ensom, and Coalition on Physical Punishment of Children and Youth, *Joint Statement on Physical Punishment of Children and Youth* (Ottawa: Coalition on Physical Punishment of Children and Youth, 2004), available through http://www.cheo.on.ca/en/physicalpunishment.

8

The Significance of Robust Theologies of Childhood for Honouring Children's Full Humanity and Rejecting Corporal Punishment

MARCIA J. BUNGE

Although Christians worldwide generally agree that they are called to love and care for children, they sometimes disagree about the best approaches to raising them. One particular area of debate is whether or not children should be physically punished. Christians living in countries in which such acts are culturally normative and/or allowed by law openly debate whether they are appropriate. Even in countries in which physical punishment is illegal and perhaps rarely debated in the Church or public life, individual Christians do not always agree with the law. They might follow the law but believe that physically punishing children out of love is in line with biblical and Christian values and can at times be appropriate. Thus, the corporal punishment of children is still up for debate within many individual Christian families and congregations across denominations and ecclesiastical institutions worldwide.

This debate is dominated by not only references to passages in Proverbs (which were probed in Chapters 6 and 7) but also by underlying assumptions about children. Sometimes these assumptions reflect simplistic views of children that diminish their complexity and integrity, thereby undermining genuine and productive debate and discussion. Current and past debates about spanking among Christian communities in the United

States, for example, both today and in the past, often refer to children in one-dimensional terms. Some speak of children mainly as innocent and vulnerable, thereby rejecting corporal punishment but often underestimating adult responsibilities for teaching and guiding children and helping them develop morally and spiritually. Others have tended to view children primarily as sinful and in need of instruction, thereby emphasizing the need to guide, discipline, and at times physically punish them but underestimating the vulnerabilities of children and the lessons that they might teach adults. These and other examples of simplistic assumptions about children, which can be found in churches and cultures around the world, tend to derail our conversations about physical punishment, undermine our commitment to children, and have serious consequences for children themselves.

Thus, in addition to discussing interpretations of Proverbs, Christians worldwide can enrich the debate about the physical punishment of children by placing it within broader theological frameworks for thinking about our overall conceptions of and commitments to children. Such frameworks are called "theologies of childhood." Whether or not we acknowledge it, Christians and non-Christians alike carry assumptions about and conceptions of children that influence their treatment of them. Theologies of childhood help Christians evaluate critically their assumptions about children, broaden their conceptions of them, strengthen their commitments to them, and guide ethical decision making about challenges facing children.

The aim of this chapter is to introduce the task and sources of theologies of childhood, to outline one example of a theology of childhood, and to draw implications for directly addressing debates about the physical punishment of children. Building on research I have pursued on views of children in the Bible and Christian theological traditions,[1] I have articulated a particular theology of childhood that highlights six conceptions of and commitments to children. All six of these perspectives, when held together rather than in isolation, broaden our conception of children and strengthen our commitment to them. I have discovered the significance of these six perspectives for my own relationships to children and youth and for a range of child-related issues in the Church, such as parenting, faith formation, and child advocacy. In this chapter, I focus directly on the issue of physical punishment. Building on this theology of childhood and insights from the social sciences, I show that the physical punishment of children is inconsistent with central Christian conceptions of and commitments to children. Thus, the Church worldwide should reject all forms of physical punishment of children, even so-called mild forms, and advocate for laws to prohibit it. By considering just one example of a theology of childhood, we can see the power and potential of vibrant theological understandings of children for informing the debate about physical punishment as well as other issues regarding child well-being.

The Task and Sources of Theologies of Childhood

The task of any theology of childhood, simply stated, is to develop more biblically and theologically informed conceptions of and commitments to children. Strong theologies of childhood, like other forms of theological reflection on particular ethical issues, such as theologies of just war, theologies of the Church, or theologies of human sexuality, tend to build on four primary sources: (1) the Bible, (2) insights from the Christian tradition (thought and practice), (3) knowledge from disciplines outside theology (such as from the social sciences, humanities, and natural sciences), and (4) the experience of individuals and communities past and present. In addition to building on these and other common sources of theological reflection, a person's theology of childhood will also be informed by his or her distinct religious tradition, particular faith community, and specific cultural and political context. Thus, theologies of childhood, like all forms of contemporary theology, are bound to be diverse and to take varied approaches in the worldwide Church.

Just as Christians have served churches by building on these sources to develop theologies on a number of subjects of common concern, Christian thinkers serve the entire Church by crafting theologies of childhood. Many contemporary theologies today, such as liberation theologies, feminist theologies, and black theologies, have strengthened the Church's commitment to and understanding of groups that have often been voiceless, marginalized, or oppressed. In the same way, those who seek to carry out the task of theologies of childhood focus on one of the most voiceless and vulnerable groups on the planet: children and youth. Special attention to children and childhood is an urgent theological task because although children are part of every community, many contemporary forms of theology worldwide today offer little serious reflection on their lives. Even among contemporary feminist and womanist theologies, little attention is given to children.[2]

A Robust Theology of Childhood

Informed by my own studies of the Bible and the Christian tradition, I have discovered that although Christians past and present have often viewed children in narrow and even destructive ways, the Bible and the Christian tradition express six insightful and central perspectives on children and our obligations to them. By holding these six perspectives in tension, rather than in isolation, we can broaden our conception of children and strengthen our commitment to them in families and in all areas of the Church. Here I briefly describe these six perspectives (which I have used and discussed extensively in my work)[3] and then draw new and direct implications for physical punishment specifically.

1. Children Are Gifts of God and Sources of Joy

Adults are to enjoy and be grateful for them

The Bible and the Christian tradition often depict children as gifts of God and sources of joy who ultimately come from God and belong to God. Since they are gifts of God and sources of joy, adults are to enjoy and be grateful for children. Many passages in the Bible speak of children as gifts of God, signs of God's blessing, or sources of joy. In Genesis 21:6–7, Sarah rejoices at the birth of her son, Isaac. In Luke 1:14, the angel promises Zechariah and Elizabeth that their child will bring them "joy and gladness." In the gospel of John 16:21, Jesus says, "When a woman is in labour, she has pain. . . . But when her child is born, she no longer remembers the anguish because of the joy of having brought a human being into the world."[4]

Many Christian theologians have emphasized this biblical theme. For example, the seventeenth-century Moravian bishop, theologian, and educator Johannes Amos Comenius states that children are dearer than "gold and silver, than pearls and gems."[5] Martin Luther, the sixteenth-century reformer, who was the biological father of three sons and three daughters and took in four orphans, speaks of children throughout his writings as "treasures from heaven," "blessings from God," and "great gifts."

2. Children Are Fully Human and Made in the Image of God

Adults are to treat them with dignity and respect

The Bible and the Christian tradition also emphasize that children are whole and complete human beings who are made in the image of God. They are fully human. Thus, adults are to treat children, like all people, with dignity and respect. The basis of this claim is Genesis 1:27, which states that God made humankind, male and female, in God's image. It follows that children, like adults, possess the fullness of humanity. Regardless of race, gender, age, or class, they have intrinsic value.

Although some of us might consider it self-evident that infants and children are human beings, in many places and times, including today, many have considered them not fully human. Over the centuries, children have been described and perceived as property, animals, beasts, pre-rational, pre-human, almost human, not quite human, or on their way to being human. Roman law, for example, considered children to be property, and a father could legally allow unwanted infants to die. Contrary to Roman law, early Christians, like Jews, consistently rejected infanticide. Early theologians such as Cyprian said all people, even infants, are "alike and equal since they have been made once by God." All share a "divine and spiritual equality."[6]

3. Children Are Vulnerable Orphans, Neighbours, and Strangers
Adults are to provide for, protect, and seek justice for all children

Many biblical passages emphasize that children are also orphans, neighbours, and strangers; they are among the most voiceless and vulnerable and are often victims of injustice. The Bible also commands adults to provide for, protect, and seek justice for *all* children, including orphans, the poor, and the marginalized. Adults are to care not only for their own children but also for all children in need. Numerous biblical passages explicitly command us to love and to seek justice for the most vulnerable—widows, orphans, and strangers. Deuteronomy 10:18–19, for example, states: God "executes justice for the orphan and the widow" and "loves the strangers, providing them food and clothing. You shall also love the stranger, for you were strangers in the land of Egypt." Christian obligations to children are also grounded in Jesus's command to "love the Lord your God with all your heart" and "your neighbour [even your enemies] as yourself" (Luke 10:27; see also Matthew 22:37–40 and Mark 12:30–31). In the gospels, Jesus shows compassion directly to children. He welcomes them, receives them, touches them, and heals them. He takes them up in his arms and blesses them.

Informed by these and other passages, many Christians around the world help feed and clothe children and advocate for children's rights and for political policies that protect children and families. This commitment to children is a task shared by Christian families and congregations, and a host of national and international faith-based organizations, agencies, hospitals, clinics, and child advocacy and lobbying ministries. There are many powerful stories in the past and today of Christians who looked outside their doorways, saw children in need, and responded. In many cases, they started with nothing, but their efforts blossomed and thrived.[7]

4. Children Are Developing Beings Who Need Instruction and Guidance

Adults are to instruct, guide, and bring them up in the faith, helping them to love God and neighbour

A fourth central view of children expressed in the Bible and Christian traditions is that children are still developing and need instruction and guidance; adults are to bring up children in the faith, helping them to love God and their neighbours as themselves. Several biblical texts address these responsibilities. For example, Christians, like Jews, refer to the famous lines from Deuteronomy 6:5–7: "You shall love the Lord your God with all your heart, and with all your soul, and with all your might. Keep these words that I am commanding you today in your heart. Recite them to your children and talk about them when you are at home and when you are away, when you lie down and when you rise." This text and others encourage us to teach and talk about faith with children and youth in our daily lives.

There are also many examples in the Christian tradition of theologians who took seriously the spiritual formation and education of children. One finds attention to children throughout this history of Christianity, such as in the works of John Chrysostom in the fourth century; Martin Luther and John Calvin in the sixteenth century; Comenius in the seventeenth century; and Schleiermacher in the nineteenth century.[8] All of them wrote and preached about the faith formation of children, and they wrote catechisms and other materials for use in the home to help parents teach their children. In his *Large Catechism*, Luther said, "If we want able and qualified persons as civil and spiritual leaders, then we really must spare no toil, trouble, or cost in teaching and educating our children to serve God and humanity."[9]

Parents, church leaders, and other caring adults have found ways to help nurture the moral and spiritual lives of children in a number of ways. They build trusting relationships and strengthen faith through a variety of spiritual practices, such as reading the Bible, worshipping, praying, singing, serving others, or participating in the sacraments. Such practices have a very long tradition in the Church throughout the world and across centuries. They are powerful vehicles for creating a space for the Holy Spirit to work in our lives and to open our hearts (at any age) to God and our neighbour. Christian communities also incorporate such practices into a host of creative programs, initiatives, and activities for young people, such as youth and family ministries, religious education programs, Bible camps, music camps, national youth conventions, campus ministries, service projects, and mission trips.

The tasks of teaching children and bringing them up in the faith are often discussed by Christians in relationship to the word "discipline." In Paul's letter to the Ephesians, for example, Paul warns parents, "Do not provoke your children to anger, but bring them up in the discipline and instruction of the Lord" (Ephesians 6:4). However, "discipline" is a word that is interpreted in a variety of ways across centuries and today. It is discussed in a focused way in a later chapter (Chapter 11).

5. Children Are Social Agents with Growing Moral Capacities and Responsibilities

Adults are to model for them compassion and accountability, and cultivate with them practices of mutual confession, forgiveness, and renewal

Many forms of Christianity express the notion that children are moral agents with growing capacities and responsibilities. Adults can help children by modelling for them compassion and accountability, and adults can cultivate with children practices and patterns of confession, forgiveness, and renewal.

The not-uncommon Christian view that understands children as having sinful tendencies is based on interpretations of several biblical texts. For example, Genesis states that every inclination of the human heart is "evil from youth" (Genesis 8:21), and in Proverbs we read that folly is "bound up in the heart" of children (Proverbs 22:15). The Psalms declare that "the wicked go astray from the womb; they err from their birth" (Psalms 58:3; cf. 51:5). Paul writes that all people are "under the power of sin" and that "there is no one who is righteous, not even one" (Romans 3: 9–10; cf. 5:12).

Building on such texts, Christian theologians generally underscore two related points. On the one hand, they often claim children are born in a "state of sin"; they live in a world that is not what it ought to be. Their parents are not perfectly loving and just; social institutions that support them, such as schools and governments, are not free from corruption; and the communities in which they live, no matter how safe, have elements of injustice and violence. On the other hand, theologians also claim that children possess growing moral capacities and responsibilities and that as children develop, they sometimes carry out "actual sins." As they develop, they can sometimes act in ways that are self-centred, unjust, and harmful to themselves and others; they sometime "miss the mark," hurt others, and thus bear some degree of responsibility for their actions.

Views of children as exclusively sinful have often warped Christian approaches to children and led in some cases to child abuse and even death. However, the recognition that children are driven toward autonomy, risk-taking, and experimentation corrects a simplistic view of children as pure and innocent. The latter view leaves no room for appreciating a child's own growing moral agency or levels of accountability, or for talking to children about the impact of their actions on others (Chapter 2).

Thus, language that connects children and an emerging morality, when used in the context of children's healthy psychological development, can strengthen our awareness of a child's growing moral capacities and responsibilities, and it gives us language to talk with children about human mistakes and shortcomings—theirs and ours—as well as the lifelong importance of forgiving ourselves and others. Since children, as they grow, both experience the harms caused by others and at times cause harm to others, adults can help children by modelling for them compassion and accountability, and adults can cultivate with children practices and patterns of accountability, forgiveness, and renewal. When we say to children, "I'm sorry. I made a mistake. Can you forgive me?," we teach them as much about ourselves as about them and create deep adult-child connections.[10]

6. Children Are Models of Faith and Endowed with Particular Strengths, Gifts, and Talents to Contribute to the Common Good Now and in the Future

Adults are to listen to and learn from them, honour their contributions, and provide them with an education

The Bible also claims that children are often models of faith for adults and that they are endowed with particular strengths, gifts, and talents. Thus, adults do not just teach children. From a biblical perspective, we are to listen to and learn from them, honour their current relationship with God and their contributions to families and communities, and provide them with an excellent education so that they can continue to cultivate their gifts and talents and contribute to the common good, both now and in the future.

The Bible depicts children and young people in striking and even radical ways as models of faith, positive agents of change, and prophets, such as in the stories of the boy Samuel (1 Samuel 2–4) and the young David (1 Samuel 17). In all three synoptic gospels, Jesus identifies himself with children and lifts them up as paradigms of receiving the reign of God, saying, "Truly I tell you, whoever does not receive the kingdom of God as a little child will never enter it" (Mark 10:13–16). Each synoptic gospel also gives an account of Jesus welcoming and blessing little children.[11] The Bible proclaims that children are Spirit-filled. God's Spirit is not limited by a person's age; it is already working in children and young people. Biblical passages depict children and infants praising God (Psalms 8:2; Matthew 21:15). As the book of Acts declares, God's Spirit will be poured out "upon all flesh, and your sons and your daughters shall prophesy, and your young men shall see visions" (Acts 2:17; cf. Joel 2:28–32). In these and other ways, the Bible depicts children as filled with the Spirit, models for adults, positive agents of change, prophets, and endowed with gifts and talents.

Holding All Six Perspectives in Tension

A strong and biblically based view of children holds all six perspectives in tension rather than in isolation. Although these six perspectives provide us with a rich view of children and of adult-child relationships, Christians today and in the past have often focused narrowly on one or two of these biblical themes. However, if we neglect any one of them, our conceptions of children become narrow and distorted, and we risk treating children in inadequate and harmful ways.

We can find many examples of such dangers in churches today and in the past. If we say, for example, that children are primarily gifts of God and sources of joy, then we might delight in them but neglect to nurture and guide them. If we believe that children are primarily moral agents, in need of instruction, then we might do much to educate them but neglect to delight in them and enjoy them. If we view children primarily as victims, we might not hear their own voices and recognize their own strengths and agency. If we perceive children mainly as social agents and participants, then we might recognize their gifts and strengths but neglect to protect and guide them. If we focus primarily on nurturing only our "own" children, then we might overlook the responsibility of reaching out to all children.

We can avoid these and other dangers by incorporating a complex view of children that holds together these six biblical perspectives. Even though these six perspectives are not exhaustive, they remind us of the complexity and dignity of children and help combat simplistic and distorted views of children in Christian communities of faith and in the wider culture. Children are not one-dimensional creatures who are either innocent or sinful, victims or agents. These six multi-dimensional and biblically based perspectives help us view children as (1) fully human and made in the image of God, yet still developing and in need of instruction and guidance; (2) gifts of God and sources of joy, yet also capable of selfish actions; and (3) vulnerable and in need of protection, yet also strong, insightful models of faith endowed with gifts to serve others.

This complex view of children honours the complexity of child-adult relationships and adult obligations to children, emphasizing that adults are not only to protect, provide, and teach children but also to enjoy, respect, and learn from them. Together, these six perspectives help us to maintain a multi-dimensional and vibrant view of children and to develop meaningful and textured relationships with them.

Implications for Debates about Corporal Punishment

If we consider these six perspectives and Jesus's own example, we find a strong case for rejecting corporal punishment in Christian homes and congregations—and for becoming strong advocates against it. A robust theology of childhood gives us a rich and multi-dimensional perspective that demands that we honour the full humanity of children by treating them tenderly and respectfully, teaching and learning from them, and never harming them.

Such a theology of childhood aligns with Jesus's own teaching and treatment of children. At a time when children occupied a low position in society and child abandonment was not a crime, the gospels portray Jesus as blessing children, welcoming them, embracing them, touching them, healing them, laying his hands on them, and praying for them. He also rebukes those who turn them away and even lifts children up as models of faith and says, "Let the little children come to me, and do not stop them; for it is to such as these that the kingdom of heaven belongs" (Matthew19:14). Furthermore, he equates welcoming a child in his name to welcoming himself and the one who sent him (Luke 9:48).[12]

If we also pay attention to the social sciences and to testimonies of victims of physical punishment, then the theological case against corporal punishment in any form is even more compelling. As the social scientific literature now suggests, corporal punishment is harmful to healthy child development and negatively affects lifelong health (Chapter 2). Furthermore, testimonies, interviews, and qualitative studies of those who have been abused or physically punished as children reveal their feelings of anger, shame, and fear (Chapter 3). Even "mild" forms of physical punishment are negative experiences in children's lives and do not achieve parents' goals of helping children to know right from wrong or to stay out of harm's way.[13]

If we combine insights from the Bible, the Christian theological tradition, the social sciences, and the perspectives of children, we see evidence on every side for eliminating corporal punishment. All six perspectives outlined above give grounds for rejecting corporal punishment.

First, if we truly see children as treasures and gifts of God, then would we not want to show them the delight we take in them, openly express our gratitude to God for them, and treat them with reverence and tenderness? What room is there in such a picture of adult-child relationships for slapping, hitting, swatting, and spanking?

Second, if we truly see children as fully human and made in the image of God, then would we not treat them as full and equal members of our communities, worthy of dignity and respect? How could we "bracket out" some groups of children (such as, in Canada, those aged two to twelve) for corporal punishment when we do not allow such punishment as appropriate for adults? In what way does spanking or swatting children convey to them their full humanity and dignity and our respect for them as fully human and made in the image of God? In the words of child development specialist Haim Ginott: "When a child hits a child, we call it aggression. When a child hits an adult, we call it hostility. When an adult hits an adult, we call it assault. When an adult hits a child, we call it discipline."[14] This logic just does not make sense.

Third, if we claim that we are to protect and seek justice for the most vulnerable, then would we not seek to protect all children from harm and provide the basic security they need to thrive? If the evidence indicates that even "mild" physical punishment harms child development and can lead to increasingly severe violence, then what role could it possibly play in child protection?

Fourth, if we understand that children are still developing and that we are to instruct, guide, and bring them up in the faith, helping them love God and neighbour, and if we know that physically punishing children thwarts learning, then what role can it play in our efforts to bring up our children in the faith and nurture their spiritual development? The Bible, the Christian tradition, social scientific studies of the faith formation of children, and our own experiences all point to the power of spiritual practices such as praying, studying God's word, worshipping, talking about our faith, and serving others together. Should we not be paying much more attention to carrying out these and other powerful spiritual practices in our homes and congregations than wondering how many "swats" will teach children a lesson?

Fifth, if we affirm that adults are called to help children cultivate their growing moral capacities and responsibilities by modelling for them compassion, accountability, repentance, and forgiveness, then would not all of these efforts be thwarted by hitting, slapping, or swatting them? How will we help children to develop morally if we do these things that breed anger, shame, and a sense of injustice?

Sixth, if we recognize that children can be models of faith for adults and have gifts and strengths that contribute to the common good now and in the future, then would we not actively seek to listen to and learn from them? Would we not recognize that the Holy Spirit is already moving in their lives and honour their insights and contributions? Would we not pay attention to helping them discern and cultivate their gifts and strengths and learning what they might teach us about God? Would we not stop punishing children physically, knowing that this behaviour creates distance and resentment that weaken our relationships with them?

Taking such questions into account and building on a robust theological framework for honouring the humanity of children, any appeals to selected passages in Proverbs to support use of the "rod" bear little weight. Indeed, as others have shown (including William Webb and William Morrow in Chapters 6 and 7, respectively), scholarly interpretations of Proverbs and other biblical passages actually provide grounds for rejecting the corporal punishment of children.

Conclusion

By offering just one example of a theology of childhood, this chapter illustrates the power and potential of vibrant theological understandings of children for informing our perspectives on corporal punishment, as well as other issues related to child well-being, faith formation, and child advocacy. As Christians worldwide develop robust theologies of childhood, they will provide strong frameworks for speaking meaningfully about their conceptions of and commitments to children. These frameworks can help their communities talk more effectively not only about corporal punishment but also about ways to strengthen child-adult relationships, nurture children's moral, religious, and spiritual lives, and advocate for all children. They can also help us to re-examine other theological frameworks that have historically been taken for granted in Christian contexts, and offer new ways of thinking theologically about child discipline and about children more broadly. Equipped with strong theologies of childhood, church leaders and child-focused faith-based organizations will be much more prepared to participate in public debates regarding child maltreatment and to work with others nationally and internationally to develop practical strategies for advancing child well-being (and build on the strong programs and initiatives that already exist, which Dodd presents in Chapter 15). In these and other ways, robust theologies of childhood that attend to children's vulnerabilities and strengths can empower the Church to participate effectively in child-focused debates with a range of audiences—from parents to pastors to policy makers—and to promote child well-being in families, congregations, and public life.

Notes

1 See, for example, Marcia J. Bunge, ed., *The Child in Christian Thought* (Grand Rapids, MI: Eerdmans, 2001); and Marcia J. Bunge, Terence E. Fretheim, and Beverly Roberts Gaventa, eds., *The Child in the Bible* (Grand Rapids, MI: William B. Eerdmans, 2008).

2 See, for example, reference to this point in Bonnie J. Miller-McLemore, "'Let the Children Come' Revisited: Contemporary Feminist Theologians on Children," in *The Child in Christian Thought*, ed. Marcia J. Bunge (Grand Rapids, MI: Eerdmans, 2000), 446–73.

3 See, most recently, for example, Marcia J. Bunge, "Conceptions of and Commitments to Children: Biblical Wisdom for Families, Congregations, and the Worldwide Church," in *Faith Forward*, vol. 3, *Launching a Revolution through Ministry with Children, Youth, and Families*, ed. D.M. Csinos (Kelowna, BC: Wood Lake Publishing, 2018), 94–112. See also Marcia J. Bunge, "A More Vibrant Theology of Children," *Christian Reflection: A Series in Faith and Ethics* 8 (Summer 2003): 11–19; Marcia J. Bunge, "The Dignity and Complexity of Children: Constructing Christian Theologies of Childhood," in *Nurturing Child and Adolescent Spirituality*, ed. Karen M. Yust et al. (Lanham, MD: Rowman and Littlefield, 2006), 53–68; and Marcia J. Bunge, "The Child, Religion, and the Academy: Developing Robust Theological and Religious Understandings of Children and Childhood," *Journal of Religion* 86, vol. 4 (October, 2006): 549–78.

4 Many additional biblical texts support this point. For example, Leah (Jacob's first wife) speaks of her sixth son as a dowry, or wedding gift, presented by God (Genesis 30:20). Several biblical passages indicate that parents who receive these precious gifts are being "remembered" by God (Genesis 30:22; 1 Samuel 1:11, 19) and given "good fortune" (Genesis 30:11). To be "fruitful"—to have many children—is to receive God's blessing. The Psalmist says children are a "heritage" from the Lord and a "reward" (Psalm 127:3). All biblical quotations are from the New Revised Standard Version (NRSV).

5 Johannes Amos Comenius, *The School of Infancy* (1663), ed. Ernest M. Eller (Chapel Hill: University of North Carolina Press, 1956), 59–70. The ideas of Comenius (1592–1670 CE) are influential far beyond the Church, and he is often called the "father of modern education." His popular book, *The School of Infancy*, points out the complex sensibilities and development of infants and young children and the need to nurture them at a very young age.

6 Cyprian, Letter 64.3, in *Letters*, trans. Sister Rose Bernard Donna (Washington, DC: Catholic University of America Press, 1964), 217–18. Although Cyprian is making strong claims for the spiritual and divine equality of children, he does not draw implications for their social equality.

7 In the history of Christianity and in our own faith communities, each of us can find examples of Christians who have harmed children and others who have shown them compassion. In my own Lutheran tradition, for example, we find many (sometimes neglected) stories of those who fully supported public education for all or showed compassion to children in need, such as Philipp Melanchthon (1497–1560), A.H. Franke (1663–1727), and N.F.S. Grundtvig (1783–1872).

8 See, for example, St. John Chrysostom, *On Marriage and Family Life*, trans. Catherine P. Roth and David Anderson (Crestwood, NY: St. Vladimir's Seminary Press, 1986). For introductions to views of children and childhood in the works of Luther, Calvin, Schleiermacher, and other Christian theologians, see Bunge, *The Child in Christian Thought*.

9 Martin Luther, *Luther's Large Catechism*, trans. F.S. Janzow (St. Louis, MO: Concordia, 1978), 40.

10 J. Ruckstaetter et al., "Parental Apologies, Empathy, Shame, Guilt, and Attachment: A Path Analysis," *Journal of Counseling and Development* 95, no. 4 (2017): 389–400.

11 See, for example, Mark 10:13–16; Luke 18:15–17; Matthew 19:13–15; also, Matthew 18:2–5; Mark 9:33–37; Luke 9:46–48.

12 For other relevant passages, see Mark 9:33–37; Luke 9:46–48; Matthew 18:1–5; Mark 10:13–16; Matthew 19:13–15; Luke 18:15–17; Matthew 11:25 and 21:14–16.

13 Elizabeth T. Gershoff, "Corporal Punishment by Parents and Associated Child Behaviours and Experiences: A Meta-Analytic and Theoretical Review," *Psychological Bulletin* 128, no. 4 (2002): 539–79, https://doi.org/10.1037//0033-2909.128.4.539; Elizabeth Thompson Gershoff et al., "Parent Discipline Practices in an International Sample: Associations with Child Behaviors and Moderation by Perceived Normativeness," *Child Development* 81, no. 2 (2010): 487–502, https://doi.org/10.1111/j.1467-8624.2009.01409.x.

14 Cited in Matthew Pate and Laurie A. Gould, *Corporal Punishment around the World* (Santa Barbara: Prager, 2012), 61.

PART 3: SEEKING FURTHER WISDOM

Indigenous Parenting, Positive Approaches to Discipline, and Spiritual Practices

9

THE CIRCLE OF COURAGE
Raising Respectful, Responsible Children through Indigenous Child-Rearing Practices

MARTIN BROKENLEG

Sacred Knowledge

When we Lakȟóta came to live in this world, we survived only because of the help we had from the Pté Oyáte, the Female Buffalo Nation. She supplied everything we needed. For many reasons, we use a buffalo skull in the centre of our ceremonial areas or centred in our art. When we speak of ourselves, we often use the term Pté Oyáte and not the term for the male buffalo, Tatánka. As the Lakȟóta First Nation we define ourselves as a female nation.

When buffalo are under threat, they organize themselves into a protective formation to optimize the survival of the herd. The buffalo bulls will form the outside perimeter of a protecting circle. Although strongest of the herd, these males are not the most necessary for the herd to survive. Inside that perimeter is the circle created by the buffalo cows, the next strongest members of the herd. As adult females, they are more necessary for the herd to survive and are protected by the bulls. Should the impending threat get past the males, the females will still be present to protect that which is most necessary for the survival of the herd—the young buffalo calves. When danger arises, the herd will encircle the young with care and protection, instinctively knowing they are the future of the herd. It is the major task of the adult buffalo to protect the young in order for the herd to continue.

Indigenous Peoples have learned through careful observation that the animal nations never lose their way, nor do they act in conflict with their nature. They maintain the wisdom they were given from the time of creation. Human beings are not so consistent, and so we turn to the animal nations to seek wisdom and direction in how we live. Without any perceptible communication, the buffalo herd uses its deeply embedded cultural behaviour to respond to a threat. We know that animal nations have cultural patterns, and so do communities of human beings. These cultural patterns are learned from the earliest days of our lives, and they are learned from the lived experience of our community.

Displacement

This experiential learning was severely damaged during the residential school era. By being away from family and community, Indigenous children were denied the sacred mythic wisdom learned only by living with one's family. Not only were residential school students deprived of hearing the sacred teachings of their communities, they were deprived of the lived experience that verified the truth of those teachings, the wisdom of their ancestors.

This cultural displacement mirrored the physical displacement that entire First Nations, Inuit, and Métis communities were experiencing through being removed from their homelands, where they were able to acquire all the resources needed for their survival. On their traditional territories, Indigenous Peoples know where to obtain the food they need, materials for survival, and medicines for when illness strikes. The cultural displacement generated by colonization generally, and by residential schools specifically, removed the ancient and time-tested wisdom and practices of First Peoples.

This cultural displacement continues in our time—the fourth wave of colonization. Darien Thira identifies this as "psycholonization," as wounded residential school survivors now need intense psychological and social services to cope with their intergenerational brokenness.[1] Not surprisingly, and adding insult to injury, it is professionals external to Indigenous communities who are seen as capable of providing this healing. This is psycholonization. The truth is that Indigenous people have always had the knowledge and skills necessary to thrive in the face of good times and bad. And an even bigger truth is that if we are to recover from the displacement of the residential school era, we need this ancient knowledge—this spiritual power—now more than ever.

Learning

Learning in Indigenous cultures always involves sacred principles and must come through experience. We refer to the learning of facts, rules, definitions, and principles as knowledge. Knowledge is the education of a person's mind, and it is crucial if one is going to be successful in Canadian society, which requires numerous intellectual skills in order to negotiate and take advantage of its benefits. Knowledge only requires words or experiences for concepts to be communicated and learned.

There is another kind of learning that is more valued among Indigenous Peoples, and there is no good English word for it. Some societies call this kind of learning "the virtues." Some call it "social-emotional" learning, while others call it "formation." This is the deep, holistic learning that takes place when all aspects of a person's perception work together. It is what some people mean when they refer to knowing something "in their heart." Indigenous Peoples have always valued this "learning in the heart" more than intellectual learning. In my Lakȟóta language, *wowiyúkčhaŋ* means thinking with all of one's human abilities. The mind is used, but this kind of thinking is not limited to logic. Emotions are involved, but this kind of thinking is not sentimentality. The body is involved, but the physical is not separated from the spirit. The soul and spirit of the person are involved, but grounded in an intense reality. When all of these human aspects work together, a Lakȟóta will say, "This I know 'in my heart.'"

Heart learning does not happen when only words are used. For something to be learned holistically, it must be learned by experience. Experiences teach the heart; words teach the mind. Experiential learning happens in cultural protocols. Every First Nation has protocols for nearly every human activity. Observing those protocols teaches the heart of the one who observes them. Some protocols are observed daily, while others happen on the cycle of the moon. Others are annual and governed by the sun, while still other protocols and ceremonies happen once in a lifetime. Each of these ceremonial protocols instills deep learning in the heart. It is only by keeping the protocols of one's own people that one will carry the spirit and heart of those people. The people who have the most experiential learning are those who have been around the longest—the Elders. Their learning from experience is the learning valued by Indigenous Peoples. Elders' experiences are the research and libraries of Indigenous Peoples.

Our Work to Understand Indigenous Child-Rearing

In the 1980s, Dr. Larry Brendtro and I taught at Augustana University in Sioux Falls, South Dakota. Dr. Brendtro, Professor of Special Education, was typical of the settler population of the Dakotas, Minnesota, and Iowa. His roots extended to Norway. Coming from the Šičáŋǧu Lakȟóta, called "the Sioux" by both the Canadian and American governments, my people have lived on the northern Prairies from time immemorial. I taught First Nations studies and gender studies, and I was a therapist at the university counselling services. Dr. Brendtro and I decided to develop a personal, year-long reconciliation relationship by just spending time together. We focused much of our dialogue on how Indigenous Peoples raised resilient youth in a world with no safeguards. With no social services as backup, Indigenous youth were always raised to survive in the face of any adversity. Threats of starvation, attacks from enemies, and the normal social and physical problems all human beings have were met by Indigenous youth with strength and determination.

Larry Brendtro and I developed our understanding of how Indigenous resilience was taught. Dr. Steve Van Bockern, an Augustana University professor of education, eventually joined us in our work, and the result was our little green book, *Reclaiming Youth at Risk: Our Hope for the Future.*[2] In this book, we use Indigenous child-rearing as the model of how Indigenous people develop youth and adults who can survive any threat. While First Nations, Inuit, and Métis peoples are three distinct groups with unique challenges, strengths, and histories, and while even within each of these groups there is a great deal of diversity, many of the themes used by Indigenous people are also universal. Thus, any people in the world can adapt them. Successful societies anywhere in the world can create young people who can survive problems. Of course, we cannot prevent all problems in life, but we have extensive research that tells us we can give anyone the capacity necessary to survive when problems arise. This is a crucial asset for Indigenous people, who live with intergenerational trauma as a result of the residential school era.

The Circle of Courage

We entitled the core philosophy of Indigenous resilience "the Circle of Courage," in part because we used a Lakȟóta medicine wheel as the central image around which we placed the key themes. A medicine wheel is a circle with four quadrants, each filled with one of the directional colours—red, black, yellow, and white. Of course, there is more than one way to arrange the colours, as various First Nations have done. Indigenous cultures always allow for variation. The model we use is a typical Lakȟóta form. The four resilience themes in Indigenous cultures are the experiences of belonging, mastery, independence, and generosity. We will explore each of these in turn and start to consider their application.

We now have self-esteem research from the field of psychology that parallels the Circle of Courage. Self-esteem is enhanced for children and adults through experiences of significance, competency, power, and virtue. Regular experiences with *significance* allow a person to know her or his importance to self and others. Encountering one's *competency* will show someone what she or he is capable of accomplishing. The experience of responsibility, being accountable for oneself, *empowers* the person. Engaging in acts of goodness and kindness keeps the person in contact with her or his fundamental *virtue*, or goodness. These four qualities of significance, competence, power, and virtue create inner strength in people no matter what their age, where they live, what language they speak, what race they come from, or what spiritual practice they may have. They are not necessarily the same as religious teachings, although they can be religious. The point is that these principles work even if they are not perceived to be religious. They work because they are spiritual. Resilience, whether it is understood from the perspective of psychology or the sacred understanding of Indigenous cultures, is a spiritual dynamic. It is the inner strength-of-spirit that allows a person to face hardships and problems.

Belonging

The primary human experience is belonging. Every child is born into the world knowing how to belong. Children in every Indigenous culture have access to this most sacred teaching: how to belong and be related to all things.

An Indigenous child is spiritually strong because that child is born into a traditional family of 250 to 300 relatives spread over five generations.

The typical Indigenous family is structured by generations. As a reference point, we will call the child the "Self." The first generation consists of the child's grandparents. This not only refers to the biological parents of the child's parents but includes the siblings and the cousins of those grandparents as well. In fact, everyone in that age range in the entire nation is grandparent to the Self. This sets the form of address and level of esteem toward those in this generation.

The second generation is the generation of parents. Of course, the child's biological parents are in this generation, but all of the parents' brothers, sisters, and cousins are the child's parents as well. They all assume parental responsibilities and functions. The Self has no uncles or aunts, only parents. Lakȟóta children are typically five years old before they start to distinguish their biological parents from their other parents, due to this life experience. Usually, Indigenous children are nursed and cared for by other parents in addition to their biological parents.

In the third generation, the child's own generation, all are considered brothers or sisters. The term "cousin" may be reserved for strangers about one's age. All the others in this generation are the children of the Self's many mothers and many fathers and thus are brothers and sisters.

The fourth generation in a traditional family consists of children to the Self. Sometimes the terms for niece and nephew are used for this generation but that is rare, since "son" and "daughter" identify these relationships more truly.

The fifth generation is made up of grandchildren to the Self. Like the generation of grandparents, anyone in this generation in the entire nation is a grandchild to the Self.

Together, these five generations would number between 250 and 300 people today. Indigenous cultures are diverse and varied; yet often they have a large number of rules, customs, teachings, behaviours, and attitudes that define every relationship in this family. Nothing is left to individual choice; individualism defies this communality, which is one aspect of the resilience that a child reared in a traditional family possesses. It is usual for Indigenous people to live together, travel together, and come together when there is a crisis. The twentieth-century-invented concept of the nuclear family produces the isolation, alienation, and solipsism of individualism. Growing up in a residential school would have generated the same isolation. Indigenous survival results from the communal belonging that comes from having many relatives and living with their support.

Typical Indigenous behavioural codes strengthen family relationships and result in mutual support and reciprocity. Belonging happens in our traditional families no matter what, because there are always other mothers and fathers, other brothers and sisters, and other children to raise if something happens to one's immediate family.

Reciprocity is giving back what has been given to you. This is the fundamental dynamic of Indigenous ethics and it fosters belonging. Because you have been helped, you will help others. If someone does a good thing for you, you will do a good thing for them as soon as you can. This is reciprocity, the return of good things to balance the relationship and keep it strong.

For Indigenous youth, this kinship experience affects all other aspects of life. Every plant and animal whose life is taken to nourish one's own is a relative, and one must give something back. For example, if the life of a deer is taken, blood should be returned to the earth and no portion should be wasted or anything left that is edible. If a plant is picked for medicine or for a ceremony, a handful of tobacco should be left to thank that nation for help it has given.

One's approach to all things in the spirit world is also governed by reciprocity. One must be focused and diligent in every aspect of ceremony and follow all the teachings and revelations in return for being heard and helped by the spirit world. This is important because these humans, animal nations, plant nations, and the spirit world are all one's relatives, to whom one belongs and lives well because of their help. This is not merely a poetic way of speaking; it is expressing one's life experience as realistically as possible. Indigenous people also belong to the earth; our experience is that she is alive, hearing and helping us reciprocally. We belong to a location in a way no settler can.

So how do we provide the experience of belonging to contemporary children and youth? First, we should do a belonging audit to determine what we are doing presently that provides the experience of belonging. We are probably doing some things but can always find more to do. We should say to every child how important she or he is to us, and we should say this frequently. This will teach the child's mind how important he or she is. It is how a child is treated that will give them the experience of belonging.

In schools and other institutions, we can examine our policies and bylaws to see if they are belonging responses. What do our tardiness and absence policies promote? Do our behavioural consequences promote belonging or alienation? Negative consequences are always alienating and do nothing to improve behaviour. What experience do we provide by our daily routines? Do our crisis plans promote a belonging response instead of a fear reaction?

In the home, when there is an emotional outburst, do we accept it? Emotions are a normal response for all human beings—including boys, who have been conditioned to deny them. When a rule is broken or an assigned task not finished, do we use this as an opportunity to connect? Is our use of all technology deliberately limited so we have time to just talk and be together? If we consistently provide experiences of belonging, we create a stronger person.

Mastery

Just as the desire to be connected is innate to every child, so is the drive to accomplish and master challenges. From the first days of life, infants begin to interact with and try to control their environments to meet their needs.

Wise societies provide guidance and safety, so that children learn their capabilities. Adults judge children's abilities and provide increasingly difficult tasks that allow them to understand what they are able to do—and its importance. An older Indigenous child may be asked to take time from playing to keep insects away from a sleeping infant sibling. The child is later congratulated for protecting the baby and will be taught that eventually this is the protection a parent provides. In all Indigenous communities, older children teach and protect their younger relatives in daily activities and in play. Eventually, adults teach the skills necessary for survival to youth, who then teach those skills to the younger children. This system optimizes the natural human desire to learn. Indigenous societies use these experiences to teach important survival skills and needed cultural skills. Meaningless tasks are avoided in this process.

In contemporary life, adults judiciously provide many opportunities for children to explore their capabilities. A mastery audit should consider policies, practices, and customs for the mastery experience that should be provided. Timing must also be considered. A too-helpful adult may step in to complete a task for a child, when waiting just a bit longer would have allowed the child the genuine discovery of an ability, such as being able to open a door or cope with a problem. Wise adults also find ways to encourage mastery by the back door when front-door success does not seem obvious. If back-door success can be found, we increase the possibility of front-door success. Wise adults also learn to see and define what could have been considered deficits as assets. A child who was reluctant can be congratulated on finding the right time to act. A child who completes a disagreeable task can be successful by getting through it with dignity.

Should we encounter a youth who is reluctant to improve academically, we adults must remember that this is an unnatural reaction, because the desire to learn is innate. An older student who has difficulty reading can be made an expert if he reads to younger students who may not be readers yet. Mastery is the experience of learning about one's capabilities, whether they be outward skills or inward emotional or attitudinal abilities.

Independence

Recognizing one's own inner power is a significant source of resilience. In Indigenous cultures, a child is treated with dignity from before birth, when relatives protect the pregnant mother from hearing or seeing anything troubling. Indigenous languages convey the dignity of the child through the terms used. For example, the Lakȟóta word for child, *wakȟáŋheža*, can be translated as "standing sacred." Nisgaa' terms translate into English as "prince" or "princess."

The best strategy to empower young people is true discipline, which never involves punishment of any kind. In fact, discipline and punishment are so antithetical that they cannot both exist at the same time. The fundamental difference is that discipline is educational. It shows children how to be responsible in one way, so they can be responsible in another way. Punishment has never worked; it is based on the erroneous thought that if I hurt you badly enough you will want to do things my way. This logic is faulty. The most that comes from punishment is temporary obedience—as long as an authority is watching.

As adults we must reconsider our role in raising children. Our role is not to control and manage them. Our true role is to systematically empower the young person until we are no longer needed. This is the pattern one sees in traditional Indigenous cultures. Children are lovingly taught increasingly complex tasks until they can self-manage. In Indigenous traditions, children are never punished but may be respectfully corrected in order to be successful.

In contemporary Indigenous life, responsibility must be explained to young people from their earliest years. Wise adults commit to devoting long periods of time to listening to the child in order to help the child process emotion. Then the child can engage rational thinking. Explanations are carefully used so that children understand their own dignity and responsibilities. True discipline is always educational, showing a young person how to be responsible in one way so other ways can be added. A wise adult narrows the choices available to the youth, allows the youth to make a real choice among the provided alternatives, and lets natural consequences teach. A mistake or a failure is not a disaster if it can provide feedback on how to be successful the next time. Wise adults are coaches and cheerleaders. If we maintain these roles, we will enhance the resilience of all youth by providing the experience of appropriate empowerment.

Generosity

Indigenous cultures value generosity and have many teachings and ceremonies allowing for the experience of generosity. The West Coast potlatches are ceremonies of generosity. The Prairie ceremony of feasts and giveaways to mark life changes are experiences of generosity. Many Indigenous cultures have daily customs that provide opportunities to learn generosity. An admired object will be handed to the admirer upon his departure. A young woman will give away to an Elder or to a poor person the artistic item she has worked on for a long time. A successful youth hunter will return with his game only to give it to a widow or an elderly couple as his reward for being successful.

Generosity is a natural human reaction to the sorrow of another. Newborns in hospital cry when they hear their fellow infants in distress. If we hear that a family down the street has had a tragedy we gather food, a blanket, and some money, and we go to them. It is by having opportunities to give of oneself that young people learn generosity, and this creates resilience. Schools provide service-learning projects for youth to help those who are less fortunate than the youth. Young people willingly help when there is a real need, although they will not respond well to a busywork project. Adults can provide daily opportunities for youth to assist Elders and younger children. The idealism and energy of youth can be their gift to their entire community if it is channelled well by wise adults who will acknowledge the good efforts of the youth.

Real generosity is always multi-dimensional, involving the history of the giver and the receiver, the symbols that matter to them and others, and the object or good deed that is conveyed. Indigenous people see the universe as generous in providing all things necessary for survival in the appropriate cycles of spring, salmon runs, and buffalo calving times. Being generous brings one into harmony with the generous universe.

The Circle of Courage Revisited

A medicine wheel was the image my people originally used to convey the ancient teaching of resilience. On the West Coast, totem poles are used to convey teachings, so I asked a carver to depict the resilience teachings as a pole. He discussed the matter with his Elders and carved a pole for me, reminding me that a pole is always read from the bottom to the top.

At the bottom of the pole, he carved Killer Whale as the image of belonging, because orcas are always with others in their pods. Above Killer Whale stands the image of mastery, Raven, who can do many astonishing things. Eagle stands above Raven, representing the empowerment of independence, as eagles always responsibly follow the rules of their own eagle nation. At the top of the pole, the carver placed Wolf, who never eats alone, representing generosity. One who knows the social organization of the Pacific Coastal First Nations will know that those four figures (houses) provide the basic organizational structures of every community.

In recent years, academic and research agencies have used complex processes to identify the factors that help children and youth live well. Drawing on computer analysis of five million children from across Canada and the United States, the Search Institute[3] identified the forty assets that correlate with life success in the face of problems. When the Search Institute's long-time president, Peter Benson, told us about these findings, he said, "We should have put them around your Circle of Courage because all forty assets fit somewhere on your Circle." Here we see that contemporary science has discovered the ideas our Indigenous grandmothers and mothers have been using for centuries.

For thousands of years, Indigenous Peoples have survived well on this Turtle Island of North America. We were here long before anyone crossed the Bering Strait. We have been here longer than previously thought, probably from "time immemorial." We have survived through all those generations because of our own basic way of teaching survival to our children—the themes that my co-authors and I call the Circle of Courage. Over many centuries, we have survived many hardships, and we will survive the violent legacy of the residential schools.

The task of First Nations who want to place their story in a Christian context has been to set the teachings of Jesus on the foundation of their First Nations way of thinking and understanding. This is what I sought in my own spiritual journey, as I explored the Eastern Orthodox Church. But what I found was Christianity in Greek clothing; I wanted Christianity in feathers, buckskin, and button blankets. This kind of adaptation happened in England, as Middle Eastern Christianity eventually transformed into the Church of England. This happened when Semitic-based Christianity put on Italian concepts, clothing, and theology to become the Roman Catholic Church. Eventually, if Christianity is going to nourish Aboriginal people, it will have to look, sound, taste, and smell like a First Nations ceremony. But drawing on the Circle of Courage, or other concepts such as what Shirley Tagalik describes in the next chapter as the Inuit concept of *inunnguiniq*, will enrich not just the Indigenous church but the entire church in Canada. As we move forward in reconciliation, may it be so.[4]

Notes

1 Darien Thira, "Beyond Colonization: Canadian Aboriginal Context: A Post-Colonial Perspective," Thira Consulting, 2008, accessed 26 September 2018, https://thira.ca/thira-tools/papers-articles/.

2 Larry Brendto, Martin Brokenleg, and Steve VanBockern, *Reclaiming Youth at Risk: Our Hope for the Future* (Bloomington, IN: Solution Tree, 1990).

3 Search Institute, "Developmental Assets," Search Institute, Minneapolis, accessed October 20, 2018, https://www.search-institute.org/our-research/development-assets/.

4 The ideas in this paragraph were first shared in an interview with Dr. David Benner, in David Benner, "Culture, Faith and Identity, an Interview," Dr. David G. Benner, 25 September 2015, accessed 21 October 2018, http://www.drdavidgbenner.ca/brokenleg-interview/. This website has since been closed.

10

Inunnguiniq: Inuit Perspectives on Raising a Human Being

SHIRLEY TAGALIK

She sits very quietly. Her grandmother is telling stories—retelling stories and reliving memories. These are the times she loves the best. This wrinkled face which always smiles on her is more than a grandmother. This is also her avaaq, *her namesake, her personal extension of herself. It is from this woman that she gains her position in the world. It is from this woman that she gains her personality—not as characteristics inherent in her, but as expectations about how to become who she should be, given her name and position in life. She has her family and all that those relationships mean, but she has her* avaaq *connections and a more significant set of relationships as well. She belongs to more than herself. She belongs to more than her family. She belongs to more than her* avaaq *family. She is situated in the history of all her* avaaqs, *and she thinks of herself not simply as Naujaq, but as all the Naujaqs of whom her grandmother speaks to her.*

Naujaq knows her place. She listens and hears. She never asks questions unless the moment is created by her grandmother for questioning. She watches and learns. Her eyes are always dutiful—moving with the pace of life in her household—ready for their turn. She is seldom scolded. She is not asked to do what she is not ready to do. Her world is one of play and experiencing and watching and respecting and helping.

Naujaq does not call her relations by their names; she refers to their relationship to her. She does not look rudely into the eyes of others. She does not rudely interrupt conversations. She does not rudely venture her ideas. She understands the importance of not seeing and not hearing and not embarrassing and not interfering with others. Showing respect for others is all important in her world. There is no way to say "I" or "me" or "mine" that is not tied to other words and other relationships. Naujaq would never show pride by talking about herself or by drawing attention to herself. There is no way to be apart from the collectivity of Inuit life. Being a part of that world means not standing out but standing within.

Naujaq concentrates as her tiny fingers pull at the strings webbed in her avaaq*'s gnarled hands. She focuses on the task at hand and is not distracted by the chanting teasing song her grandmother sings to her. She transfers the new string pattern successfully to her own hands and holds them up. A new pattern, a new challenge: an ancient pattern, a challenge traced through the history of a people and retraced in the lives of their youth. Naujaq lives her place in this history with eagerness and a joy for the possibilities which stretch out ahead of her as her ever-unfolding world propels her forward.*[1]

When I first arrived in Arviat (formerly Eskimo Point), it had only been fifteen years since the people had been forcibly removed from the land and relocated to the community. The children I came to teach were the first generation born into settlement life. The story of Naujaq was written in my own attempt to better understand the home life and cultural background of these children. In those early years, I continually encountered cultural divides in the classroom. For example, on my first parent-teacher night, I carefully explained to a grandmother all the "important" work the children were doing. After my detailed account, her response was, "But is he a good boy? Is he kind? Does he have friends?" This was my first indication that the markers for success were obviously different for Inuit parents than for parents in the south. Much later I came to understand the concept of *inunnguiniq*—the making of a capable human being.

For the past fifteen years, I have been very fortunate to have had the opportunity to work with Inuit Elders from across Nunavut and to document much of their knowledge about Inuit ways of being. In sharing this, I try to provide access to their voices, as it is their experience and knowledge that we all need to understand. It is their wish that this way of being be returned to their grandchildren and future generations. However, they also repeatedly state that non-Inuit, or *Qallunaat*, need to know and better understand Inuit cultural experience in order to be able to come alongside them as partners moving into our shared future. One of the most important cultural concepts that Elders repeatedly refer to as the foundation is *inunnguiniq*—the making of a capable human being. This is the Inuit socialization process.

Inunnguiniq requires teaching to the heart rather than cramming the head. It relies on being grounded in the strengths of relationships and connections. It is very clearly defined, very intentional, sets high expectations, and has been successfully equipping Inuit to thrive for generations. Elder Louis Angalik explains:

> *Inunngnuiniq* starts with child-rearing, but it continues throughout life. We cannot make a capable human being all at once. *Inunnguiniq* is a process that Inuit commit to pursuing with each child across his/her lifetime. It is important to regard *inunnguiniq* from a holistic big picture and to consider the many aspects of building a capable human being that are required to be addressed over this long period of personal development. We also must encourage a child to be able to do things on their own, so when they get older, they will become capable. We are all going to run into obstacles in life, so raising a child to know that he/she will indeed run into obstacles, run into difficulties, and preparing him/her well for the future is the best thing we can do for our children.[2]

I came to understand that in a culture where everything is shared, one is supposed to perceive and meet the needs of others without their having to ask. So a child not doing work was often a child without a pencil, which I had not supplied because I had not taken notice of their need. Often, children did not respond to questions though I was certain they knew the answers. From their perspective, it was confusing to be asked a question when I clearly knew the answer. Why ask? Knowledge, like everything, is to be shared. Questions were for the unknown and should result in solution-seeking, deep thinking that was collaborative and moved ideas forward. By asking direct questions, I was also putting children in a difficult dilemma. By answering, they might appear to be showing off or trying to seem smarter than the others. This would be shameful behaviour and might lead to conflict or bad feelings. For Inuit, this kind of behaviour was never to be indulged in. Humility is essential to maintaining harmony. By praising a child in front of others, we are also setting them apart from their peers. This is again unacceptable. We brought with us a system that rewarded what a child could remember being told. For an oral society, remembering what you have been told was expected at all times. For Inuit, real knowledge must always be attained from experience and then demonstrated in ways that help others. Knowing something has no value unless you can use that knowledge to improve the lives of those around you. Knowing is the synergy of two elements: *tukisiumaniq*, or building an understanding of life; and *silaturniq*, or experiencing the world. All knowledge is mediated by a person's character and ethics and is demonstrated by good behaviour of the individual.[3]

I was asked by an Elder, "Why do *Qallunaat* (non-Inuit) think if a child can do something 50 percent of the time, this is acceptable? If I built an *iglu* 50 percent of the time, we would be dead. Inuit expect mastery in learning. Children must continually be improving until they become masters." This is also what *inunnguiniq*—becoming capable—is about.

There are many similarities across Indigenous ways of nurturing children. Martin Brokenleg (Chapter 9) has beautifully described the concept of sacred knowledge and the foundation of learning as holistic heart learning. These beliefs are shared by Inuit. Since all people have body, mind, and spirit, it is critical to align these personal aspects with the natural and social realms and to approach all *inusirq*, or life matters, in holistic relationship. So first and foremost, *inunnguiniq* is about being in respectful relationship.[4] All teaching takes place within the strength of relationships. One's strength and success is based on the extent of one's personal connection and support networks. Within Inuit society, this success is ensured for a child by the connections created through naming, birth blessings, kinship affiliations, childhood friendships, and hunting partnerships. These multiple systems of affiliations were strongly maintained before colonization because they served the important function of connecting a child to as many personal resources and supports as possible. These relationships are nurtured through the family. A central focus of Inuit belief is to live a good life by living respectfully.[5] Understanding one's connections and responsibilities to being in respectful relationship was taught through *inunnguiniq*—teachings that were instilled and repeated throughout life so that they became strongly internalized.[6] One Elder describes a capable human being in the following way:

> *Inunnguiniq* is making a human being who will be able to help others with a good heart. Someone with a good heart and mind will always be aware of his/her surroundings. He/she will be quick to think and be able to look at the brighter side of different situations. This person is always ready to help. This is called *inuttiavak*. A person who never really pays much attention to the teaching of his parents and Elders, though they were taught, would not learn much. Little things will make him/her upset. They won't care if the tension inside of them spills out on everyone around them. Even if the parents did their best to help him/her, that will have very little effect on that person. We call this *inuttiavaungituq* (a person with bad attitude). This kind of person would be considered as potentially harmful.[7]

One can only imagine what a brutal experience residential school would have been for a child coming from this background. Coming into newly established classrooms in the 1970s was difficult enough for most children and for their parents. We colonizers had so many rules and such very different expectations. Everything was expressed in a foreign language and often in very loud voices—sometimes angry voices to which children would not immediately respond. That we had a very different way of interacting with the children in our care was made evident to me in an early interview that appeared in *Ajurnarmat* magazine: "Raising children is important to Inuit. When a child is small, they are loved by everyone. A child is encouraged to remain a child. He is praised for learning at his pace. When things are too complex for a child to learn or use, they are not encouraged to understand. The burden is too heavy for a child and [s/he] will develop a weak mind. This can only be bad for a child and confuse them."[8]

Thus for Inuit, the education of children is administered through relationship and paced in ways designed to meet their individual needs and to support their achievement and success. Inuit consider each child unique—as an individual who develops, learns, and matures at her or his own speed. Rather than speaking of a child's age in years—people do not keep track of ages—Inuit speak of children in terms of their physical development and capabilities.[9]

Children are raised in an environment where they are closely observed, and the teaching and training they receive is tailored to meet their personal needs and interests. After the creation of Nunavut, when we were engaged in designing a made-in-Nunavut education system, an Elder asked me, "Why do you put all the six-year-olds in the same classroom and expect them to learn the same thing at the same time?"[10] In his mind, this approach was guaranteed to fail. Each child is unique, so learning needs to be individualized and geared to building on each child's particular strengths and abilities. Furthermore, society does not need children who are all trained to turn out the same. The success of Inuit society relies on each individual becoming a master in a certain area and then contributing that expertise to improving the common good. There are many other lessons that our Western system of education can take from *inunnguiniq*.[11]

Inuit say that everything should be about being in respectful relationship. Learning occurs in a relationship between teacher and learner that is trusting, lasting, and focused on continual development. Inuit children encounter teachers in every aspect of their lives. Everyone is in a teaching/learning relationship, and it is understood that children also have much to teach, so they are given respect for that role in life. *Inunnguiniq* is a process that builds the character, the attitudes, and the behaviours that will enable a child to become a highly skilled contributor to the collective well-being. The process specifically stresses positive relationality. Children are trained to avoid confrontation, to resolve conflicts at their start, to never respond in anger (which is a sign of immaturity and self-indulgence),[12] to be respectful at all times, to always consider the other person's contexts, and to support the needs of others before yourself. From an early age, children are helped to be in touch with and manage their emotions. Inuit have always known that thinking comes from the heart, and that emotions cause thoughts. If the heart rules the head (and ultimately the tongue), then it is incumbent on parents to make sure that we fill the hearts of children with the good things that will help them to become the capable human beings that they are designed to become.

When parents stray from the *inunnguiniq* plan, the result could be the creation of a fragile-egg person or a hardened-rock person. The fragile egg is said to be the result of overly protective parenting that does not allow the child to take on responsibilities, learn from mistakes, be accountable to others, or become self-reliant. This kind of person needs to be looked after throughout life and has difficulty dealing with challenges, hardships, or disappointments. These egg-like people are said to be dangerous to society. Equally dangerous is the hardened-rock person who is burdened with heavy expectations or responsibilities too early in life. They experience failure and then are reprimanded for failing. Often, they are raised with harshness and not enough love and care. They may be exposed to environments characterized by anger, violence, and conflict. They tend to shut themselves off, do not engage in healthy relationships, and do not respond well to those around them.[13]

Fortunately, a rock- or egg-like person can be redeemed through a supportive, loving relationship. Elder Rhoda Karetak stresses the need for parents to be intentional in how they raise children:

> But if you are creating *inunnguiniq* (a human being), one has to work on it with consistency. Even the ones who are living right now still have to be created as human beings. This is not something that Inuit should lose. If you are persistent in working with someone, they can become able people. They can be bright and helpful, can follow instructions given to them, as long as they are treated well and taught. They can be taught how to perform important tasks. They can make sure their anger is not easily aroused by being given concrete understanding and by being encouraged to succeed. They come to understand, and other people are not afraid of them because they are known to be able to work well.
>
> When you look at those who have no desire to obey other people, they have been brought up not to respect anything, not really loved enough to be trained, just growing up in any old way, and just following anything they see. These are things we need to think carefully about. Anyone can be raised in this way, but they will never have a good life.[14]

In the closely knit camps of the past, where everyone was required to support each other, these kinds of people would be very difficult and unpredictable. Making sure that every child became a capable human being was a collective responsibility. Parents who were missing the mark would be sanctioned and supported in improving their parenting style through a process called *aajiiqatigiingniq*. This process engaged everyone in providing whatever advice and supports were necessary to address wrongdoing and lead to a successful outcome. In this kind of system, discipline is essential. However, when Elders speak about punishment, they say that they were seldom aware of it being applied. Because respectful relationship was emphasized so strongly, children were quick to obey and follow the teachings and expectations. When a child was getting out of hand, usually a stern look or a nod of the head was enough to bring a child in line. Pond Inlet Elder Joannasie Muckpa described it this way: "My uncles also used to admonish and discipline me, but they did it with such love that it immediately made you want to obey them. If you discipline harshly, the child will be resistant and will not want to listen or be able to listen because they are already too upset. Even discipline can be administered in a calm way that builds connection and confidence and promotes harmony within the family. There were always some situations that led to anger. This anger would be diffused so that harmony was restored."[15]

Physical violence was not acceptable in traditional Inuit society. Those who were acting violently would be admonished and counselled to change their behaviour. If change was not observed, they would be sanctioned through the *aajiiqatigiingniq* process. The group would set out the expectations for change, each member would agree to provide specific supports, and the person would be closely counselled until they succeeded. If the person did not change, then serious sanctions would be applied. For example, the wife of an abuser might be taken from him or children who were being abused would be given to loving families, usually relatives. Keen observation of all social relationships was everyone's responsibility:

> You will know when a little child is raised with love and respect by the way they act. They will be happy and respectful of others. Children who are raised in good homes are attentive and will learn faster. The ones who are raised with a parent shouting at them or neglecting them will have very low self-esteem.
>
> If parents are always shouting at each other or at their children, their young minds will become confused and they will never know what is expected. A young child will be afraid

> all the time if parents are spanking them very hard. They will become afraid to be touched even as an adult.[16]

As so poignantly described by Brokenleg (Chapter 9), these societal systems, which served Inuit for thousands of years, were crushed by colonization. Western systems were put into place, with catastrophic results for Inuit. An aim of this book is to begin to address some of the destruction wrought by residential schools. However, residential schools were only a small part of the systemic abuse that Inuit endured. These systemic abuses are ongoing as colonizing continues through the systems now entrenched in our communities:

> When our parents were pressured to change, this caused our society to leave behind our traditional ways of child-rearing . . . when school first began, the kids were uprooted and, as a result, their foundation shattered. Up to now we hear about those people who were uprooted . . . they are suffering psychologically. They have higher positions in the workforce, . . . but they have been deprived of their roots. First of all, a young person has to know that s/he is an Inuk, not a white person—an Inuk who has his or her own personality like no other.[17]

The process of *inunnguiniq* was primarily the role of parents and grandparents. A core cultural value was to establish healthy families. This required husband and wife to work closely together and share child-rearing responsibilities in consistent ways. *Inunnguiniq* was viewed as a collective responsibility and applied by all members of the camp. Children developed a strong sense of belonging to the group and looked upon many group members as teachers, mentors, and advisors. A core expectation for Inuit, so strongly held that it was expressed as *maligarjuat,* meaning a big law, was to continually work for the common good. The successful application of this rule required that every member of the society become an effective and capable contributing member. Igloolik Elder Atuat Akkitirq said:

> We were taught to respond quickly and willingly. We would respond so quickly that sometimes we would put our boots on in the porch. At times, we were not too happy to do some of the chores we had to do when we were young, but we knew they were for our own good. Being strict with children is not abuse. Sometimes parents had to make their children strong by

> being strict with them and make them work so they can learn to care for themselves as adults. This is why we should teach our children what it was like in the past. This way they would know when they are taught to be strong rather than think they are being abused. This way they will not become weak adults. Children will grow up and get married and raise a family. They will need to know how to care for them. Problems will arise, and they will have to face them and solve them. Some will have to fight for their rights too. These are the things we need to discuss so we can pass them on.[18]

Much has been said about the very negative impact of the school system on Indigenous children. The impact on parents and community was equally devastating. The role of parents and grandparents was to raise the next generation that would care for and sustain their society. They were stripped of this role and identity overnight. Their deep sense of loss was made worse when the colonizers described Inuit culture as backward, savage, and incompetent, and asserted that Inuit needed to be taken over and retrained. Suddenly every aspect of Inuit life was being administered by non-Inuit—*Qallunaat* were now in authority and were very aggressive in ensuring that Inuit followed their rules. According to Clyde River Elder Peter Paniaq,

> While we were growing up, there were principles applied in our instruction. Inuit children from very different territories were raised very similarly because the training was based on the Inuit cultural beliefs that had been in place for millennia. These beliefs were highly valued and so we were taught with very strict expectations. Rules to live by, such as never causing fear in an animal, are not being followed today since colonization. For example, scaring a polar bear away would never have been practised. A polar bear that came into a camp would be killed. A polar bear encountered on the land would be avoided. These rules were grounded in Inuit laws. The new hunting regulations imposed by the government caused Inuit to go against Inuit laws. The breaking of Inuit laws and values was an intentional attempt to bring Inuit under government control.[19]

Often, Inuit who had lived successfully and independently on the land suddenly had every aspect of their lives taken over by new authorities. They were unable to hunt because all their tools and weapons were removed at the time of forced relocation. Their dogs were shot. Their children were removed to schools, where they were repeatedly told that their parents were incompetent. The start of formal education marked a change in the respect shown to parents by their children. Inuit who believed that children were children as long as the parents lived were now being told that at sixteen years of age children did not have to listen to their parents any longer, and that their children could be taken away from them. They were told where to work, what to eat, what not to hunt, how to keep clean. They learned to live in fear. I encountered this when I went to visit the families of my students. If I knocked on a door, the family knew it was a *Qallunaaq* coming. Often, I would enter to find that children had hidden in case I was a Royal Canadian Mounted Police (RCMP) officer or social worker come to take them, or a nurse come to jab them with a needle. Once I understood this, I never knocked again. This fear was well-founded. The 1960s were a decade when Inuit, especially children, were being removed from families regularly, just as in other jurisdictions. Sometimes this was a child welfare issue, sometimes it was for tuberculosis or another illness. Too often these children were never seen again. To this day, whenever we meet with Elders, they mention their fear that a social worker will take the child from the family. This is a very raw legacy of colonization of which we need to be cognizant. As Paniaq points out,

> What happens in childhood is carried throughout life and so we have to be very careful what we expose children to and how we care for children throughout their lives. When a child is hurt, it will be very hard to let go of that hurt and to heal. It will stay with him/her into later life if someone is not careful to help resolve the issue with the child through healing. There are things that cannot be done alone and learning to forgive is one of those. Learning to forgive others and resolving conflict is something that is also taught early in life. In Inuit cultural practice, anyone experiencing hardship or prolonged unhappiness was closely observed and counselled so that issues could be resolved quickly, and the person could return to productive

> living. Punishment was reserved only for those who were persistent in their wrongdoing and who had become a danger to others.[20]

The aim of residential schools was to take the Native out of the child. This aim has been carried forward in the colonizing systems that are protected and continue in our communities to this day: education that uses Western curriculum and non-Indigenous languages, health delivered according to a medical model, services that treat mental illness rather than provide healing, child welfare that continues to "scoop" Inuit children, justice and legal systems that are entrenched in a punitive model, and governance that is based in elected systems rather than a recognition of Inuit definitions of leadership. Colonization continues to marginalize Inuit even in their own lands. As Norman Attungala of Baker Lake stated, "We agreed to this life because we thought it would be better. Today, we should be weeping with contentment rather than with anger if those promises had been kept. In this new life, it is more difficult to find contentment today. We used to live a life where everything was connected. Today's life is tangled and without clear purpose."[21]

On a positive note, the settlement of land claims in Inuit jurisdictions has contributed to reclamation of Inuit cultural knowledge and identity. It is the ultimate irony that Inuit would ever "lay claim to land" when cultural beliefs were that land cannot be "owned," but colonization has forced Indigenous people to walk in new ways in order to dig themselves out of the colonial oppression that sought to bury their cultural identities. Access to authentic culture is a starting point for decolonization. In Nunavut, we have been documenting *Inuit Qaujimajatuqangit* (IQ, cultural knowledge).[22] IQ can be described as what Inuit have always known to be true, a set of beliefs that support cultural systems and processes that have always served Inuit and have remained mostly unchanged over thousands of years. It is the centrality of this belief system that enabled Inuit to be highly successful in adapting and adjusting to a changing world without compromising central values or social systems. Inuit Elders advocate for the reclamation of these long-held cultural systems in order to return Inuit to the strength and resilience of the past and to send them solidly into the future. *Inunnguiniq*, the raising of a capable human being, is one such system being actively reclaimed.

Elders have identified that the most effective intervention in this revitalization process will be with parents—that if parents can reclaim and apply *inunnguiniq*, they will begin to see themselves as Inuk again. Since the Inuit world view is entirely holistic, the process of *inunnguiniq* should be understood within the context of other core cultural beliefs and processes. By applying the principles and beliefs that underlie *inunnguiniq*, Inuit will reconnect with and apply the values and beliefs of all IQ. As colonizers, we need to step back and allow this to happen. We need to be supportive of these efforts to rebuild cultural strengths and make way for reinstating cultural systems to replace our largely ineffective colonial ones. This is how we can begin to decolonize ourselves. Reconciliation occurs in partnership, by working for shared understanding and by being respectful of authentic Inuit culture. When we take this time to step back, listen to, and learn about these cultural beliefs, we will find that we have much of value to learn.

Today, Inuit communities include many strong Christian believers. Elders sometimes tell me that some Inuit were quick to accept Christianity because the beliefs were so similar to their own. Like most Indigenous groups, Inuit believe there is a Creator or Protector over all things. Their laws and beliefs were given to them and have been maintained across thousands of generations. They know that these beliefs should not change over time, because they are always perfect for living successfully. It would be unlike the God we know to create humankind and then disperse them across the world without direction or a set of laws to follow. It seems presumptuous to think that a very small group of "chosen people" are the only ones under God's loving care. When missionaries appeared, many Inuit were happy to know that the sacrifice of Jesus had freed them from all the restricting taboos they had lived with in the past. It is unfortunate that the *Qallunaat* who came to share this news often did not take the time to find out more about the shared beliefs that could have built unity across peoples.

For most Indigenous Peoples, one's purpose in life is to live well, according to specific laws. Brokenleg (Chapter 9) describes the Medicine Wheel and the four cultural understandings that are foundational to the Lakȟóta belief system. Inuit refer to four laws, or *maligarjuat*, that must be followed in order to live a good life. These are (1) continually working for the common good; (2) living in respectful relationship with all things; (3) maintaining balance and harmony; and (4) continually planning and preparing for the future.[23] Unlike the ten commandments of the Judeo-Christian tradition, these laws never were written down; they were ingrained in the heart of every child and demonstrated in lived application, across the circumpolar Inuit world and throughout millennia. The strength of Indigenous belief systems is remarkable, but Indigenous people would tell us that these beliefs are simply true; they need never change and must always be followed. We continue to miss remarkable opportunities to learn when we ignore and marginalize Indigenous belief systems. Now is the time to change.

> *Naujaq's grandmother has died. Naujaq misses her grandmother and sings her song softly at night. Her grandmother's place is empty, and her things are gone, but Naujaq sees and hears her everywhere. She went to the funeral and then back to school. Naujaq carries her grandmother with her. She carries her name with her. She sings her songs in her heart. Naujaq is becoming what an* avaaq *should become. She decides that she will not wear a hat so that her learning and thoughts can be shared with her grandmother. She feels a strange sense of peace. She is Naujaq—herself and her other. She is never alone.*

Notes

1 Originally appeared in Shirley Tagalik, *The Arviat Language Research Project: Language Beliefs as an Influencing Factor in the Quality of Oral Language in Arviat* (Montreal, QC: McGill University, 1998), Master of Education monograph.

2 Louis Angalik, personal communication, 2004.

3 For a more detailed description of this, please see National Collaborating Centre for Aboriginal Health (NCCAH), *Inunnguiniq: Caring for Children the Inuit Way* (NCCAH and the Public Health Agency of Canada, 2009–10), 4, accessed 21 October 2018, https://www.ccnsa-nccah.ca/docs/health/FS-InunnguiniqCaringInuitWay-Tagalik-EN.pdf.

4 Shirley Tagalik and J. Joyce, *Relationality and Its Importance as a Protective Factor for Indigenous Youth* (Arviat, NU: Centre of Excellence for Children and Adolescents with Special Needs, 2005).

5 NCCAH, *Inunnguiniq*, 2.

6 National Collaborating Centre for Aboriginal Health (NCCAH), *Inutsiaqpagutit: That Which Enables You to Have a Good Life: Supporting Inuit Early Life Health* (NCCAH and the Public Health Agency of Canada, 2010), 4–5.

7 Atuat Akittirq, personal communication, 2007.

8 Rachel Qitsualik, ed., "The Inuit Educational Concept," special edition, *Ajurnarmat*, no. 4 (November 1979), Inuit Cultural Institute.

9 John Bennett and Susan Rowley, eds., *Uqalurait* (Montreal: McGill-Queen's University Press, 2004), 11.

10 Louis Angalik, personal communication, 2001.

11 For a more detailed description of this, please see NCCAH, *Inunnguiniq*.

12 Jean L. Briggs, *Never in Anger: Portrait of an Eskimo Family* (Cambridge, MA: Harvard University Press, 1970).

13 For a more detailed description, please see Joe Karetak, Frank Tester, and Shirley Tagalik, eds., *Inuit Qaujimajatuqanit—What Inuit Have Always Known to Be True* (Halifax: Fernwood Press, 2017).

14 Rhoda Karetak, personal communication, 2005.

15 Shirley Tagalik, "Inuit Knowledge Systems, Elders and Determinants of Health—Harmony, Balance and the Role of Holistic Thinking," in *Determinants of Indigenous Peoples' Health in Canada: Beyond the Social*, ed. Margo Greenwood, Sarah de Leeuw, Nicole Lindsay, and Charlotte Reading (Toronto: Canadian Scholars' Press, 2015), 25–32, 28.

16 Qaujigiartiit Health Research Centre (QHRC), *Inunnguiniq Parenting Curriculum* (Iqaluit, NU: QHRC, 2013), 139–40.

17 Quotation from Peter Kattuqaq (2000), as cited in QHRC, *Inunnguiniq Parenting Curriculum*, 138.

18 Atuat Akittirq, personal communication, 2007.

19 Peter Paniaq, personal communication, 2010.

20 Paniaq.

21 Tagalik, "Inuit Knowledge Systems," 29.

22 Karetak, Tester, and Tagalik, *Inuit Qaujimajatuqanit*.

23 National Collaborating Centre for Inuit Health (NCCAH), *Inuit Qaujimajatuqangit: The Role of Indigenous Knowledge in Supporting Wellness in Inuit Communities in Nunavut* (NCCAH and the Public Health Agency of Canada, 2009–10). https://www.ccnsa-nccah.ca/docs/health/FS-InuitQaujimajatuqangitWellnessNunavut-Tagalik-EN.pdf.

11

Rethinking Christian Theologies of Discipline and Discipleship

MARCIA J. BUNGE

Throughout this volume, a strong and interdisciplinary case has been made against the corporal punishment of children. Consideration of the residential schools, Indigenous cultural values, social scientific research findings, biblical and theological scholarship—including robust Christian theologies of childhood—have all led to the same conclusion: the corporal punishment of children poses substantial risks to children and has no place in homes, religious communities, or public institutions. Thus, Christian churches must do all they can to stop this practice.

If corporal punishment is not an acceptable way to guide children, those in Christian communities who care about children might then ask the following questions: What are the best ways to guide and discipline children and young people? Are there forms of discipline that do not include corporal punishment? And what does "discipline" in a Christian context even mean? Should we avoid the word altogether, or should we reclaim it from those who have defined it too narrowly as physical punishment? If the latter, then what shape should discipline take?

We need to address the question of discipline seriously because both inside and outside churches, debates about corporal punishment are often linked to diverse understandings of discipline. In everyday language, "discipline" is sometimes used in positive ways to refer to mastery, effort, and training. We admire, for example, a great musician or sports hero who is "disciplined." In popular discussions of child-rearing, however, "discipline" is often equated with "punishment," including corporal punishment. For instance, in the United States, where I live, conservative churches devote significant attention to the discipline, teaching, and guidance of children, and generally tie these important topics to corporal punishment.[1] For this reason, Christians who reject corporal punishment sometimes avoid the word "discipline" altogether, yet in the process they sometimes also neglect to focus sufficient attention on the importance of teaching and guiding children.

Given the various uses of "discipline" in discussions of Christian parenting, as well as the findings of social scientific studies of healthy child development, the aim of this chapter is to examine more closely biblical and theological notions of "discipline" and "discipleship." In the Bible, these words are translations of various Greek terms. When we examine more carefully their meanings and use in particular biblical passages, we find some surprises. By exploring the Bible and the history of Christianity with attention to ways that Christians have sought to cultivate discipleship and "the discipline and instruction of the Lord" (Ephesians 6:4), we find very little attention paid to corporal punishment. Rather, as we see in the Bible, in Jesus's teaching and example, and in the history of Christianity as well as in contemporary research findings and reflection on our own experience, true discipleship and the "discipline of the Lord" are cultivated by following Jesus's command to love and serve the neighbour (including our enemies) and by carrying out central spiritual practices such as worshipping, praying, forgiving, and reading the Scriptures. By examining the terms "discipleship" and "discipline," this chapter can serve both as a resource for thinking in fresh ways about the discipline of children and as a precursor to the next chapter in this volume, in which Charlene Hallett and Ashley Stewart-Tufescu describe the evidence-based practice of "positive discipline."

Disciple and Discipleship

The Greek word for "disciple" is μαθητής (*mathētēs*), and it refers broadly to a student, pupil, learner, or adherent of a particular leader or movement. In the gospels, we see Jesus calling his disciples to know him, to be in relationship to him, and to heal, preach, love, and forgive. Jesus appoints twelve disciples "to be with him, and to be sent out to proclaim the message" (Mark 3:14).[2] Paul says God calls us "into the fellowship of his Son, Jesus Christ our Lord" (1 Corinthians 1:9). After healing all who were trying to touch him, preaching to a great crowd of disciples, and teaching them to "love your enemies, do good to those who hate you" (Luke 6:27), Jesus powerfully states, "A disciple is not above the teacher, but everyone who is fully qualified [or "fully trained"] will be like the teacher" (Luke 6:40).

It is noteworthy for Christians today who seek to be, and to raise their children to be, disciples of Jesus that physical punishment does not appear in the New Testament picture of discipleship. Jesus never recommends hitting, spanking, or physically punishing one's self or others as a way to be a faithful follower or to love God and the neighbour. Rather, he calls his followers to be close to him and to be like him. Furthermore, the practices Jesus carries out and encourages his disciples to emulate are loving others (including one's enemies), repenting, forgiving, praying, serving the poor, fasting, caring for and healing the sick, washing one another's feet, being humble, attending to the Word of God, and spreading the good news.

Furthermore, we find no instances of Jesus hitting or spanking children. Rather, if we look at even just a few of the verbs used to describe Jesus's interactions with children, we see his warm, active, and caring engagement. He blesses, heals, and takes them up in his arms. He claims, "Whoever welcomes one such child in my name welcomes me" (Matthew 18:1–5; Mark 9:37). Here the Greek word for "welcomes" or "receives" (*δέχομαι*; *dechomai*) can mean "warmly receptive or welcoming" or "receptive with a high level of involvement." When children are brought to Jesus so that he might bless and pray for them, the disciples try to stop them, but Jesus rebukes the disciples, saying, "Let the little children come to me, and do not stop them; for it is to such as these that the kingdom of heaven belongs" (Matthew 19:14). In another passage found in all three synoptic gospels, Jesus uses a strong word meaning "cause to stumble" or "offend" and related to the English word for "scandal" (*σκανδαλίσῃ*, *skandalisē*) when he says, "If any of you *put a stumbling block* [*σκανδαλίσῃ*] before one of these little ones who believe in me, it would be better for you if a great millstone were hung around your neck and you were thrown into the sea" (Mark 9:42; cf. Luke 17:2; Matthew 18:6).

Discipline

Given this notion of disciple and discipleship, what can we learn further about the concept of discipline in the New Testament? None of the teachings or sayings of Jesus in the gospels refer to "discipline." References to "discipline" are found only in some letters of the New Testament, where the word is often a translation of the Greek word παιδεία (*paideia*), which cannot be responsibly translated as "physical punishment."

Paideia is a Greek term that generally refers to instruction, training, education, upbringing, or guidance.[3] *Paideia* has been used in ancient Greek philosophy and even at some liberal arts colleges today to speak about the kind of wide-ranging education that can lead to excellence, virtue, and contributions as a citizen.[4] Thus, for the ancient Greeks and for thinkers past and present, *paideia* refers to a broad and holistic education that includes training in moral, physical, and intellectual life. Even though some Greeks did physically punish children as part of their upbringing, *paideia* itself is not a term that can be translated or understood merely as "physical punishment" but is much more closely associated with well-rounded understandings of education, formation, and training.

In the often-quoted passage from Ephesians 6:4, for example, the word translated as "discipline" is *paideia*, and it is used in the phrase, "discipline of the Lord." Here, "discipline and instruction," especially "discipline and instruction in the Lord," cannot be equated with physical punishment. The passage even includes a warning not to provoke children to anger or exasperate them: "Do not provoke your children to anger but bring them up in the discipline [*paideia*] and instruction [*nouthesia*] of the Lord" (Ephesians 6:4).

Colossians also warns parents not to provoke their children, "or they may lose heart" (Colossians 3:21).[5] This text and others speak of the qualities of those who find new life in Christ. In Colossians, the warning not to provoke anger, for example, is preceded by a long description of the new life in Christ and the admonition to "clothe yourselves with compassion, kindness, humility, meekness, and patience," and "above all, clothe yourselves with love, which binds everything together in perfect harmony" (Colossians 3:12,14). In Paul's letter to the Galatians, he also speaks of being "clothed with" and unified in Christ (Galatians 3:26–27). He describes the fruit of the Spirit as "love, joy, peace, patience, kindness, generosity, faithfulness, gentleness, and self-control" (Galatians 5:22–23), and he warns: "If anyone is detected in a transgression, you who have received the Spirit should restore such a one in a spirit of gentleness" (Galatians 6:1).

The verb *paideian* is used in 2 Timothy to speak of "training in righteousness" (2 Timothy 3:16), and here, too, there is no reference to physical punishment. Rather, the passage emphasizes that "training in righteousness" takes place by studying Scripture. "All Scripture is inspired by God and is useful for teaching, for reproof, for correction, and for training [*paideian*] in righteousness" (2 Timothy 3:16). The Greek word translated as "for correction" is ἐπανόρθωσιν (*epanorthōsin*), which refers to restoring to an upright state or straightening of the conduct of one who is crooked.

Some references to "self-discipline" or "self-control" can also be found in New Testament letters in relation to both discipleship and leadership, and they are translations of other Greek terms. For example, Titus 1:8 uses the Greek adjective ἐγκρατῆ (*enkratē*), translated as "self-disciplined," "disciplined," or "temperate," to help describe one of the important qualities of a church leader, along with "hospitable," "a lover of goodness," "prudent" (also translated as "sensible"), "upright," and "devout." In 2 Timothy, self-discipline and love are contrasted with cowardice: "For God did not give us a spirit of cowardice, but rather a spirit of power and of love and of self-discipline [*σωφρονισμοῦ* (*sōphronismou*)]" (2 Timothy 1:7).

The only passage in the New Testament that appears to link discipline (*paideia*) with suffering and possibly physical punishment are a few verses in Hebrews (12:5–9) that quote directly from Proverbs. Here the author of Hebrews speaks of the "discipline [*paideias*] of the Lord" and quotes Proverbs 3:11–12. However, in these passages of Hebrews, the author is not speaking about training or teaching children, and the one here who disciplines is not parents but God. As we learn from the work of William Morrow (see Chapter 7), the author of Hebrews is addressing early Christians who have experienced persecution. The author acknowledges their suffering and encourages them to keep the faith. Although this text has much to say about enduring suffering and God's action in the world, this passage does not prescribe the corporal punishment of children.[6]

The Power of Spiritual Practices for Christ-Centred Discipline and Discipleship

Given even this brief exploration of discipleship, discipline, and Jesus's own teachings and example, we have ample biblical support to reject physical punishment as a proper form of Christ-centred discipline. Although some Christians have inflicted harsh physical punishment as a way to "discipline" children or help them become disciples, the primary and biblically based spiritual practices encouraged by Jesus and among diverse forms of Christianity around the world, past and present, for becoming or raising disciples do not include physical punishment. Rather, the most important practices are loving others, praying, repenting, forgiving, studying the Word of God, worshipping together, sharing bread and wine in remembrance of Jesus, being baptized, spreading the good news, and serving those in need.[7]

Such spiritual practices are biblically based, carried out by Jesus himself, and rooted in the Christian theological tradition, and they are the focus of several studies of healthy spiritual development and faith formation. For example, prominent social-scientific studies of the spiritual and religious lives of children and teenagers do not indicate that physical punishment promotes healthy child development or spiritual growth. Rather, social scientists who have studied Christian communities, such as Christian Smith, Robert Wuthnow, or Eugene Roehlkepartain, point to other factors that help children grow and develop in their faith and cultivate a larger sense of purpose, such as worshipping, praying, and carrying out service projects together.[8] Wuthnow states, for example, that "effective religious socialization comes about through embedded practices; that is, through specific, deliberate religious activities that are firmly intertwined with daily habits of family routines."[9] Respected religious educators who have developed faith formation programs and resources for the Church also say nothing about corporal punishment, focusing instead on cultivating warm and caring child-adult relationships, talking about faith, and carrying out spiritual practices with children and youth in the home and congregation.[10]

Even psychologists and sociologists who study the positive role of religion, religious communities, and spirituality in the lives of children do not suggest or find that physical punishment is a positive approach to spiritual development. Lisa Miller is one of the growing number of psychologists who are interested in the positive role that spiritual life can play in children's intellectual, physical, social, and emotional development.[11] Building primarily on recent scientific studies in the field of positive psychology that focus on mental health, happiness, and human flourishing, Miller finds that children with a robust spiritual life are less likely to abuse alcohol or drugs or to engage in risky sexual behaviours. They tend to develop a more resilient way of coping with setbacks, failures, and adversity. They are also less likely to suffer from depression as adults. In the final chapter of her book, Miller offers several concrete suggestions for parents who seek to cultivate a child's spiritual development but does not suggest physical punishment. Rather, she encourages parents to speak openly and authentically about their own spiritual experiences, carry out spiritual practices in the home, serve others, and delight in the natural. She also suggests talking more intentionally about spiritual dimensions of daily life, thereby enriching children's language environment and providing them with a robust spiritual and ethical vocabulary that gives meaning and helps set one's moral compass. In these and other ways, Miller believes parents can connect deeply with their children and enrich their own and their children's spiritual lives.[12]

Our own experiences and the experiences of young people in our midst also testify to the power of such spiritual practices for faith formation and healthy development. I have taught college students for over twenty years, and whenever I have asked them to reflect on experiences that positively shaped their spiritual or moral development, no student has mentioned corporal punishment. Most of them write about positive role models such as their parents or youth leaders, and experiences such as participating in mission trips or service projects, being a part of a warm and supportive religious community, leading worship, attending Bible camps, praying and sharing concerns with their parents, or talking about faith with their parents, mentors, or friends.

Even if one believes that corporal punishment truly does no harm, what positive role can it possibly play in nurturing a child's spiritual development? Do adults who were physically punished talk about it as one of the most powerful and positive ways that they deepened their faith or connected more deeply with their parents? As Joan Durrant and Bernadette Saunders have shown (Chapters 2 and 3, respectively), physical punishment is much more likely to breed shame and resentment and to erode parent-child relationships.

Conclusion

The Bible, many church leaders past and present, social scientists, and our own experiences all testify to the power of meaningful spiritual practices in the home and the community for cultivating faith and discipleship. In line with such practice, any positive model for cultivating discipleship and discipline will certainly also attend to children's basic needs for food, water, shelter, adequate health care, education, belonging, acceptance, affection, and love. It is this kind of positive discipline, not pain and suffering, that leads to authentic discipleship and human flourishing.

Notes

1 For example, Focus on the Family and its founder, James Dobson, have paid attention in important and positive ways to strengthening families, child development, and faith formation. Nevertheless, even the most recent version of Dobson's hugely popular book (originally called *Dare to Discipline*), *The New Dare to Discipline*, rev. ed. (Carol Stream, IL: Tyndale Momentum, 2018), claims that physical punishment is biblically based and condones spanking under certain conditions.

2 All biblical passages quoted in this chapter are taken from the New Revised Standard Version (NRSV).

3 See the entry for *paideia*, for example, in F. Wilbur Gingrich and Frederick W. Dancker, *A Greek-English Lexicon of the New Testament and Other Early Christian Literature*, 2nd ed.), rev. and augmented from Walter Bauer's 5th ed., 1958 (Chicago: University of Chicago Press, 1979).

4 Luther College in Decorah, Iowa, for example, uses the word *paideia* as the title of a signature offering in its general education program. The *Paideia* Program focuses on writing, critical thinking, and the close reading of primary texts, and aims to ground students "for success in education and life." In the program, "both students and faculty read, think, discuss, and write about the questions and choices that matter." See "Paideia," *Luther College,* accessed 9 October 2018, www.luther.edu/paideia/.

5 Other translations of this passage include "lest they become discouraged" or "disheartened." The Greek word here is ἀθυμῶσιν, which literally means "spiritless" or "without a spirit."

6 Note that in one resource about biblical notions of the discipline of children on the Focus on the Family website, the primary biblical passages discussed are from Hebrews 12 and Proverbs. See Chip Ingram, "What the Bible Says about Discipline," Focus on the Family, accessed 9 October 2018, www.focusonthefamily.com/parenting/effective-biblical-discipline/effective-child-discipline/what-the-bible-says-about-discipline.

7 Some of the classic texts on faith formation in the history of Christianity include St. John Chrysostom (fourth century), *On Marriage and Family Life,* trans. Catherine P. Roth and David Anderson (Crestwood, NY: St. Vladimir's Seminary Press, 1986); Martin Luther (sixteenth century), *The Large Catechism of Dr. Martin Luther, 1529: The Annotated Luther Study Edition*, ed. Kirsi Stjerna (Minneapolis: Fortress Press, 2016);

and Horace Bushnell (nineteenth century), *Christian Nurture* (New York: Charles Scribner, 1861).

8 See, for example, Christian Smith and Melinda L. Denton, *Soul Searching: The Religious and Spiritual Lives of American Teenagers* (Oxford: Oxford University Press, 2005); Robert Wuthnow, *Growing Up Religious: Christians and Jews and Their Journeys of Faith* (Boston: Beacon Press, 1999); the Search Institute's attention to "Developmental Assets," accessed 10 October 2018, www.search-institute.org/our-research/development-assets; Eugene C. Roehlkepartain et al., eds., *The Handbook of Spiritual Development in Childhood and Adolescence* (Thousand Oaks, CA: Sage, 2006); Karen M. Yust et al., eds., *Nurturing Child and Adolescent Spirituality: Perspectives from the World's Religious Traditions* (Lanham, MD: Rowman and Littlefield, 2006). See also the ongoing studies of the Search Institute, accessed 10 October 2018, www.Search-Institute.org; and the "National Study of Youth and Religion," University of Notre Dame, accessed 10 October 2018, www.youthandreligion.nd.edu.

9 Wuthnow, *Growing Up Religious,* xxxi–xxxii.

10 Additional resources on the spiritual development and faith formation of children in Christian communities include Merton P. Strommen and Richard Hardel, *Passing on the Faith: A Radical New Model for Youth and Family Ministry* (Winona, MN: St. Mary's Press, 2000); Kara Powell, Brad Griffin, and Cheryl Crawford, *Sticky Faith: Youth Worker Edition* (Grand Rapids, MI: Zondervan, 2011); John Roberto, Kathie Amidei, and Jim Merhaut, *Generations Together: Caring, Praying, Learning, Celebrating, and Serving Faithfully* (Naugatuck, CT: LifelongFaith Associates, 2014); Vern Bengtson, *Families and Faith: How Religion Is Passed Down across Generations* (New York: Oxford University Press, 2013); Catherine Stonehouse and Scottie May, *Listening to Children on the Spiritual Journey: Guidance for Those Who Teach and Nurture* (Grand Rapids, MI: Baker Academic, 2010); and Jerome W. Berryman, *Godly Play: An Imaginative Approach to Religious Education* (San Francisco: HarperSanFrancisco, 1991).

11 Lisa Miller, *The Spiritual Child: The New Science on Parenting for Health and Lifelong Thriving* (London: Picador, 2015).

12 For more about the spiritual lives of children and adolescents generally, see, for example, S. Cavalletti, *The Religious Potential of the Child* (New York: Paulist Press, 1983); R. Coles, *The Spiritual Life of Children* (Boston: Houghton Mifflin, 1990); David Hay and Rebecca Nye, *The Spirit of the Child* (London: Fount, 1998). Various not-for-profit institutes and projects are also holding conferences on children's spirituality, such as The International Association for Children's Spirituality, which has sponsored an annual international conference since July 2000 and also launched the *International Journal of Children's Spirituality* in 1996; see www.childrenspirituality.org.

12

WALKING THE PATH TOWARD RECONCILIATION

One Mother's Transformative Journey from Parenting with Punishment to Parenting with Positive Discipline

CHARLENE HALLETT AND ASHLEY STEWART-TUFESCU

Charlene's Story (by Charlene Hallett)

Twenty-four smacks on the bum. Spanking was so normal in my childhood home that sometimes, to take my mind off the pain while it was happening, I would count the smacks. Twenty-four smacks was the most I remember getting. I had been playing with a dollhouse in the main floor hallway, blocking the road to the front door, living room, and stairs all at once. I left that area and went to my mom's room near the back of the house. Not long after, I heard her yell for me, "Charlene! Charlene, where are you? Get out here!" I froze. I knew that sharp tone. "What have I done?" I wondered. Not wanting to find out the answer, I hid between the wall and the deep-freezer in my mother's room. This space was no more than a foot wide, but I slipped in there and dared not stir. She was still yelling my name, but she was on the move now. I knew she was searching for me. We lived in a three-storey house on Winnipeg's Pritchard Avenue then, so it took her a while to find me. She came into her room and, seeing nothing (she probably did not suspect that someone could hide in that terribly tight spot), left nearly as quickly as she had entered. Then I could hear her on the second floor, still yelling. This had turned very bad now, and I knew I was only making it worse by hiding. My seven-year-old brain went into self-protective mode and told me that if I came out of hiding, I would get hurt. I stayed put. The longer she looked and called for me, the more terrified I became. And then, after what seemed like forever, she was in her room again. But this time, she did not turn and leave. I could hear her steps coming closer to my hiding spot. Our eyes locked. She had found me. I remember feeling that I took flight in that moment when she grabbed me from between the wall and the deep-freezer and threw me on her bed. Then came the spanking, the squirming, the crying, the counting. One. Two. Three . . . Twenty-four smacks.

After thirty-five years, it is still hard to let the pain of that memory go. I felt so scared, defenceless, and hurt. All because I had left the dollhouse in the way and she wanted me to move it. I cannot know if responding from the start would have saved me from a spanking. Her tone was predictable; the fallout was not. This event is seared into my childhood memories. But my mom has no memory of it—which is probably for the best. Sometimes the mind needs to block out the most painful parts of our past, and my mom has lived through a lot of pain. She does not discuss much of the physical punishment she endured as a child, whether at home or in the residential school she briefly attended, but she has spoken of it and acknowledged that it affected the way she parented. Essentially, it was the only way she knew. Thinking about how violence was so normalized in her childhood and remembering that day in her room all those years ago makes me feel tense and emotional. I feel sad that my mom did not experience the warmth she deserved in her childhood and that because of this, she did not fully know how to provide that kind of nurture to her own children.

I have considered how my experience that day would make my own children feel, and how their dignity would be impacted. It is because of this experience—the fear I felt while hiding from my mom, coupled with the pain and degradation of the spanking—that I made a commitment to myself long before my children arrived that I would never subject them to physical punishment.

Then, when I was thirty-seven years old, it happened: I spanked my son. He was just about four years old and had taken to expressing his own frustration by hitting. This behaviour was new to my husband and me, as our two older daughters had not behaved this way. I was slow to realize that he was not *giving* me a hard time. Rather, he was *having* a hard time. It was one day along this learning curve, while both he and I were low on patience and high on frustration, that I lost control of my own emotions and spanked him. Hard. He was scared and shocked as I left him crying in the living room, only to go around the corner and burst into tears myself. I felt guilty, out of control, and out of tools. Nothing about my actions felt good or right, and I had to acknowledge the absurdity of trying to teach my child not to hit by hitting him. I realized that the only message I was sending was that the biggest, strongest person in the room is the one to fear. Was that the message I wanted him to take out into the world as he grew from a boy into a man? This incident forced me to reflect on all of this. Yet just a week later, I spanked him again. It was then, as I made myself stay with him and look into his eyes, that I intimately recognized the expression of fear that filled them—another moment seared in my consciousness—and I vowed to both of us that I would never do that again. I knew that I had to stop spanking him, as this only perpetuated the cycle of violence I had experienced as a child, a cycle I was desperate to break. It was time to get serious about finding a healthier way to raise my children, and I knew I could not do this on my own. I also knew that if I was going to do better in the future, I would need to find the courage to address my past.

Part of confronting this intergenerational transmission of violence in my own parenting meant looking at my personal family history. We are an Indigenous family in this country known as Canada. I have participated in many circles where discussions of intergenerational trauma have taken place, and I can personally speak to its reality and impact. Colonialism was not designed to respect or nurture healthy Indigenous families, ones that are strong in connection, culture, and spirituality. Instead, the intention was to "civilize the savages." When that did not work to the colonizers' satisfaction, the new goal became separating children from their families, communities, and all that they knew. This was, in large part, the rationale for the residential schools, whose impact has lasted for generations. I feel the pain through my blood and bones when I think about the children being stolen, ceremonies being outlawed, languages being stifled, and families left devastated. I can say that the hurt of all that, whether I am always conscious of it or not, lives in my DNA. That is what intergenerational trauma means to me. However, something more powerful is alive there, too, and courses through my veins with more force and grit: resilience. I wholeheartedly feel the strength, courage, and gentleness of my ancestors. They guide and protect me, and it is my role as a parent to do the same for my children. Raising a healthy family, one free from violence and threat, is an act of decolonization, and I am eager to do my part.

While on this journey to decolonize my parenting, I began to seek a deeper connection with traditional Indigenous approaches to raising children. I learned through watching others, watching videos, reading, and talking with community members. I have listened to Indigenous midwives and doulas who are bringing back traditional birthing practices to communities. I have spoken with families who are reviving their language(s) with their children. I have sat with Elders who describe a time when children were treated as sacred beings, and tell us how we need to remember this and let our actions reflect it. All these teachings informed the way I would parent my children. I began to embrace the Seven Sacred Teachings—love, humility, truth, honesty, wisdom, courage, and respect—as I have learned them from the Anishinaabeg people in this territory. Doing so has helped me to nurture a more positive and meaningful connection with not just my own children but with my ancestors and all of creation. Golden are the conversations I have had with my children about humility, the difference between truth and honesty, the gift of being loved, what it means to be respectful, and much more. Embodying these teachings in our day-to-day living has had a monumental impact within our family, as my husband and I work hard to uphold our commitment to raise our children without violence.

In addition to (re)connecting with my roots, I thought I might benefit from more formal parenting supports. It was through my association with a local parenting group that I became aware of Positive Discipline in Everyday Parenting (PDEP),[1] a parent support program I took soon after. The principles of PDEP are rooted in respect, empathy, and the rights of children. This resonated deeply with me from the start. The program's philosophy aligned so beautifully with the traditional ways of parenting I was trying to reclaim. Within this approach, there is no room (or need) for spanking, yelling, or punishing. I appreciate the way the program taught me to be accountable for my actions by reminding me to consider whether my actions move me closer to or further away from my long-term parenting goals. After all, it is a lifelong connection with my children that I am working to maintain.

Learning more about what my children were thinking and feeling at each stage of development enabled me to empathize with what they were experiencing. My boy had just started kindergarten when I took the PDEP Facilitator training. He was still working through some big emotions and I felt ill-equipped to help him. While I had already discovered quite a few tools for positive discipline by immersing myself in reading and attending family centres, the PDEP program is where my real transformation occurred. Any trepidation I felt about taking on this new approach or my ability to change was overshadowed by my hope for something better. I undertook the gradual process of unlearning what was unhealthy and re-learning how to communicate and resolve conflict in a more constructive way. I have found this to be an ongoing and humbling process. I mess up often (as my children can attest), but perfection is not the goal. Instead, and much more realistically, some goals are to be kind to myself and my children when we do mess up, to apologize, to learn from our mistakes, to try again, and to nurture our roots and relationships. My hope is that my children—and all children—grow with an understanding of how sacred they are and that they will feel this not just through our words but also through our actions.

I can cite many examples of how PDEP has helped to reaffirm my commitment to responding to parent-child conflict without punishment. One such opportunity came when one of my children had used harsh words with a classmate to the extent that she (my daughter) believed that her words could be considered bullying. This was disappointing to hear and out of character for her. Rather than criticizing or punishing her before she had a chance to explain, I decided to listen to her. After all, it took courage for her to come to me, and with humility to admit her mistake. As I listened, she spoke of the pressures she felt to fit in with her peers. She described the feeling of not being able to put aside what she had done to her classmate. We talked about our consciences and how that nagging inside is our spirit's way of guiding us to do what is right. Living in an honest way is the best way. Talking out her feelings was the first step in alleviating the guilt she was feeling. Making things right with the girl she had wronged would be the next step. She recognized that until that happened, the nagging inside would continue. My daughter took the girl aside at school and made it right, doing this of her own volition. When I consider what would have happened had I struck her, berated her, or made her feel badly about her actions, I realize that she would have learned that I cannot be trusted to talk about hard things. That is not what I want. When I tell my children that they can tell me anything, my actions must match my words.

There have been many incidents where my children have come to me to discuss something that is bothering them, including their mistakes, and now (after much practice) we can usually talk about it calmly. As they have grown, we have had to deal with bigger issues. For example, when I picked up my fifteen-year-old from a party recently, I detected the unmistakable odour of alcohol when she entered the vehicle. In that moment, I was very grateful for the principles of PDEP, because I had to draw on them deeply right then. My daughter admitted to drinking, and we talked about her choice to do so. She apologized more than once on the ride home, so I reminded her that what she did was not done *to* me, nor was it a reflection *of* me. This was her choice. Nonetheless, she was sorry she had done something that could potentially diminish my trust in her. The conversation carried over into the next day, while she nursed a hangover and kept up with her chores. It also continued when I saw her friends. Because I have established a trusting and respectful environment in our home, I was able to have a frank conversation with all of them about safety, responsibility, pressures, curiosity, and more. That was a very good outcome of a bad decision. We have all made bad decisions, but as I like to remind my children, onward we go.

We will never stop learning. We will never stop loving. And we will always seek out ways in our home to combine the PDEP tools with the traditional ways of parenting from my own community that I have come to value. Learning about the impact of residential schools, colonial violence in Canada, and intergenerational trauma has opened my eyes to what many Indigenous families have lived through and overcome, including, in various ways, my own family. This knowledge also softened my heart enough to put aside the anger and hurt I felt toward my mother for too many years. She and I continue to work hard at building the connection that we both craved but did not create during my childhood and adolescence. Doing so has motivated me to focus on the way I treat my own children—while they are still young and while I still have influence over their everyday lives—and to take the time to enjoy them, embrace them, and empower them. Children have the right to a life free from violence, and it is in all of us to make this a reality. My own healing comes from earnestly working toward my long-term goals. I know that I cannot change the past, but I can do my part to ensure that my children do not carry this pain into their futures.

Positive Discipline in Everyday Parenting: A Transformative Tool for Reconciliation and Parenting without Punishment (by Ashley Stewart-Tufescu)[2]

Charlene's narrative of her transformation illustrates the vital role of formal parenting supports, which she found to be highly compatible with the traditional Indigenous teachings she has received. PDEP was not only instrumental in supporting Charlene in fulfilling her promise to herself to raise her children without violence, but also in helping her to work toward her long-term goal of halting the intergenerational transmission of punitive violence and colonial parenting practices within her family.[3] The program deepened her understanding of what "discipline" means: embrace the idea of listening to children's perspectives in times of conflict; understand how their thoughts, feelings, and behaviours are related to their mental, physical, emotional, and spiritual development; respond to them with warmth, love, empathy, and trust; and guide them with structure, wisdom, respect, and humility. With practice and patience, the PDEP principles have helped Charlene gradually make the transition from punishing her children to guiding and nurturing their healthy development.

PDEP has four main principles. First, it is important as parents to identify and focus on our long-term goals. Much of a parent's day is spent focusing on short-term goals, such as getting the dishwasher emptied, getting out the door on time, and getting homework done. In the frustration that is so common in those moments, we often respond with anger and threats of—or actual—punishment (spanking, taking things away, isolating the child). Over time, those responses damage our relationships with our children and impede our progress toward what we really want to achieve. In my experience of delivering PDEP programs all over the world, I have discovered that parents everywhere share similar hopes and dreams for their children. They hope their children will grow up to be kind, compassionate, non-violent, honest, responsible, and good communicators and problem solvers. When we strike or otherwise hurt our children, we are losing an opportunity to show them how to remain kind when angry, how to communicate when frustrated, and how to solve problems without aggression. When parents become aware of the difference between short- and long-term parenting goals, their focus begins to shift.

Second, it is important to be aware of the two most important tools for teaching—"warmth" and "structure." *Warmth* is the emotional climate of a home that ensures children's physical and emotional safety. In such a climate, children are not afraid to admit mistakes, to seek help, or to tell the truth. *Structure* is the information and support that children need to succeed. PDEP is based on the notion of "scaffolding" children's learning. This requires the parent to assess what the child understands and is capable of doing now. Then the parent can figure out the next step in the child's learning and provide what the child needs in order to understand.

Third, to provide warmth and structure appropriately, we need to have a good understanding of how children think, feel, and see the world. For example, it is important to understand that the developmental process underlying toddlers' negativism, preschoolers' desire to choose their own clothes, and teenagers' preference for peers over parents is the same one—the innate human drive for autonomy. When we see a child's behaviour as reflecting this basic human need rather than as non-compliance, we can provide warmth and structure in a way that keeps the child safe, teaches the child important skills, and strengthens the parent-child relationship.

Fourth, a true "disciplinary" response that teaches rather than punishes requires thought. In PDEP, we call this "problem-solving." Rather than reacting with a slap, a threat, or another punishment, parents learn how to think through the situation and to respond in a way that will preserve the relationship and teach the child what they actually want the child to learn.

This approach is not a quick fix. It requires courage to confront destructive parenting practices to which we might have been exposed or that we might have internalized. It requires humility to learn from mistakes (both ours and others') and the willingness to try new approaches. Parents, in their commitment to make this shift, put their trust in the program's facilitator, whose role it is to guide them on their transformative journey. The first step in Charlene's transformation was identifying her long-term parenting goals and contrasting them with the fear she felt during her childhood as a result of physical punishment. For many, making the transformation from punishment to discipline requires a complete shift away from what is easy and familiar, a decision to walk a different parenting path that might not be supported by one's family, community, or society. In the beginning, Charlene was apprehensive about explaining this new parenting approach to those closest to her because it was so different from how she and her siblings had been raised. She also struggled with her own doubts about the effectiveness of positive discipline in the long term. She has described having intense conversations with someone who was convinced that spanking children, especially boys, was necessary. She struggled when she was around others as they physically punished their children. It took great faith and a strong commitment for Charlene to walk this new and sometimes lonely path toward transformation.

For Charlene, responding to challenging situations with positive discipline came more easily when she better understood the developmental reasons underlying her children's behaviour. PDEP is carefully designed to help parents understand developmental processes, enabling them to see the world through the eyes of their maturing, growing, curious children. A parent who can consider a situation from a child's perspective is better equipped to guide and teach the child, responding in a way that is developmentally appropriate. For example, instead of viewing a young child's hitting or biting as aggression and punishing it, the parent understands that a young child does not yet have the language to express frustration and anger, or even an understanding of what those feelings are. In PDEP, parents learn that instead of reacting to the child's behaviour with punishment, such as biting them back or forcing them to sit alone in isolation to "think" about the wrongs they have committed, the parent responds with warmth (safety and security) and structure (information and communication). Warmth might take the form of empathizing with the child's feelings and ensuring that the child feels safe. Structure might involve labelling these feelings with words and modelling a constructive and safe way for the child to express and manage these intense emotions. When Charlene's adolescent daughter experimented with alcohol, rather than punishing her, Charlene took the time to speak with her and to understand the reasons behind her decision. She paused to consider how peer pressure and risk taking might have influenced her daughter's behaviour. She then created a secure environment in which to discuss with her daughter (and her daughter's friends) the importance of safety, responsibility, and independent decision-making in the face of peer pressure. In this challenging parenting situation, Charlene was able to use the PDEP approach to transform a situation that could have been fraught with anger, fear, and relationship damage into an important learning opportunity for her daughter, her friends, and (as Charlene reminds me) for herself, too.

PDEP as a Bridge toward Transformation in Diverse Religious Contexts

PDEP has supported many parents in gradually making the shift from punishment to discipline. The program has been delivered in over thirty countries, including in some deeply religious contexts where corporal punishment is normative, prescribed, and widely practised. For example, PDEP has been successfully implemented in Protestant Hutterite communities in Canada. In one instance, the program was sought out by a Hutterite colony in Manitoba in response to a child welfare case involving a nearby Mennonite community. More than thirty-five children from that insular community of Old Order Mennonites were apprehended by child welfare services and placed into foster care when it was discovered that they had been physically abused in the name of discipline, in keeping with that community's interpretation of biblical scriptures.[4] This situation sparked debate about corporal punishment within some Hutterite communities in the surrounding area. A group of Hutterite colonies came together and re-evaluated the necessity of corporal punishment in raising children. They sought out non-violent approaches to disciplining children in their homes and their schools, which led them to invite me to deliver PDEP to all of the parents living in several colonies. One of these parents went on to become a certified PDEP facilitator in order to continue sharing the approach with other Hutterite parents.

PDEP has also been widely implemented with parents in Muslim-majority countries. In Gaza and the West Bank, it has been effective at reducing parents' support for physical punishment, and both mothers and fathers living in that context perceive the program as highly relevant to their parenting experiences.[5] PDEP also has been effective in reducing caregivers' support for punishment in the Muslim-majority countries of Bangladesh[6] and Indonesia.[7] In Latin America, PDEP has been widely implemented with Catholic and evangelical Christian families in numerous countries, without the need for adaptations or cultural contextualization. Together, parents from diverse religious contexts, countries, and communities have found PDEP to be *relevant* to their parenting experiences, *effective* at shifting their approval of physical and other emotional forms of punishment, and to have a *positive impact* on their ability to parent without punishment.[8]

Supporting Parents' Transformation from Punishment to Discipline

The evidence is clear that physical punishment of children is harmful to their physical, emotional, and spiritual development (Chapter 2) and is incompatible with a Christian theology of childhood, discipline, and discipleship (Chapters 8 and 11). Yet it is simply not enough to tell parents and other caregivers to stop using it. If we are serious about decolonization and reconciliation and about helping parents make this gradual transformation away from punishment, then we have a collective responsibility to educate parents and other caregivers about alternative approaches to resolving parent-child conflict. This responsibility is extended to all Christians, who are in a position to work together to develop healthy, effective, and non-violent approaches to discipline in raising children and youth. Indeed, because of the ways that some Christian theologies have been used to propagate corporal punishment in Canada (see Chapters 4–8), Christians are in a unique position to disrupt the colonial narrative that has fuelled their theologies around child discipline, and counter these practices from within the place of faith, in their own communities.

To begin, church leaders, Christian parents and others may find it useful to reflect on how the PDEP principles are consistent with the biblical vision that Marcia Bunge has presented (Chapter 8) of children as social agents with strengths, gifts, and agency who also need guidance and protection in a way that honours their dignity as full human beings and bearers of God's image. Bunge (Chapter 11) draws from the teachings of Jesus to further explain that being a disciple is about being in relationship. It is about loving one's neighbour, practising forgiveness, and serving others. She argues that discipline in the New Testament is a holistic concept associated with education and formation—not punishment. Crawford and Sheldon (Chapter 13) point to spiritual practices rooted in the Christian tradition that have similar objectives to PDEP. We hope that collectively, all of these chapters provide tangible tools to move beyond theological reflection to a genuine and sustained change in practice, for the well-being of not only our children but also our families and communities.

The central message of this chapter is highlighted by the lessons we can learn from Charlene's transformative journey: all parents—Indigenous or not, Christian or not—can raise children without violence, fear, or humiliation. But we must not expect that parents and other caregivers can make this significant and long-term transformation without supports.

There is an opportunity at hand for Christian communities to invest in parenting supports (both within and outside those communities) as an act of reconciliation. PDEP is an important bridge to guide parents on the transformative journey away from parenting with punishment and toward parenting with positive discipline. Our children—in all their splendid curiosity, wonder, and value—are surely worth the effort.

Notes

1 See Joan E. Durrant, *Positive Discipline in Everyday Parenting,* 4th ed. (Stockholm: Save the Children Sweden, 2016). PDEP was developed by Dr. Joan Durrant, who is one of the editors of this volume. For the sake of transparency, she earns no royalties from the program, and all facilitators commit to delivering it on a not-for-profit basis.

2 Dr. Stewart-Tufescu is a Positive Discipline in Everyday Parenting Master Trainer. She earns no royalties for this work.

3 For more information about PDEP, see "Positive Discipline in Everyday Parenting," Positive Discipline in Everyday Life, accessed 6 December 2019, http://www.positivedisciplineeveryday.com/.

4 See Canadian Broadcasting Corporation, "Mennonite Child Abuse Arrests Have Community Reeling," CBC News, 21 June 2013, accessed 9 October 2018, https://www.cbc.ca/news/canada/manitoba/mennonite-child-abuse-arrests-have-community-reeling-1.1373140.

5 Ashley Stewart-Tufescu and R. Aljawi, "Transporting a Violence Prevention Parenting Program to a Conflict Setting: Positive Discipline in Everyday Parenting in the Palestinian Territories," presentation at the International Society for the Prevention of Child Abuse and Neglect, Prague, Czechoslovakia, September 2018.

6 L. Khondkar, C. Ateah, and F. Milon, "Implementing 'Positive Discipline in Everyday Parenting' among Ethnic Minorities, Urban Slums, and Brothel Areas of Bangladesh," presentation at the International Society for the Prevention of Child Abuse and Neglect, Calgary, AB, August 2016.

7 A. Stewart-Tufescu et al., "Evaluating the Positive Discipline in Everyday Parenting Facilitator Training Program with Community Health Workers in Indonesia," presentation at the International Society for the Prevention of Child Abuse and Neglect, Prague, Czechoslovakia, September 2018.

8 J. Durrant et al., "Parents' Views of the Relevance of a Violence Prevention Program in High, Medium, and Low Human Development Contexts, *International Journal of Behavioral Development* 41, no. 4 (June 2017): 523–31; Khondkar, Ateah, and Milon, "Implementing 'Positive Discipline in Everyday Parenting.'"

13

WHOLE-PERSON DISCIPLINE
The Spiritual Nurture of Children

AMY CRAWFORD AND ANDREW SHELDON

Jesus had such respect and reverence for what is within the heart of a child that he became a child himself. When people began to follow him, they noticed the special relationship he had with children. He seemed to know who they really were, and they seemed to know who he really was, without being told. The children came to him. His disciples tried to stop them, but he told them, "No—let the children come." He welcomed them into his arms and blessed them.

Bishop Mark MacDonald (Chapter 1) describes the contrast that is the systemic evil of colonialism, identifying the evil perpetrated in the schools as particularly egregious because it was directed at children in such a violent way. The purpose of much of this volume has been to argue against the abuses that happened in the residential schools in Canada, and that happen to children around the world, through the practice of corporal punishment. Such acts stand in stark contrast to the story of Jesus taking, welcoming, and honouring children. Sadly, they are acts to which churches often have been an animating partner over centuries.

This third section of this volume takes a turn away from corporal punishment to thinking about what children actually need to flourish. Surely it is more than not being hit. Martin Brokenleg (Chapter 9) and

Shirley Tagalik (Chapter 10) share their experiences and wisdom related to Indigenous child-rearing practices that honour children. Marcia Bunge (Chapter 11) presents fresh theological work on discipline that helps us all to understand it as being not about rules and obedience but about the flourishing of the child. Charlene Hallett and Ashley Stewart-Tufescu (Chapter 12) describe a practical approach to discipline that parents can use in the home and that is compatible with both Christian teachings and the Seven Sacred Teachings. In the present chapter, we turn back to the rich canon available through Christian scriptures and our spiritual tradition. Bunge (Chapter 11) is clear that a robust theology of discipline demands far more than the ability to know right from wrong. Discipline, she argues, is about making disciples. To truly accomplish this goal, not hitting children must be considered as only an *early* step in this journey. The nurturance of children, who are already recognized by Jesus as fully formed spiritual beings, is core to our Christian calling. As Rebecca Nye, one of the leaders in work on children's spiritual formation, suggests, "maybe 'child protection' policies should include measures to protect the withering of children's spiritual potential!"[1] Spiritual formation is the focus of this chapter.

Advancing a High View of Children

Current and emerging understandings of children's spirituality advance a "high view" of children, one that is in keeping with the life and ministry of Jesus. The term "high view" is borrowed from a typology developed by Jerome Berryman, in which he contrasts a "low view" of children, that is indifferent, ambivalent, and ambiguous with a "high view" that considers them even as means of grace.[2] We begin this chapter by advocating for a high view of children. This includes their centrality in our lives as people of God, their spiritual capability to know God innately and instinctively, and their position as exemplars of what it is to be a spiritual person. Following that, we will explore how such an understanding would alter a low view of children and thus alter our behaviours. Finally, given this alternative way of seeing children, we offer some practices that will facilitate the care, nurture, and protection their dignity demands.

Historically, the church has been an animating partner in perpetuating a low view of children, and in so doing has relied on particular interpretations of scriptures or particular theologies to buttress that view. This is ironic when one considers the arguably high view that Jesus had of children. In the gospels, it appears that Jesus affirms both the centrality and the spiritual capability of children. Consider an account in the gospel of Matthew: "At that time the disciples came to Jesus and asked, 'Who is the greatest in the kingdom of heaven?' He called a child, whom he put among them, and said, 'Truly I tell you, unless you change and become like children, you will never enter the kingdom of heaven. Whoever becomes humble like this child is the greatest in the kingdom of heaven. Whoever welcomes one such child in my name welcomes me" (Matthew 18:1–5).[3]

Consider too what we read in the gospel of Luke: "An argument arose among them as to which one of them was the greatest. But Jesus, aware of their inner thoughts, took a little child and put it by his side, and said to them, 'Whoever welcomes this child in my name welcomes me, and whoever welcomes me welcomes the one who sent me; for the least among all of you is the greatest'" (Luke 9:46–48).

These are profound words. Reflect especially on the notion of "taking." We have another later instance of Jesus "taking" something: on the night before he died, Jesus took bread; he took wine. In this earlier case, Jesus took a child and said something profound about the child's centrality and capability of being an exemplar of Christian faith. The one form of "taking"—of bread and wine—has become the central act around which Christians gather on a regular basis. The other form of "taking"—of the child—has often been consigned to church basements and less-than-adequate programming. Yet even in his own time, these words of Jesus turned conventional wisdom inside out and upside down. We need to hear them again with open minds and hearts and "see clearly that this is a parable of action about where to look for spiritual maturity."[4]

In recent years, many individuals have embraced the importance of Jesus's words and have put forward a view of children that challenges much of the received tradition that has pervaded the Western church. Rebecca Nye is an influential voice in this respect. She questions the thinking that informs so much Christian parenting and programming, noting that "some still seem to treat children as spiritually empty and passive vessels until and unless adults intervene."[5] In contrast to this view, Nye cites a Finnish study that found that 80 percent of seven-year-olds and 60 percent of eleven-year-olds reported experiences of being aware of God's existence. Only 30 percent of adults reported similar experiences.[6] On the basis of her own research, Nye concludes that "spiritual awareness is especially natural and common in childhood."[7] With this in mind, we wonder how seeing children as full of God and full of spirit would inform how we structure children's programming, how we teach the faith, and how we parent. Surely, it would say something to us about the belief that physical punishment is a necessary factor in the formation of a child. Is that how we are to treat someone who is offered to us as an exemplar of Christian discipleship?

Practices to Nurture Children's Spiritual Growth

We now consider some practices that adults and caregivers can introduce into their lives with children that both reflect a high view of children and nurture their spiritual growth. Nye reminds us that spirituality starts with God. It is not something parents or caregivers must initiate. What adults can do is appreciate and support the ways that God and children have of being together.[8] As life gets busier and participation in religious organizations declines, parents and caregivers can still support their children's spirituality in simple ways, without adding more activities, pressure, and guilt to family life. Once parents and caregivers see the children in their care as spiritual beings having their own relationship with God, they can begin to nurture that relationship in three simple ways: providing opportunities for authentic play; creating a culture of "storying" together; and creating and implementing communal rituals and traditions.

Authentic Play

Over the past eighty years, psychologists, sociologist, educators, and theologians have emphasized the importance of play to children's physical health, mental well-being, and social and spiritual development. Johan Huizinga's *Homo Ludens*, Mihaly Csikszentmihalyi's *Finding Flow*, Stuart Brown's *Play*, Catherine Garvey's *Play*, and Jürgen Moltmann's *Theology of Play* are just a few titles in a rich repository underscoring the importance of play.[9] Each of these authors recognizes that play is inherent to human existence and that individuals and society are poorer for a lack of it. In *Dangerous Wonder*, Mike Yaconelli writes, "Play is an expression of God's presence in the world; one clear sign of God's absence in society is the absence of playfulness and laughter."[10]

Genuine play is different from organized sports and activities that are tightly monitored by adults. In *Free to Learn*, Peter Gray summarizes the research of several play theorists with five agreed-upon characteristics of play:[11]

1. Play is self-chosen and self-directed. Children define play as voluntary. Even fun and enjoyable experiences are not play if one is obliged to engage in them.
2. Play is motivated by means more than ends. Children engage in play for its own sake; its outcomes or goals are not what is most important to them.
3. Play is guided by children's own rules. Rather than being simply free-form activity, play has rules known to the child. For example, to adults, children's rough-and-tumble play may look wild or chaotic, but the players abide by a shared understanding of what is and is not allowed.
4. Play is imaginative. It takes place in a fantasy world and a state of suspended reality.
5. Play is conducted in an alert, active, but non-stressed frame of mind. Players are attentive to and focused on the process of the play.

Jerome Berryman emphasizes the centrality of play in facing the existential issues of human life, including fear of death and loss, alienation and being alone, desire for and fear of freedom, and the need for meaning and purpose in life. Through play, children enter into a creative process that helps them find ways to deal with these issues.[12]

It is important to stress that "play" is different from "activity." Children in contemporary Western society do not lack opportunities for activity; indeed, in many cases their lives are overflowing with activity. The organization of children's activities is often the domain of the adults in their lives. When it comes to play, children lead. Prescribed play is not true play. For children, play is their work, which merits our respect. When parents and caregivers allow children time and space for authentic play, they are quietly nurturing their children's spiritual development by providing opportunities to come close to a playful God who will accompany them through the joy, suffering, and everyday experiences of life.

The Power of Stories

Stories have played an important role in human history since the beginning of time, helping us learn our history, values, and culture, and form our identity. They also play a role in children's discoveries of their sense of identity and meaning as spiritual beings, formed in the image of

God. In his study of faith development, James Fowler found that when the imagination of a young child is grasped by a story, he or she can be profoundly influenced by that story. He noted that for elementary-age children, meaning is carried in narrative. Children know much of what they know about God through stories.[13] Berryman observed that by entering the stories of scripture, children can affectively and intuitively grasp truths about God that are deeper than what they could comprehend if those truths were only presented in theological words.[14]

But we are not speaking simply of storytelling. Berryman advocates for an approach to "storying" as it is articulated by Kevin Bradt,[15] who describes "storying" as an interplay, a relationship between the teller and the listener. Stories give children another way of knowing and encountering what is true and authentic in life.[16] Storying supports the relationship between God and the child and gives parents and children a way to see and know one another more deeply. But perhaps most important is storying as a collaborative venture. In the context of home and church, storytelling often involves an active adult as storyteller and a passive child as hearer. This is not to suggest that the child does not react and respond to adults' stories, but such reactions and responses can be unsolicited. In storying, there is an intentional engagement of the child in co-creating the story with the teller.[17]

In Godly Play, an innovative method for the spiritual nurture and faith formation of children, the engagement of children's participation is exemplified by the practice of "wondering." The storyteller shares a story and then asks wondering questions. These are genuine open-ended questions that invite children to find meaning in the story for themselves. "I wonder what part of this story you like the best?" "I wonder what part of this story is the most important?" "I wonder if there is anything in this story you can take out and still have all the story you need?" "I wonder where you are in this story, or what in this story is about you?"[18]

In *Stories of God at Home*, Jerome Berryman provides six Godly Play stories to tell at home and recommends six storybooks to read with children.[19] Some find these six stories to be a useful starting place, while others prefer to simply tell stories of their own choice and use wondering questions like the ones above.[20] Tell your children the stories you want them to know about God. Tell them the stories of your family, your values, your culture—especially those that they beg to hear over and over again. Invite their participation. As Berryman notes, "Reading out loud with your family takes no preparation but pays large dividends. It will deepen the meaning and resiliency of your family and help improve empathy and self-esteem to meet future challenges."[21]

Rituals and Traditions

A third practice concerns the importance of rituals and traditions. Children love having the same story retold numerous times, not only because of their need to make meaning but because they value ritual. In her book *Formational Children's Ministry*, Ivy Beckwith notes that rituals can have transformative power.[22] They can change the way we think, feel, and find meaning in day-to-day interactions and experiences. David Hay, Helmut Reich, and Michael Utsch further argue that a primary way spirituality is expressed is through rituals. Children who may not yet have language to describe their spiritual experiences can express them through simple actions, hand gestures, or even facial expressions.[23] Creating simple family rituals can support children in their ways of being together with God and help them know that the adults in their lives see and value their spirituality. Rituals can be traditions that represent the family and connect to previous generations, routines that are unique to a family, or ways of marking life transitions. Rituals are also a conduit for passing on values and beliefs.

Besides creating traditions around major holidays or life celebrations, parents and caregivers can make the evening meal a family event. Finding at least one night a week when the whole family commits to eating together is a good start. Parents can make mealtimes special by lighting a candle or using a special table covering. Family behaviours—things you do only with each other—can also become important rituals to support spirituality. A dance party in the kitchen as the dishes are being done can become a way of expressing joy and gratitude for the gifts of family and bodies. A special hand signal or facial expression can be developed to remind children that they are loved by God and loved by their family. It is important that parents and caregivers discover the rituals that children find meaningful, the traditions that matter to them, the actions they may want to adopt as their own. This cooperative engagement in the home can then be integrated into our communal life, as churches begin to engage children in the creation and implementation of community rituals, liturgies, and commemorations.

Conclusion

These three simple practices—play, storying, and ritual making—can support children in their relationship with God and in their relationship with their parents and caregivers, and they can help adults to see children as spiritual beings, created in the image of God. What is most important is the collaborative nature of these three practices, and ensuring that children are full and equal participants. Far from undermining parents' authority, a collaborative approach engages children as capable partners in the faith journey. Just as Jesus "took" a child into the centre and proclaimed that for adults to reach full spiritual maturity they must become like a child, these practices enable adults to live more faithfully in childlikeness—while providing an opportunity for the child to carry a vital spirituality into adulthood.[24]

We now come full circle. In advocating for a high view of children and in promoting these collaborative practices we have, in a sense, levelled the playing field. We learn that although it is still and always the case that adults have something to offer children in terms of their faith formation and spiritual nurture, children also have something to offer the adult. Such an understanding surely precludes harmful attitudes and behaviours toward children, such as physical punishment.

Let the children come. And know that they need the adults in their lives. They need us to acknowledge their centrality and respect their spiritual capability; to value them for who they are and not just who they might become; and to appreciate their vulnerability and offer grace, not judgement. Our children need opportunities and space to do the play which is their work; to hear the stories that have sustained the people of God for generations; and to ask their questions and to make their meaning. They need adults to provide them with religious language that gives content and context to what they innately know and feel; to invite them into full participation in those traditions and rituals that sustain and enhance our common life; and to provide them with community where they are loved, protected, and valued. Above all, they need us to be present to them, to embrace them, to listen to them, to give a helping hand, even a gentle nudge. In so doing, we will bless the children, and they will bless us.

Notes

1 Rebecca Nye, *Children's Spirituality: What It Is and Why It Matters* (London: Church House Publishing, 2009), 9.

2 The term "high view" is borrowed from a typology Jerome W. Berryman uses in his book *Children and the Theologians: Clearing the Way for Grace* (New York: Morehouse Publishing, 2009).

3 All biblical citations in this chapter are taken from the the New Revised Standard Version (NRSV).

4 Berryman, *Children and the Theologians*, 15.

5 Nye, *Children's Spirituality*, 9.

6 Nye, 9.

7 Nye, 9.

8 Nye, 5.

9 Johan Huizinga, *Homo Ludens: A Study of the Play Element in Culture* (London: Routledge and Kegan Paul, 1949); Mihaly Csikszentmihalyi, *Finding Flow: The Psychology of Engagement with Everyday Life* (New York: Basic Books, 1997); Stuart Brown, *Play: How It Shapes the Brain, Opens the Imagination, and Invigorates the Soul* (New York: Penguin, 2009); Catherine Garvey, *Play: The Developing Child*, enlarged ed. (Cambridge, MA: Harvard University Press, 1990); Jürgen Moltmann, *Theology of Play* (New York City: HarperCollins, 1972).

10 Mike Yaconelli, *Dangerous Wonder: The Adventure of Childlike Faith*, 3rd ed. (Colorado Springs, CO: NavPress, 2003), 79.

11 Peter Gray, *Free to Learn: Why Unleashing the Instinct to Play Will Make Our Children Happier, More Self-Reliant, and Better Students for Life* (New York: Basic Books, 2013), 140–52.

12 Jerome W. Berryman, *Godly Play: An Imaginative Approach to Religious Education* (San Francisco: HarperSanFrancisco, 1991), 57.

13 James W. Fowler, *Stages of Faith: The Psychology of Human Development and the Quest for Meaning* (New York: HarperCollins, 1981), 149.

14 Berryman, *Godly Play*.

15 Jerome W. Berryman, *Stories of God at Home: A Godly Play Approach* (New York: Church Publishing, 2018); Kevin M. Bradt, *Story as a Way of Knowing* (London: Sheed and Ward, 1997).

16 Bradt, *Story as a Way of Knowing*, 4–5.

17 Berryman, *Stories of God at Home*, 6.

18 Jerome W. Berryman, *The Complete Guide to Godly Play*, vol. 1 (Denver: Living the Good News, 2002).

19 Berryman, *Stories of God at Home*.

20 Face-to-face storying with your family can be an antidote to the face-to-screen interaction that is ubiquitous in contemporary life. Sherry Turkle notes that "research shows that those who use social media the most have difficulty reading human emotions, including their own." The face-to-face collaborative aspect of storying can help re-establish the dynamic human connection that is at risk in today's digitized world. It also engages children as full participants, valued for what they offer and not just what they consume. See Sherry Turkle, *Reclaiming Conversation: The Power of Talk in a Digital Age* (New York: Penguin Books, 2015), 25.

21 Berryman, *Stories of God at Home*, 122.

22 Ivy Beckwith, *Formational Children's Ministry: Shaping Children Using Story, Ritual, and Relationship* (Grand Rapids, MI: Baker Books, 2010).

23 David Hay, K. Helmut Reich, and Michael Utsch, "Spiritual Development: Intersections and Divergence with Religious Development," in *The Handbook of Spiritual Development in Childhood and Adolescence*, ed. Eugene C. Roehlkepartain et al. (Thousand Oaks, CA: Sage, 2006), 54.

24 Nye offers a much broader perspective on what the connectedness between childhood and adult spirituality looks like. See Nye, *Children's Spirituality*, 11.

PART 4: MOVING TOWARD RECONCILIATION

Reflections on the *Theological Statement* and (Re)Imagining Our Shared Future

14

DEVELOPING THE THEOLOGICAL STATEMENT ON CORPORAL PUNISHMENT
The Process

KACEY DOOL

What the World Was Not to Know

I am Métis. I have no religious affiliation. My family has been seriously impacted by the residential school system and by the cultural dislocation caused by Canada's assimilation policies. So in 2016, when two of my professors, William Morrow and Valerie Michaelson, invited me to consider a job as a research assistant with this project, I was surprised. Knowing a bit about my family history, they acknowledged that I might not want to be involved in a project related to the Christian church.

Rewind to 2015. My professor in my "Childhood and Religion" course has handed out a list of possible topics for our final assignment. I take it home and read it aloud to my mother: Harry Potter and the Hero's Journey; Rites of Passage; the Residential Schools in Canada . . . My mom looked at me thoughtfully and then said these five words: "I think we should talk."

My mother left the room. When she returned a few minutes later, she brought her copy of Sylvia Van Kirk's *Many Tender Ties: Women in Fur-Trade Society, 1670–1870*. Van Kirk's research provides a historical and personal chronicle of Indigenous women's involvement in the fur trade, by means of intermarriage with traders of the North West and Hudson's Bay Companies. This particular copy was as worn as if it had made its own northern trek from Winnipeg (my mother's home) to Kingston. The book describes how, in order to gain access to territory and forge loyalties between communities, European traders and "Indian" women engaged in "marriage à la façon du pays,"[1] resulting in families that blended the practices of both cultures. Their children were commonly referred to as "mixed-blood."[2] The children and subsequent generations who were born out of these inter-community marriages were distinguished as Métis or Bois-Brûlés—separate from other First Nations bands. Many were descendants of French-Canadian traders and Indigenous women.[3]

While these Métis children initially were raised with the Traditional Knowledge of their mothers,[4] as early as 1800s the House of Commons of Great Britain, following the model of the Law of the Poor, established the London Committee to oversee colony governance. This committee initiated policies intended to isolate and remove Indigenous children from their birth homes. The policy was that in order to "estrange [them] from Indian influences . . . the children . . . should be boarded at a school where they could be isolated from Indian women."[5] In particular, it was the hope of English and French officials to "impress upon their daughters 'the Ideas and habits of Civilized life,'"[6] steering their "mixed-blood" daughters toward European practices and identities in order to achieve an assimilated Eurocentric community. By pushing their daughters to become increasingly white and European in their identities, the traders placed "them in a vulnerable position by making them increasingly dependent upon white male protectors."[7] With growing distance from their traditional cultures and communities, many daughters of the fur trade were forced into relationships of reliance and subsumed into a white Eurocentric system that was necessary for their survival.

Enter Margaret Taylor. Born in Rupert's Land to Jane, a Cree woman, and George Taylor, the sloopmaster for the Hudson's Bay Company at York Factory (located on Hudson Bay in what is now northern Manitoba), Margaret was esteemed by her father for being "widely admired not only for [her] beauty, but for [her] 'civilized' womanly qualities."[8] George Simpson, Governor-in-Chief of Rupert's Land and Governor of the Northern Department, took Margaret as his sexual consort, then abandoned her at York Factory in favour of a Christian British woman in 1826. Five years later, following the directive of Governor Simpson that "mixed-blood" women should be married to Hudson's Bay Company servants,[9] Margaret married Amable Hogue. It is here that the endeavours of the British and French officials to forge lasting relationships between Indigenous and European communities began to show their institutional corruptions. Margaret was trapped between two worlds: abandoned by General Simpson for being too 'native,' but having lost connection to her Cree heritage and family, she was an outsider in both settler and Indigenous communities. It is also here that my matrilineal family's legacy begins. And it was while undertaking my class research project that I began uncovering the truths of my family's Métis ancestry.

Growing up, I had heard occasional passing comments about my being an "Indian Princess," my aunts and uncles teasing one another about who was the most "red," and even receiving the gift of moccasins at birthdays. However, I had never heard of the residential schools, let alone the assimilation and ethnocide inflicted on my ancestors. As I began to uncover the horrors experienced by First Nations, Métis, and Inuit communities across Canada, my project evolved from an academic exercise to a personal journey marked by pain and confusion. As Margaret Taylor had learned to forget her Indigeneity, so had the women and children in my family for generations before me. They hid their books, their language, and themselves to avoid the horrors of assimilation policies, including the residential school system. While *we* knew we were Métis, the world was not to know. Even I did not really know until that after-school conversation with my mother in 2015.

My First Steps on the Road to Reconciliation

It was in this context that I became the research assistant for the project that grew into this book. The focus of the project was to organize a forum that brought together Indigenous leaders, child health researchers, Christian theologians, church leaders, and community members to acknowledge the church's involvement in the marginalization and maltreatment of Canada's Indigenous populations, and to participate in the reconciliation process. Christian theology played a large role in the administration of the residential schools. For many Indigenous children, this resulted in a violent destruction of their dignity, culture, and identity through the infliction of corporal punishment.

Our specific objective was to respond to the Truth and Reconciliation Commission's Call to Action 6: "We call upon the Government of Canada to repeal Section 43 of the Criminal Code of Canada."[10] Section 43 allows schoolteachers, parents, or those standing in the role of parents to use physical punishment or "force by way of correction." The forum, held in October 2017, brought together participants from diverse professional, personal, and cultural backgrounds to create a dynamic and knowledgeable community of individuals committed to engaging in the process of reconciliation, and to respecting children's rights to dignity, respect, and protection.

The irony of my working on this project did not escape me, but I was compelled to see it through. Why? Simply because all children deserve to be protected and to be treated with dignity and respect. Participating in the organization of this forum became my own first steps on the road toward reconciliation.

The Process of Finding Common Ground

As the planning of the forum began, we recognized that we were creating a space where people from very different perspectives and histories would gather to discuss issues and experiences of deep personal meaning. Some of those people would have experienced deep and lasting trauma as a result of their connections to the residential schools. Others would have deep commitments to the religious faith that underpinned those schools. We had to make space for honesty, reflection that could be painful, and respectful expression of diverse and heartfelt perspectives.

The planning process was as enlightening as it was hard work. On 12 April 2017, the planning team met for the first time at the National Office of the Anglican Church of Canada in Toronto, hosted by Mark MacDonald, then National Indigenous Bishop of the Anglican Church. We shared our personal and professional backgrounds with one another, and as we embarked on taking this step toward reconciliation together, an atmosphere of comradery and solidarity emerged. With Indigenous, public health, theological, and church leadership voices heard and celebrated around the table, our work began.

Some six months later, twenty-eight forum participants were seated around tables at the Sheraton Conference Centre, just a few blocks away from Queen's University in Kingston, Ontario. With the addition of specialists in positive discipline and child-centred theologies, frontline social workers, local religious leaders, students, and participants of various Indigenous backgrounds, a larger mosaic of experience, expertise, and passion emerged. As event coordinator and research assistant, I was entrusted with consulting Traditional Knowledge holders in the Kingston community to ensure respectful representation of Indigeneity at the forum. The wisdom gained through this process allowed me to develop further appreciation and understanding of my own Métis identity. With the thoughtful guidance of Paul Carl of the Indigenous Education program at Queen's University, I was given the great honour of performing the Indigenous Welcome at the forum. As we stood in a circle together, acknowledging our time together on traditional Anishinaabe and Haudenosaunee territory, with reverence and gratitude to the ancestors who allow us to live and learn upon that sacred space, our diverse perspectives were brought together.

Over the course of two intensive days, which included an informative and inspiring public lecture shared by Mark MacDonald and Marcia Bunge, our response to Call to Action 6 was developed collaboratively. Working in teams of four to six participants, who were systematically rotated in order to provide a balanced set of experiences and expertise at each table, the groups began to document their reflections on a series of presentations delivered by Indigenous leaders, Christian theologians, and child health researchers and practitioners, reconsidering the corporal punishment of children within the context of reconciliation.

The Sacred Circle of Life

While planning the forum, and in my search to generate an atmosphere conducive to reconciliation at the event and to better understand my own background, I communicated with various Indigenous Knowledge holders. Paul Carl urged me to listen to my heart and focus on where it was leading me, on the understanding that all actions carried out with a good heart have good intentions. Through this conversation, I was drawn to teachings of the Four Sacred Directions of the Medicine Wheel. The Medicine Wheel is a powerful tool for facilitating spiritual and personal growth, and it is flexible enough to be used in a variety of ways across Indigenous communities. At its basic level, the circle of the Medicine Wheel represents the continuity and interconnectedness of humanity, the environment, and the cosmos; the spinning of the wheel symbolizes the ever-changing nature and forward motion of time.[11] When reading the Medicine Wheel, it is important to move in a clockwise direction, in keeping with the universe, following the rotation of the moon around the earth.[12] At its next level, the circle is divided into four quarters, with four identifiable equidistant points representing the four sacred directions—north, east, south, and west.[13] The quadrants of the Medicine Wheel also symbolize the four seasons (spring, summer, fall, winter), the four sacred colours (yellow, red, black, and white), and the stages of the life cycle (childhood, adolescence, adulthood, late life).[14]

Acting as the Medicine Wheel's central axis is the self, represented by the colour green, demonstrating a balanced self in connection with Mother Earth.[15] Indigenous scholar Frank Black Elk explains meaningful interpersonal and intrapersonal development as that which "respects the sacred circle and all other beings in it, [so that] every step [we] take can be ceremony that celebrates [our] connection with the Creator."[16] In this sense, the Medicine Wheel is a reflection of the internal lifelong journey of self-understanding and spiritual strength, which is as never-ending as the passing of time, changing of seasons, or growth of a human being.

During the forum, Bishop MacDonald reminded us of how the four quadrants of the Medicine Wheel correspond to the stages of life, with the two bottom quadrants representing adolescence and adulthood, and the top two quadrants representing childhood and later life. He noted that the responsibility of adolescents and adults is to support, protect, and revere the children and Elders of the community as those closest to the Creator. The Medicine Wheel requires all generational voices to be respected and represented equally, including those of children. The discussions that took place at the forum reflected the many meanings and teachings of the Medicine Wheel. This contributed to individual, community, and spiritual growth; reminded us of our role in supporting the needs, wisdom, and inherent dignity of children and Elders; and focused us on our responsibility to protect our fellow beings who are travelling with us in the sacred circle of life.

At the end, from a forum that brought many diverse voices together to explore issues both academic and deeply personal, the *Theological Statement* (see page 11) was generated, inspired by the reflections and discussions that had taken place over two days of intensive exploration of the meaning of reconciliation. The statement was created through a collaborative process that ended in consensus on every point it contains. The wish of forum participants is that it will provide impetus for placing children at the centre of academic, political, religious, and personal conversations, and remind adults of our role in supporting children during their life journey while providing love, care, and protection. The statement is a tangible step toward Bishop Mark MacDonald's prophetic vision of a violence-free future for all children in Canada (Chapter 1).

Conclusions and Contentions

The process of reflection and dialogue regarding the treatment of Indigenous Peoples in Canada is not without tension. As Peter Robinson describes (Chapter 5), residential schools "were set up as protected enclaves of European culture, with the express intention of amalgamating First Nations, Inuit, and Métis children into that culture." Due to the intertwining of cultures that took place during the most intensive period of assimilation, Christian rhetoric and religion have had a strong influence on many Indigenous communities and families. The profound complexities of the relationships among Indigenous, settler, and Christian communities—like the experiences that Shirley Tagalik (Chapter 10) describes among Inuit—speak to my own personal and professional experiences. Brought up within a Christian settler society with Catholic influences from my extended family, largely because of the Christianization process experienced through the colonization of Canada, I live with one foot in each world, straddling the line between settler society and Traditional Lifeways. It is paradoxical for an Indigenous individual to engage with the same political and religious institutions and leaders that historically led to the colonization of her own people. The enduring legacy of pain left by the assimilation policies executed by the Christian church has left lasting imprints. But at the same time, the spirit and strength of Christian leaders—both Indigenous and settler allies—who are pursuing a reconciled future, are beacons of hope.

Clarence Hale (Chapter 18) personifies this same paradox. In the wake of his experiences with intergenerational violence and his struggles to find his identity, Clarence has found solace and strength within the Christian church and community. He recognizes that relationships of trust and reconciliation require everyone to take a seat at the table. I am inspired by the healing and grace that is manifest in Clarence's journey, in particular as I pursue my own Indigenous identity in a setting as drenched in colonial history as the Queen's University School of Religion. Not only has the university honoured and memorialized key architects of Canada's assimilationist policies such as Duncan Campbell Scott and Sir John A. Macdonald, its Theological College trained many of the Christian leaders responsible for the practical implementation of residential schools.[17] Today, we move together toward a shared future of reconciliation. The halls we walk down are haunted by the horrors of the past but also drive us toward a future that will respect the identities and rights of Indigenous Peoples in Canada.

When I sit down with my mother today, she reflects on her own advocacy for the rights and dignity of First Nations and Métis communities, and with relief she sighs, "I knew one day others would understand." The resilience and strength of the human spirit demonstrate their power through the process of reconciliation. If future generations can be imbued with this spirit of respect and recognition, perhaps the prophetic imaginings that Bishop MacDonald articulates in Chapter 1 will become a reality.

Notes

1 Sylvia Van Kirk, *Many Tender Ties: Women in Fur-trade Society, 1670–1870* (Norman: University of Oklahoma Press, 1980), 4.

2 Van Kirk, 95.

3 Van Kirk, 95.

4 Van Kirk, 95.

5 Van Kirk, 103–4.

6 Van Kirk, 95.

7 Van Kirk, 106–7.

8 Van Kirk, 106.

9 Van Kirk, 188.

10 Truth and Reconciliation Commission of Canada, *The Truth and Reconciliation Commission of Canada: Calls to Action* (Winnipeg: Truth and Reconciliation Commission of Canada, 2015), 1.

11 Sharilyn Caillou, "Peacekeeping Actions at Home: A Medicine Wheel Model for a Peacekeeping Pedagogy," in *First Nations Education in Canada: The Circle Unfolds,* ed. Marie Battiste and Jean Barman (Vancouver: UBC Press, 1995), 51.

12 Best Start Resource Centre, *A Child Becomes Strong: Journeying through Each Stage of the Life Cycle* (Toronto: Best Start Resource Centre, 2010), 6, accessed 9 October 2018, https://www.beststart.org/resources/hlthy_chld_dev/pdf/CBS_Final_K12A.pdf.

13 Caillou, "Peacekeeping Actions at Home," 51.

14 Best Start Resource Centre, *A Child Becomes Strong*, 6.

15 Annie Wenger-Nabigon, "The Cree Medicine Wheel as an Organizing Paradigm of Theories of Human Development," *Native Social Work Journal* 7 (November 2010): 147.

16 Caillou, "Peacekeeping Actions at Home," 51.

17 Queen's University Truth and Reconciliation Commission Task Force, *Yakwanastahentéha Aankenjigemi Extending the Rafters: Truth and Reconciliation Commission Task Force Final Report* (Kingston, ON: Queen's University, Office of the Provost, 2017), 5.

15

AN INTERNATIONAL PERSPECTIVE ON THE CANADIAN *THEOLOGICAL STATEMENT*

Context, Tools, and Encouragement

CHRIS DODD

> Through omission, denial and silence we have at times tolerated, perpetuated and ignored the reality of violence against children in homes, families, institutions and communities, and not actively confronted the suffering that this violence causes. Even as we have not fully lived up to our responsibilities in this regard, we believe that religious communities must be part of the solution to eradicating violence against children, and we commit ourselves to take leadership in our religious communities and the broader society.[1]

Religious communities have a vital role to play in creating a violence-free world for children. As multiple chapters in this volume demonstrate, churches in Canada have not always done this well, even to the point of participating in extreme harm. Yet as we also read throughout this volume, our way forward is in keeping with the gospel of Jesus, who shows us that another way is possible.

Jesus's regard for children was at the centre of the new, transformative social order that he initiated through his life and ministry. Remarkably, at a time in history when children held a very low status, Jesus made them visible as valued human beings. In response to the disciples' question, "Who is the greatest in the kingdom of heaven?" Jesus put a child in their midst and told them they should become like children if they were to enter the kingdom of heaven (Matthew 18:1–3). In Matthew 18:5, the disciples were asked to receive children and to treat them as they would treat Jesus. While the disciples rebuked those who brought children to Jesus, he listened to children and gave them time, respect, dignity, and blessing (Mathew 19:13–15).

All recorded encounters between Jesus and children were kind, respectful, and gentle. For Jesus, children not only enter the kingdom of heaven; they seem to own it (Matthew 19:13–14). The kingdom of heaven *belongs* to them.[2]

To move forward in reconciliation and in championing the well-being of children in Canadian churches is to participate in this new social order initiated by Jesus. For Canadian churches, this is an encouraging moment, one that maps readily onto an exciting international movement. The purpose of this chapter is to provide context, tools, and encouragement for change in Canada. In terms of context, some examples are given of initiatives from different world regions that support those emerging in Canada. In terms of tools, a number of resources are provided to facilitate action.

Context

Around the world, there have been initiatives by religious communities to address physical punishment of children for many years. This section provides some examples of actions that have been taken to prompt change in various regions of the globe.

Global Consultation on Violence against Children

The involvement of religious communities in the global movement to end violence against children gained momentum during the UN Secretary-General's Study on Violence against Children between 2003 and 2006 and the publication of the *World Report on Violence against Children* (2006) that resulted from that study.[3] Recognizing the pivotal role religious communities can play in addressing violence against children, in May 2006 the international organization Religions for Peace partnered with UNICEF to convene a Global Consultation of religious leaders and experts in Toledo, Spain. Its purpose was to provide a faith-based perspective on the landmark global study. Fifty religious leaders and experts from thirty countries discussed the impact of violence on children and the importance of faith-based communities taking leadership to protect children from violence.

The objectives of the Global Consultation were threefold: (1) to submit a final set of recommendations to the Violence against Children Study Secretariat for inclusion in the report to the UN General Assembly; (2) to develop key messages and action commitments for religious communities to address violence against children; and (3) to prepare a draft declaration for religious leaders on violence against children, to be formally adopted at the next World Assembly of Religions for Peace. Participants were challenged to draw on their unique strengths and spiritual insights to find solutions to the urgent problem of violence against children, generate strategies to protect them, and speak out as advocates and champions for children's rights and well-being around the world.

All participants agreed that human dignity is sacred and that no one has the right to violate it. At the same time, they acknowledged that religious communities have often neglected their obligations to protect children from violence. A central message resulting from the consultation was that corporal punishment of children is incompatible with the universal and religious principles of respect for human dignity, compassion, justice, equality, peace, and non-violence, professed by the major world religions. A key outcome of the consultation was *A Multi-Religious Commitment to Confront Violence against Children*, known as the Kyoto Declaration after its ratification by over 800 religious leaders at the Eighth World Assembly of Religions for Peace in Kyoto, Japan, in August 2006.

The Kyoto Declaration continues to be an invaluable guide for religious communities. Since its publication, growing numbers of Christians and people of all religious traditions have been in the forefront of the global movement to eliminate all corporal punishment of children and to end its legal justification. The preamble of the Kyoto Declaration states:

> We find strong consensus across our religious traditions about the inherent dignity of every person, including children. This requires that we reject all forms of violence against children and protect and promote the sanctity of life in every stage of a child's development. Our religions share principles of compassion, justice, love and solidarity that are great strengths in dealing with the difficult presence of violence in human society . . .

> Our faith traditions take a holistic view of a child's life, and thus seek to uphold all the rights of the child in the context of its family, community and the broader social, economic and political environment.[4]

The Kyoto Declaration explicitly recommends that religious communities work with governments to protect children. Article 6 states: "We call upon our governments to adopt legislation to prohibit all forms of violence against children, including corporal punishment, and to ensure the full rights of children, consistent with the Convention on the Rights of the Child and other national and regional instruments. We urge them to establish appropriate mechanisms to ensure the effective implementation of these laws and to ensure that religious communities participate formally in these mechanisms. Our religious communities are ready to serve as monitors of implementation, making use of national and international bodies to maintain accountability."[5]

Another outcome of the Global Consultation was the resource *From Commitment to Action: What Religious Communities Can Do to Eliminate Violence against Children*.[6] A major strength of this initiative was the recognition that violent punishment of children is not associated with any one religion or tradition. The resource advocates for multi-religious collaboration, bringing together people of diverse communities to work in solidarity, sharing their strengths, insights, and commitment to children. Such collaboration enables communities to share training, skills, and resources, positioning them well to form partnerships with other organizations and institutions in promoting children's rights to protection.

Southern African Catholic Bishops' Conference; Ninth All Africa Conference of Churches' General Assembly

In 2013, the Southern African Catholic Bishops' Conference (SACBC) Parliamentary Liaison Office submitted a report to the South African Parliament entitled *The Use of Corporal Discipline in the Home*. This report states that "there is nothing in the Catechism of the Catholic Church which supports the right of parents to use corporal punishment."[7] The SACBC report calls for discipline that teaches children vital life skills and appropriate ways of dealing with anger and frustration, builds emotional intelligence, fosters the ability to compromise, and encourages self-reflection. It describes positive discipline as that which "engenders tolerance and a sense of human dignity, justice, and bodily integrity."[8] Addressing the 27th Special Session of the United Nations General Assembly (New York 2003), Cardinal Alfonso Lopez Trujillo said that full recognition of a child's dignity had been lost and must be recovered. Cardinal Trujillo stated, "The true measure of a society's greatness is the extent to which the society recognises and protects human dignity and human rights and ensures the well-being of all its members, especially children."[9]

The 173 member organizations of the All Africa Council of Churches (AACC) represent more than 120 million Christians in forty African countries.[10] The council's Ninth General Assembly was held in Mozambique in 2008. The theme of the meeting was "The Church Awakens: New Hope for the African Child." The primary conclusion drawn from this meeting was that the church must place children in the centre by ensuring that children's issues are integrated into the church's core activities, and that children and youth participate in decision making. The assembly adopted ten resolutions, including a commitment that all AACC member churches would ensure that their countries' laws would not allow any form of corporal punishment of children.[11]

Caribbean Coalition for the Abolition of Corporal Punishment of Children

At a meeting held in Jamaica in 2012, religious leaders from Aruba, Guyana, Jamaica, and the Cayman Islands actively supported law reform to prohibit corporal punishment in all settings. In a joint statement of commitment, they clarified that discipline is about teaching and guiding children by example, through empathy, compassion, understanding, respect, and kindness. They emphasized that physical punishment is incompatible with core religious values and that laws have an important role in eliminating violence against children:

> We believe that the adoption of legislation to prohibit corporal punishment of children in all settings is a crucial step towards a compassionate, non-violent society. Corporal punishment of children has for too long been a common part of our tradition and culture. But physical punishment as a form of discipline is incompatible with the core religious values of respect for human dignity, justice and non-violence and evidence of the harm it causes both in the short and long-term is well documented. . . .

> As Christians, our reading of the Bible is done in the light of Jesus' teaching and example. Jesus treated children with respect and placed them in the middle of the group, as in Matthew 18:1–5: "Whoever welcomes one such child in my name welcomes me." The word "discipline" is for many people synonymous with physical punishment. But the word comes from the same root as "disciple" . . . Positive non-violent discipline is about guiding children and teaching by adult example. It is based on empathy, compassion and an understanding of how children develop. Positive discipline is both respectful and kind and it is the best way to promote self-discipline.[12]

National Conference, Iran

In the spirit of the Kyoto Declaration's call for inter-religious cooperation to combat violence against children, leaders from diverse religions met with experts and policy makers and UNICEF in the holy city of Qom, Iran, in October 2011 to discuss the country's progress on corporal punishment in family and educational settings. This conference was the first of its kind in Iran, and it highlighted the important role religious communities can play in ending violence against children. Following the opening ceremony, participants took part in working-group discussions to identify mechanisms through which religious leaders can work together to end corporal punishment of children.

An important outcome of this conference was a *Declaration* in which religious leaders made a commitment to take action toward ending violence against children and to promote positive, non-violent discipline. The *Declaration* invites

> all religious leaders and their followers to make efforts based on religious teachings, to utilize all their capabilities to build the culture of respecting children's dignity and the principle of the best interest of the child, and to confront violence against children, particularly violence in the form of corporal punishment in the home and educational settings . . . [and calls on] all guardians and custodians of home and school settings to make use of modern violence-free educational methods and to make every effort to confront corporal punishment in these settings as, based on the viewpoint of divine religions, home

> and school are considered as two sacred and fundamental pillars of the society, and children spend most of their time in these two settings.[13]

Church of Scotland General Assembly

On 24 May 2016, Commissioners of the General Assembly of the Church of Scotland voted in favour of calling on Scottish government ministers and parliamentarians to acknowledge the recommendations of the UN Committee on the Rights of the Child and remove the defence of "justifiable assault" from the Criminal Justice (Scotland) Act 2003: "We now add the Church's voice to many other organisations to call upon the Scottish Government to remove the defence of justifiable assault, granting children the same rights that every adult enjoys in this area. Bringing up children is one of the most challenging privileges any of us can face. But in performing this privilege we must not negate the rights of the child. As parents, as a Church, as a society we want the best for our children. As a Church we will work with parents and others to support them in doing that."[14] On 3 October 2019 the Children (Equal Protection from Assault) (Scotland) Act was passed by the Scottish Parliament, meaning children in Scotland now have the same protections against assault as adults.[15] On 28 January 2020, a second member of the United Kingdom—the Welsh National Assembly—passed the Children (Abolition of Defence of Reasonable Punishment) (Wales) Act, achieving equal protection from assault for children.

The General Assembly encouraged the Church and Society Council to join campaigns seeking to end corporal punishment of children. Commissioners also urged officials to work with the church's social care arm, CrossReach and Safeguarding service, to provide access to resources supporting the development of positive, non-violent parenting skills.

Anglican Bishops, New Zealand

In 2007, New Zealand removed its criminal defence to the corporal punishment of children. Among the most vocal of the many groups supporting this change were the Anglican bishops of Aotearoa/New Zealand, who issued a public statement:

> As Christians, our primary role model is Jesus Christ. As fallible humans we struggle with the issues of power and authority, and with their use or misuse. In the face of the abuse of power,

> Christ brings freedom, forgiveness, compassion, mercy and ultimately self-sacrifice. The way of Jesus was non-violence. He declined to sanction violent punishment against offenders, preferring instead to look to the root causes of ill-behaviour and to offer people a new start. This is how we must relate to our children. As Christians, our reading of the Bible must always be done through the lens of Christ's teaching and life. There has been a lot of talk of "Spare the rod and spoil the child," an attitude that can be sanctioned by scriptural proof texts such as Proverbs 13:24. . . . However, it is inappropriate to take such texts out of their ancient cultural context, and out of the broader context of Scripture, so as to justify modes of behaviour in a modern situation very different from that for which they were given. Such texts need to be read in the light of the way Christ responded to children, placing them in the middle of the group with respect and care, as in Mark 9:37: "Whoever welcomes one such child in my name welcomes me."[16]

World Council of Churches

Putting "the child at the centre" was the subject of discussion during "Ecumenical Conversations on the Churches' Advocacy for Children's Rights" at the World Council of Churches' (WCC) Tenth World Assembly held in Busan, South Korea, in 2013. Following the discussions, an outcome document—*Putting Children at the Center*—reflecting the issues raised during the conversations was signed by member churches and partners of the WCC. The document states: "We affirm that [children's] dignity comes from their creation in God's own image. They are precious human beings with rights that need to be guaranteed and protected by our families, our societies and our churches. When Jesus put a child in the centre . . . he not only demonstrated extraordinary respect for children, he upheld the inherent human dignity of the child and challenged his disciples to learn from children."[17]

This document calls on churches to work "with others in the global movement to prohibit and eliminate corporal punishment of children," use scripture to promote non-violence in living with children, and advocate for the rights of children to governments and others who influence policy.[18]

Canada: A Christian Theological Statement in Support of the Truth and Reconciliation Commission's Call to Action 6

In October 2017, a forum held at Queen's University in Kingston, Ontario brought together a multi-denominational group of theologians, church members and leaders, clergy, and students. Their purpose was to generate a response to the Truth and Reconciliation Commission's Call to Action 6, which calls for repeal of the law allowing corporal punishment of children in Canada.[19] The forum's outcome document was a *Theological Statement* supporting Call to Action 6 and recommending specific actions for churches to take in order to end physical punishment of children (see page 11). This statement is based on common values and theologies that transcend traditional denominational boundaries. It is notable for being the first faith-based document to place corporal punishment in the context of colonialism and the churches' relationships with Indigenous Peoples.

Resources

Prohibiting and eliminating all corporal punishment of children calls on all of us to recognize children as people in their own right and to act to end the suffering of children who endure violent and humiliating punishment. Through their many roles and functions as spiritual advisers and pastors, teachers and theologians, preachers and leaders of worship, community leaders and activists, Christian leaders and their communities can work with others to address these practices which may have been part of tradition and culture for generations. They are also in a position to lead the movement that will transform children's lives. The following resources can support their efforts.

Ending Corporal Punishment of Children: A Handbook for Working with Religious Communities

Ending Corporal Punishment of Children: A Handbook for Working with Religious Communities[20] provides links to tools and resources for engaging with and enlisting the support of religious communities and faith-based institutions toward the prohibition and elimination of corporal punishment of children. It recognizes the pivotal role that religious communities play and seeks to broaden their involvement as active partners in the global movement toward achieving children's right to equal protection under the law. It includes information on (1) the relationship between religion and corporal punishment; (2) the prevalence of corporal punishment and its impact on children's lives; (3) children's right to protection from all corporal punishment; (4) challenging corporal punishment and taking action within religious communities; and (5) working with religious communities toward law reform to protect children. This resource is a collaboration between the Churches' Network for Non-violence (CNNV), Global Initiative to End Violence against Children, and Save the Children.

Ending Corporal Punishment of Children: A Handbook for Worship and Gatherings

With contributions from a number of church leaders, *Ending Corporal Punishment of Children: A Handbook for Worship and Gatherings*[21] contains prayers, reflections, vigils, and liturgies reflecting Jesus's teachings about children and promoting non-violent adult-child relationships. It can be used both privately and collectively; adapted for the local context; or used to trigger ideas for further studies or reflections. It includes a set of downloadable posters.[22] Again, this resource is a collaboration between the Churches' Network for Non-violence (CNNV), Global Initiative to End Violence against Children, and Save the Children. Contributors were Vivian Kityo, Director of Uganda Wakisa Ministries; Katy Lloyd; Thabo Makgoba, Archbishop of Cape Town and Primate of Southern Africa; Sir David Moxon, Archbishop Emeritus, Archbishop of Canterbury's Representative at the Holy See; Lorraine Olden, Australia; John Pritchard, former Bishop of Oxford; CNNV Worship Resources Working Group; and the late Colin Bennetts, formerly Bishop of Coventry.

From Commitment to Action: What Religious Communities Can Do to Eliminate Violence against Children

This guide,[23] which is the result of a partnership between UNICEF and Religions for Peace, aims to channel the collective energies of religious communities to advance a shared vision of a future free of violence against children. It outlines practical ways that religious leaders, theologians, educators, community mobilizers, and others can work toward ending violence against children. It also includes concrete suggestions for working effectively with governments, civil society, and UN agencies.

Churches' Commitments to Children

The ecumenical World Council of Churches (WCC) outcome document *Putting Children at the Center* (see above) precipitated a broad consultative process that led to the publication of the resource *Churches' Commitments to Children.*[24] This widely disseminated living resource outlines specific actions and strategies that churches are encouraged to adopt in response to challenges affecting children's lives, including the promotion of child protection. The WCC has developed complementary toolkits, manuals, and protocols, and a digital platform to facilitate collaboration and networking.[25]

Partnering with Religious Communities for Children

Created by UNICEF, this guide[26] focuses on creating alliances with other sectors to protect children and bring about cultural transformation regarding violence against children. It provides information on how to create partnerships between religious communities and civil society organizations based on shared values; identifies barriers to collaboration and potential entry points; and provides direction on how to build on each other's strengths.

Ending Corporal Punishment of Children: A Handbook for Multi-Religious Gatherings

Ending Corporal Punishment of Children: A Handbook for Multi-Religious Gatherings[27] was written in consultation with religious leaders and faith-based communities, based on the premises that (1) the major religions profess respect for the inherent dignity of every person, including children; and (2) the universal principles of compassion, justice, equality, and non-violence are central to religious teachings. It acknowledges the many opportunities of faith-based communities to promote prohibition and elimination of corporal punishment of children, including through religious and spiritual observances such as pilgrimages, prayers, retreats, vigils, and religious and spiritual teachings. Many of the materials are suitable for personal and collective use and can be freely adapted for the local context or used to generate ideas for further reflection and discussion. The handbook also contains a guide for reflection and discussion marking the tenth anniversary of the Kyoto Declaration (see above). It was produced by the Churches' Network for Non-violence and Save the Children.

Churches for Children

The Canadian *Christian Theological Statement* (see above, and this volume, page 11) is posted on the Churches for Children website, where church communities and individuals can endorse it, demonstrating their support for its recommendations.[28] The website also provides resources, including guides, links, and sermons and prayers that can be adapted for use in various contexts.

Encouragement

Jesus's model of putting children at the centre affords every child a central place in the church community and wider society and promotes respect for the child's dignity. It views the whole child in the context of the wider environment and acknowledges the interests, rights, and needs of the child as well as valuing children's perspectives. Meaningful child participation ensures children are not merely passive recipients of "discipline" but are engaged in the processes of problem solving and conflict resolution. Recognition that every child has accumulated knowledge, skills, views, and ideas—and that she or he can contribute to solving problems—is a vital component of fostering their emerging capacities (see Chapters 9–13).

Protecting children, and facilitating their healthy development, is the most natural commitment for Christians—and everyone can play a part. The following suggestions provide some ways of taking action in the local church and community:

- Create opportunities for church communities to reflect on religious teachings and principles that relate to the care and protection of children. Discuss how corporal punishment of children is incompatible with religious principles of compassion, justice, equality, and non-violence.
- Learn about, promote, and model positive non-violent discipline, as described in Chapter 12.
- Promote the meaning of "discipline" as teaching and guidance—not punishment (see Chapter 11); offer resources and support for parents and children, including opportunities for parents to take part in positive parenting groups.
- Speak out about the harmful effects of corporal punishment and the benefits of positive non-violent parenting.
- Explain why the legality of corporal punishment is incompatible with the teachings of Jesus, based on the theological resources provided in this book.

- Ensure religious texts, teachings, and liturgies are used to promote respect for children—not to condone violence against children.
- Hold vigils, prayer gatherings, and other events dedicated to ending corporal punishment of children.
- Use opportunities in the life of the community, such as marriage preparation and baptism, to promote non-violent parenting.
- Identify child protection risks in the church. Ensure accountability and reporting mechanisms are in place.
- Develop child-centred policies to underpin child protection and safeguarding. These should contain guidelines for putting a church charter or mission statement into action.
- Ensure child protection and safeguarding policies explicitly denounce corporal punishment.
- Encourage religious communities to actively support law reform campaigns and to work with others, including government, non-government organizations, and multi-faith councils, toward prohibition and elimination of all corporal punishment of children.
- Work with others to enable children and adults to be conversant with the UN *Convention on the Rights of the Child*. Discuss similarities between the *Convention* and Christian teachings.
- Use the ideas found in Chapter 13 to nurture the positive spirituality of children in Christian churches and homes.
- Emulate Jesus's interaction with his disciples in Matthew 18:1–5 and Matthew 19:13–15, placing children at the centre of the community. Enable the meaningful participation of children and make provision for their voices and opinions to be heard.
- Be attentive to other ways that colonial ideologies continue to harm Indigenous Peoples, including by sustaining harmful inequities and disparities in health and educational outcomes.
- Take tangible action to become an Agent of Reconciliation in your own community. If you aren't sure what this means, a good place to start is by reading the Truth and Reconciliation Calls to Action. The website #Next150challenge will also give you many meaningful and constructive ideas: https://next150.indianhorse.ca/challenges/94-calls-to-action.

Notes

1 Religions for Peace, *A Multi-Religious Commitment to Confront Violence against Children*, Adopted at the Religions for Peace VIII World Assembly in Kyoto, Japan, 28 August 2006, https://www.unicef.org/violencestudy/pdf/Final%20Declaration%20VAC-28%20Aug-Kyoto.pdf.

2 John Pritchard, "Jesus with children: what do we learn," in Churches' Network for Non-violence (CNNV) and Global Initiative to End All Corporal Punishment of Children, *Ending corporal punishment of children: A Handbook for Worship and Gatherings* (Nottingham UK: The Russell Press Limited, 2015).

3 Paulo Sérgio Pinheiro, *World Report on Violence against Children* (Geneva: United Nations Secretary-General's Study on Violence against Children, 2006).

4 Religions for Peace, *A Multi-Religious Commitment*, Preamble.

5 Religions for Peace, Article 6.

6 Religions for Peace and UNICEF, *From Commitment to Action: What Religious Communities Can Do to Eliminate Violence against Children* (New York: UNICEF and Religions for Peace, 2010).

7 Southern African Catholic Bishops' Conference (SACBC) Parliamentary Liaison Office, Submission by the Southern African Catholic Bishops' Conference Parliamentary Liaison Office on "The Use of Corporal Punishment in the Home," 2013, 4. http://www.sacbc.org.za/wp-content/uploads/2012/02/The-Catholic-Church-in-Southern-Africa-Protection-Policy-and-Procedures-for-Minors-.pdf.

8 SACBC Parliamentary Liaison Office, "The Use of Corporal Punishment in the Home," 6.

9 Independent Catholic News (ICN) https://indcatholicnews.com/news/9531.

10 All Africa Conference of Churches (AACC-CETA), "The All Africa Conference of Churches (AACC)," accessed 20 June 2018, http://aacc-ceta.org/en/about/10-about-aacc.

11 Keith Vermeulen, "Resolutions from the 9th All Africa Conference of Churches' General Assembly: Developments in Africa," *Article 19* 5, no.1 (July 2009): 9–11, accessed 20 July 2018, https://hdl.handle.net/10520/EJC21044.

12 Global Initiative to End All Corporal Punishment of Children and Global Movement for Children in Latin America and the Caribbean, *Prohibiting Corporal Punishment of Children in the Caribbean: Progress Report 2012* (London, UK: Global Initiative to End All Corporal Punishment of Children, 2012), 20.

13 UNICEF, *Declaration: Conference on the Role of Religions and Religious Leaders in Confronting Corporal Punishment of Children in the Family and Educational Settings*, 20 October 2011, 2–3, accessed 20 September 2018, https://www.unicef.org/iran/Declaration_Interreligious_Conf._on_VAC2011_UNICEF_Iran_-_FINAL.PDF.

14 Church of Scotland, "General Assembly Calls for Law Amendment to Protect Children," Church of Scotland: News and Events, 24 May 2016, http://www.churchofscotland.org.uk/news_and_events/news/2016/general_assembly_calls_for_law_change_to_protect_children.

15 The Scottish Parliament, *Children (Equal Protection from Assault) (Scotland) Bill*, 4 February 2020, https://www.parliament.scot/parliamentarybusiness/Bills/109156.aspx.

16 Anglican Church in Aotearoa, New Zealand, "Removing the Loophole: Anglican Bishops Support Repeal of Section 59," 2, Churches' Network for Non-violence, 1 May 2007, http://www.churchesfornon-violence.org/New%20Zealand%20Bishops%20statement.pdf.

17 World Council of Churches (WCC), *Putting Children at the Center*, churchesfornonviolence.org, 4 February 2020, http://churchesfornon-violence.org/wp/wp-content/uploads/2012/02/Putting-Children-at-the-Center.pdf.

18 WCC, *Putting Children at the Center*.

19 Truth and Reconciliation Commission of Canada, *The Truth and Reconciliation Commission of Canada: Calls to Action* (Winnipeg: Truth and Reconciliation Commission of Canada, 2015), 1.

20 Churches' Network for Non-violence and Global Initiative to End All Corporal Punishment of Children, *Ending Corporal Punishment of Children: A Handbook for Working with Religious Communities* (CNNV, 2015).

21 Churches' Network for Non-violence and Global Initiative to End All Corporal Punishment of Children, *Ending Corporal Punishment of Children: A Handbook for Worship and Gatherings* (CNNV, 2005).

22 Churches' Network for Non-violence, "What Can Christians Do towards Ending Corporal Punishment of Children?," Churches' Network for Non-violence, accessed 9 July 2018, http://churchesfornon-violence.org/wp/wp-content/uploads/2012/02/Handbook-posters.pdf.

23 Religions for Peace and UNICEF, *From Commitment to Action*.

24 UNICEF and World Council of Churches, *Churches' Commitments to Children: Churches Uniting for Children in the Pilgrimage of Justice and Peace* (Geneva: World Council of Churches, 2017), accessed 20 September 2018, https://www.oikoumene.org/en/resources/documents/wcc-programmes/public-witness/rights-of-children/churches-commitments-to-children.

25 World Council of Churches, "Resources and Tools Available for the Implementation of Churches' Commitments to Children," Oikoumene.org, last modified 2018, https://www.oikoumene.org/en/resources/documents/wcc-programmes/public-witness/rights-of-children/resources-available-to-support-member-churches-in-the-implementation-of-each-principle; World Council of Churches, "WCC Develops Digital Map for Churches' Commitments to Children," Oikoumene.org, 19 October 2017, https://www.oikoumene.org/en/press-centre/news/wcc-develops-digital-map-for-churches-commitments-to-children.

26 UNICEF, *Partnering with Religious Communities for Children* (New York: UNICEF, 2012), https://www.unicef.org/eapro/Partnering_with_Religious_Communities_for_Children.pdf.

27 Churches' Network for Non-violence, Global Initiative to End All Corporal Punishment of Children, and Save the Children, *Ending Corporal Punishment of Children: A Handbook for Multi-Religious Gatherings* (Nottingham: CNNV, Global Initiative to End Violence against Children, and Save the Children, 2016).

28 *A Christian Theological Statement in Support of the Truth and Reconciliation Commission's Call to Action #6*, *Churches for Children*, accessed 9 July 2018, https://www.churchesforchildren.net/what-has-happened.

16

"ON SPARING THE ROD AND SPOILING THE CHILD"

Preaching on Call to Action 6 and the Repeal of Section 43 of the Criminal Code

JOHN H. YOUNG

In this chapter, I shall begin with some reflection on why tackling the matter of corporal punishment of children in a sermon would be a good thing for Christian clergy to do. Second, I shall indicate a text I would use for such a sermon, and outline how I would approach preaching such a sermon. The final part of this chapter will be a sample sermon on the selected text.

Why Might One Preach about Corporal Punishment of Children?

In the not-too-distant past, corporal punishment of children was simply an accepted "tool" for parents and teachers in Canada; it was not until 2004 that teachers were prohibited from using it. Today, parents and those standing in the place of parents still have access to a legal defence if they physically punish the children in their care. In the wake of the Truth and Reconciliation Commission (TRC) report, growing public awareness of the frequency and severity of the physical abuse Indigenous children suffered in the residential school system has heightened reflection on both that specific history and corporal punishment of children more generally. Across Christian denominations in Canada, in any congregation with a regular attendance of several dozen or more, one is likely to find members who are struggling with this issue. Preaching on this subject may help to bring about some reflection and respectful dialogue within the congregation.

In most Christian denominations, the Bible is a key authority in shaping theology. Individual Christians' particular understandings of Scripture and its influence on the development of theology, both individually and denominationally, also help to shape the actions Christians take as they seek to live their lives in a manner congruent with the faith they profess. In the section that follows, I suggest a scriptural text and approach to preaching on this topic.

A Text for Preaching

> Do not withhold discipline from your children; if you beat them with a rod, they will not die.
>
> If you beat them with the rod, you will save their lives from Sheol.
>
> PROVERBS 23:13–14[1]

Preaching on This Text

The reference in this text to beating a child with a rod will likely shock members of the congregation when they hear it read. It would be important to point out that in the ancient world, where mutilation was an accepted punishment (Chapter 6) and where slavery existed, the Hebrew Scriptures (or the Old Testament, in the Christian canon) generally placed a higher value on life than was true in neighbouring societies, placed more restrictions on the use of corporal punishment, and gave slaves greater protection. As a follow-up to this point, it would be helpful to remind the congregation of the degree to which societal views on corporal punishment have changed over recent generations. Acts that were acceptable as recently as two generations ago, such as striking children with leather straps in schools, would not be acceptable today. Recognizing this point will encourage congregational members to think about taking the next step, namely, ending corporal punishment altogether.

In preaching on this text, it would be important to acknowledge the necessity of discipline. The passage from Proverbs, at its heart, is concerned with discipline. The passage does not advocate the corporal punishment of children for its own sake. Those who wrote the passage and those who incorporated it into Scripture did so because of the importance they placed on the discipline of children. This point is one upon which most, if not all, members of the congregation will likely agree. Thus, a key question to pose in the sermon would be: If we are able to exercise good and appropriate discipline of children without the use of corporal punishment, why would we not do so? We know that corporal punishment poses dangers to children's emotional health. We also know that Section 43 has permitted gross physical abuse of children in the past. If the primary rationale for corporal punishment is discipline, and if we know that discipline is really about teaching and guidance, and that we can promote children's health and development more effectively without corporal punishment, why would we want to continue to permit it?

A Sample Sermon

On Sparing the Rod and Spoiling the Child

To spank or not to spank: many parents still wrestle with that question. Parents and others involved in the care of children ponder how to keep them safe once the child reaches the age of being able to get places and do things. These days, discussion of the topic may take a wider view, influenced by Call to Action 6 of the Truth and Reconciliation Commission, which calls for Section 43 of Canada's Criminal Code to be repealed. Section 43 gives parents and those acting in the place of parents a legal defence if they punish children physically; in other words, if they take an action that, if done by one adult to another, would be an assault. The Truth and Reconciliation Commission's call to repeal Section 43 stems from wide-ranging accounts of the physical abuse children suffered in the residential schools—as well as in many homes and schools across this country—physical abuse made legal by that Section of the Criminal Code. Section 43 makes *every* child vulnerable to physical assault by those entrusted to care for them.

I chose to preach today on this particular passage from Proverbs. I did so because it is a text, one of several in Scripture, that is often perceived to support the physical punishment of children. In considering the question of whether to physically punish children today, and the larger question of whether to repeal Section 43, it is useful to ponder this text.

The passage is a relatively short one, running but two verses. When I first reread this text, thinking about this sermon, I was struck by the words "beat them with a rod." In contemporary Canadian society, even most parents who believe that corporal punishment is sometimes necessary would not think of using a rod. Using a stick—after all, a "rod" is a stick of some size—would result not just in pain but almost certainly in bruising and possibly in serious injury. But the text of Proverbs, albeit written in a different day and era, uses this term. We might well say something like, "but that is not what is important about this text," or "there is a more important principle involved," but the language of the passage is nonetheless prescriptive.

So, what ought we to make of this passage? Some of us, particularly those of us who are older, may have memories of being physically punished when we were children. Certainly, such was true for me. My mother had no hesitation about spanking me in my preschool days. She was a typical parent in my northeastern New Brunswick village in the 1950s. She saw spanking as a necessary means of correction, and it was the form of physical punishment she most frequently used. The strap was still used in my village school, though its use was quite rare in my school days.

My parents were active church members. That said, I doubt that their approach to parenting, and to the use of corporal punishment, was the direct result of this text from Proverbs 23 or a similar one from Proverbs 13:23, which says, "Those who spare the rod hate their children, but those who love them are diligent to discipline them." Rather, they took their cues from the conventionally accepted wisdom of that period about how one ought to parent. Regardless, texts such as today's lesson from Proverbs, or Proverbs 13:23 that I quoted a moment ago, helped to undergird the view that corporal punishment was acceptable, even though in my childhood striking a child with a rod would not have been. Several sources contributed to create the parenting standards of that time. These texts from Proverbs were one source—one source among many, but they were one source.

What might we make of these verses, then? What wisdom might they offer at a time when an increasing number of experts argue strongly against corporal punishment and when a body such as the Truth and Reconciliation Commission calls for the repeal of the law that permits it? The passage in Proverbs 23 is part of a larger section of that chapter focused on the education of youth, most likely the children of well-to-do members of society who would have been expected to occupy positions of leadership as adults. The focus of this larger section is on the development of what we would call character—the moral or ethical side of how people lead their lives. Some of that larger section contains plain and good advice about how to live in harmony with others. But enhancing the weight of this particular section of Proverbs is a theological dimension. There is an emphasis on living a life pleasing to God, for, as the text just beyond today's reading puts it, we should "always continue in the fear of the Lord" (Proverbs 23:17).

So why does today's reading advocate corporal punishment? The answer is found in the universal importance of discipline. The purpose of the discipline of children, according to this passage, is "to save their lives from Sheol." In early Israelite history Sheol was a somewhat shadowy netherworld where the dead resided. As time passed, the concept of Sheol developed an increasingly negative connotation. "Saving their lives from Sheol" meant developing the good character that could lead to a long and good life.

If I think back to my childhood, my parents exercised discipline for two reasons. First, I needed to learn quickly that certain things were to be done or avoided for my own safety. For example, I needed to learn not to go racing out onto the provincial highway that ran through our village. My physical well-being depended on my learning certain things. Those lessons were enforced early on by discipline, some of it physical.

The second reason my parents exercised discipline was to develop my character as they would have understood that concept—to make me into a good and reliable person. I learned, painfully, that lying was not permissible. Hurting other people or animals was wrong. Fighting brought punishment if I was perceived to have started the fight, although self-defence was permitted. The destruction of someone else's property brought both physical punishment and the necessity of compensatory action. Rules about when to be home and what kinds of activity were acceptable were enforced. I could go on, but my point is that discipline, and in this case physical punishment, was used with the intent to help me develop good character.

Parents in our time and place share the two concerns my parents had. We too want to ensure that our children are safe, that they quickly learn to avoid danger. We also want them to develop good character, to grow up to be good and reliable people. What today's parents want is consistent with the rationale behind the text in Proverbs.

The question with which we need to wrestle is whether physical punishment is necessary to accomplish these goals. When Proverbs became part of Scripture, corporal discipline was a given. That said, the contemporary biblical scholar William Webb makes clear that the people of Israel were more reserved in their practice of corporal punishment than were their contemporaries in surrounding empires and cultures.[2] We also know that the level of corporal punishment meted out to children in our own country has declined over the years. It is not just that the strap is no longer used in schools. Few parents would now think of punishing a child with a rod, something that would have been common a few generations back. Webb demonstrates in his study that many of the leading figures who continue to support corporal punishment now advocate a very limited use of it. For example, even the conservative organization Focus on the Family now advocates a much more limited form of corporal punishment than was the case in materials they published four decades or so ago.[3] Webb regards this reduction both as a very good thing and as an example of how, over the centuries, Christians and Jews have allowed other knowledge to influence their interpretations of biblical texts and their implications for daily living.

If levels of the corporal punishment of children have been greatly reduced over the years, the question at some point needs to become, "Can we get rid of it totally?" Do parents need to be able to physically punish their children? Two important points need to be made here. First, those who call for the elimination of corporal punishment are not saying that the discipline of children is unnecessary. Very few parents, and an even smaller percentage of those who study parenting, would assert that discipline is unnecessary. Discipline is necessary. But there are many ways to teach children—more effectively—without hitting them (see Chapter 12). The intent of Proverbs 23 can be fulfilled without resorting to the harsh corporal punishment it advocates, or even the more limited form we generally see in this country. And surely the intent is what matters. As long as we can achieve the same outcome, who would advocate for physical punishment? Good evidence exists that one can parent effectively and teach children effectively without resorting to corporal punishment.

On a related point, what effect does it have on a child when a parent to whom the child looks for safety and security suddenly becomes a source of pain and violence? The parent who is striking the child does not think of it that way. The parent thinks, "I am carrying out a necessary disciplinary act." But how does the child see the action? A key person on whom a young child depends for security, protection from danger, and affection suddenly (from the child's perspective) causes pain and becomes a threat (see Chapter 3). That the parent does not intend this to be the child's experience is beside the point. While some of us may have endured physical punishment as children without obvious lasting traumatic effects, not all of us were so fortunate. We do not know how much of the depression and insecurity with which many contemporary adults struggle is rooted in early experiences of corporal punishment, especially severe and frequent experiences. What we do know is that many people have suffered permanent emotional damage and scarring. Why would we risk such effects if there is another equally—if not more—effective way to teach our children?

According to an old saying, "Time makes ancient good uncouth." Love for others and caring for others, especially those who are most vulnerable, are themes that run throughout Scripture and that have brought about change, as seen within both Testaments and through the ages since. Changing viewpoints on slavery may be the most well-known example, but it is not the only one. Now it is time to consider whether the corporal punishment of children should undergo one last change—its elimination. May we indeed seek the end of all harmful acts against children in the light of Scripture, in the light of history, in the light of contemporary knowledge and experience, and in light of our commitment to reconciliation. And to the God who created us, the God made known to us in Jesus the Christ, and the God present to us through the Holy Spirit, be all honour, glory, and praise, Amen.

Notes

1 This text, and all other biblical quotations in this chapter, are drawn from the New Revised Standard Version of the Bible. Dr. Young is pleased for others to borrow this sermon in part or in its entirety. Please give credit for any sections that are used.

2 William J. Webb, *Corporal Punishment in the Bible: A Redemptive-Movement Hermeneutic for Troubling Texts* (Downers Grove, IL: InterVarsity Press, 2011), 78–85; 99–118.

3 Webb, 25–29, especially 29.

17

AN OPPORTUNE TIME
Corrupt Imagination and Distorted Lives

MICHAEL THOMPSON

The imagination is the drama in which bodies are invested.
WILLIAM T. CAVANAUGH

For our struggle is not against enemies of blood and flesh, but against the rulers, against the authorities, against the cosmic powers of this present darkness, against the spiritual forces of evil in the heavenly places.
EPHESIANS 6:12 (NRSV)

Truly I tell you, unless you change and become like children, you will never enter the kingdom of heaven.
MATTHEW 18:3 (NRSV)

But understand this: if the owner of the house had known in what part of the night the thief was coming, he would have stayed awake and would not have let his house be broken into.
MATTHEW 24:43 (NRSV)

When an adult hits a child in order to change the child's behaviour, we need to pay close attention. That action, still all too common, can reveal a way of thinking that confounds our society and has done for a very long time. Our society has been in the grip of an imagination—a system of meaning and significance—that presents itself as "just the way things are." That we so seldom examine that imagination with its assumptions about how the world works, that we somehow acquiesce without either understanding or consent, is a dangerous spiritual failure, because by accepting one particular construct as "the way things are," we allow it to fade into the background. But when an adult hits a child in order to change that child's behaviour, that construct emerges into plain sight, if only for a moment or two. That is long enough, if we slow down the action and look at it with care, for us to discover how deep, pervasive, destructive, and illusory that construct is. Seeing that invites us to commit ourselves to a way of seeing and being that can nourish and support us in the hard work of being human bodies seeking to make a good journey through time and across space in the company of other human bodies.

This is fertile ground, of course, for spiritual traditions. Spiritual traditions are, after all, about the impact of unseen reality on our lives. It has always been part of spiritual traditions to acknowledge that if there are unseen realities whose impact on our lives is positive and life-giving, there are also unseen realities that corrode and corrupt human life. This is, I think, what Paul is saying to the Ephesians when he writes about the "principalities and ruling forces and masters of the darkness." Earlier in the same letter, Paul writes that Christ, in his ascension, "made captivity captive." This is not evidence of a primitive world view that needs to be laid aside in the wake of the Enlightenment, but a deep insight into the power of an imagination to shape and direct our lives. It speaks accurately of our captivity to unseen realities—to an imagination, a spirituality, even, that for the most part functions with neither our consent nor our awareness.

William Cavanaugh invites us to recognize that this "imagination" finds expression in our treatment and use of bodies. How we invest our bodies, and the bodies of others, is shaped by this imagination, this spirituality. How we move as bodies through time and across space in the company of other bodies expresses an imagination, a spirituality. Even if that spirituality presents itself as describing "just the way things are," it is the work of our souls to become conscious of it and to determine whether the "default" spirituality, the pervasive imagination that poses as reality, is worthy of our investment of bodies. The freeze-frame image—of an adult hitting a child—pries open the door behind which this imagination has been hiding, insists that we see and acknowledge it, and requires us to make a spiritual choice, to search out the imagination, the spirituality, that can nourish us and, in the words of Jack Biersdorf, "heal our purpose."[1]

Bishop Mark MacDonald (Chapter 1) points out that when we reduce our response to evil to a search for culprits, we overlook the systemic nature of evil—its capacity to hold in the same captivity those who are identified as culprits and those who are identified as victims. When an adult hits a child, we have an opportunity to understand that captivity and to seek the alternative of freedom.

When I was a child, the language used when an adult hit a child was that it was "for your own good." Stories told by children in the study reported by Bernadette Saunders in Chapter 3 (this volume) confirm that I was not alone in this experience. On the—thankfully rare—occasions upon which this particular "good" was visited on me, I don't think that I believed that it had anything at all to do with my own good. I am pretty sure, even at the age of six or seven years, that what I knew I was experiencing was the adult—my father—imposing pain to ensure that his will prevailed over mine. At the same time, I am sure that he truly was investing both my body and his in an imagination that he trusted as true and good. The other thing he said—"This hurts me as much as it hurts you"—was closer to the mark. Even so, the sentimental truth—that it was painful to inflict pain—did not, I think, create for him the reflective stillness that might have helped him to see the imagination that had captivated us both, or to seek the freedom of an alternative to that default imagination. In the end, he was left with the illusion that hitting me was a good way to help me make better choices, and I was trapped in the contradiction of words and actions, knowing it made no sense for this person who loved me to deliberately cause me pain, with no opportunity to address the confusion that ensued.

What is, then, this imagination, this spirituality that holds us in such captivity that it can cause someone to inflict deliberate pain on a beloved child? It is this: that some people believe that they are equipped to understand, without enquiry, what is "good for" other people, and are empowered—even if as a painful duty—to impose it on them.

The impact of the residential schools on survivors, their families, and their communities provides a clear and heartbreaking occasion to see and understand this toxic imagination at work. In the residential schools, this imagination functioned as a sort of matryoshka, the Russian doll in which one doll nests inside another. On the outside, the fundamental premise of the schools themselves was that white leaders were equipped to be certain, without enquiry, of what was good for Indigenous children and empowered to impose it on them. Prime Minister (and Minister of Indian Affairs) John A. Macdonald had this to say in the House of Commons in 1883:

> When the school is on the reserve, the child lives with its parents, who are savages, and though he may learn to read and write, his habits and training mode of thought are Indian. He is simply a savage who can read and write. It has been strongly impressed upon myself, as head of the Department, that Indian children should be withdrawn as much as possible from the parental influence, and the only way to do that would be to put them in central training industrial schools where they will acquire the habits and modes of thought of white men.[2]

One layer deeper, we encounter the witness of survivors to the pervasive adult use of physical punishment on children. *The Survivors Speak: A Report of the Truth and Reconciliation Commission* is one of the places in which we hear sobering direct testimony of survivors to the physical punishment they endured.[3] It is the tip of the iceberg. If the imagination is, as Cavanaugh describes it, "the drama in which bodies are invested," the shattered bodies of children—indeed, their very presence, by forced removal, in these schools—bears terrifying witness to the pervasive, deep, and destructive imagination that, until the first courageous survivors came forward, was largely unexamined.

Perhaps even more tragically, there is another horror hidden inside the matryoshka, a transfer of physical abuse from one generation to another. It begins as the children's experience of the use of force as modelled by adult authorities who run the schools becomes normative. A 2014 study by the Aboriginal Healing Foundation of lateral (student-to-student) physical abuse in the residential schools quotes one student as saying that "being chronically abused at a young age tends to make people think that it is normal [pause] I can think of some men [Survivors] that simply thought, 'Well, that is what you do with people.'"[4] This "new normal," which had not been in any sense normal in Indigenous households before the schools, was carried by the traumatized survivors back into their communities, infecting them with the belief that abuse is "what you do with people."

While in many cases it was "modelling" that generated lateral violence, in a significant number of instances, students reported to their service providers that they were explicitly empowered and even directed to use force against other students: "Just under one-quarter of service providers recount histories of some of their clients who described how the residential school staff would actually give permission to certain students to abuse others and, in some cases, [it] was even encouraged." Several share stories about how "staff gave the student abuser permission to handle or deal with the children in any way to maintain control over the student," and another describes how some were given "encouragement by staff to act as enforcers."[5]

Through the direct experience of students as victims, physical and sexual abuse was imitated by students within the residential schools themselves in the form of lateral violence. The violence then moved from the schools to the communities by way of the lives of traumatized survivors. In this way, the toxic imagination that abuse is "what you do with people" has found its way into Indigenous communities to the depth that Paul describes in his letter to the Ephesians—that "our struggle is not against enemies of blood and flesh, but against the rulers, against the authorities, against the cosmic powers of this present darkness, against the spiritual forces of evil in the heavenly places."[6]

In the course of participation in gatherings of the Truth and Reconciliation Commission, in meetings that include the churches and the government (as defendants) and survivors of the schools, and in work with Indigenous leaders and non-Indigenous allies to effect change in the relationship between Indigenous Peoples and non-Indigenous Canadians, one thing has been absolutely consistent: those who have been on a healing journey in response to the trauma of the schools do not call for punishment, but for justice. They are not fixated on culprits, but on a systemic imagination about power that distorts every life it touches.

Churches have, of course, participated in that distortion, aligning themselves with those who use their power to dominate. In all of the places to which churches have travelled on the coattails of colonialism, they have offered a covering fog of religion to support the idea that the colonizing power is equipped to know what is "good" for the colonized and empowered to invest the bodies of the colonized in that "good." In return, churches participated in the privilege that colonization secured. A distorted spirituality was created to support a destructive process, a spirituality that could justify children being removed from their families and communities, from their cultures, traditions, languages, and loves, all for the purpose of assimilation, of "killing the Indian in the child."[7]

This dynamic by which religious authorities borrow power from the dominating powerful and, in return, endow the powerful with a distorted spirituality that frames their use of power as right and godly, is more like a chronic illness than a tragic exception. It appears to be active, for example, in the relationships among Rome, the Temple, the wealthy, the peasant population, and Jesus of Nazareth.[8] It leaps out from the motto of David Livingstone—"Christianity, Commerce, and Civilization"—inscribed on his statue at Victoria Falls. It is worth noting that Livingstone did indeed harbour good intentions in his opposition to the slave trade. It is not that Livingstone, or the religious authorities in Jerusalem at the time of Jesus, or the church leaders who invested so deeply in the residential school system are "culprits." In Chapter 1, Mark MacDonald writes: "That there were many well-intentioned individuals in the schools is without doubt. The truth remains that all participated in a system of great evil."

He writes, also, of the "moral slumber" that allows systemic evil to flourish. If the image of an adult hitting a child awakens us from that slumber by disclosing what is always there but not always noted, what will it take to keep us from falling back asleep? The answer depends, to a large degree, on knowing and understanding why borrowing power at the cost of distorting and corrupting our spiritual collateral is attractive. One way of moving toward that knowledge and understanding is to reflect on the temptations of Jesus in Luke's gospel.[9] The first temptation is to deny the goodness of God's work, to renovate creation so that it can be useful to Jesus: "Jesus, full of the Holy Spirit, returned from the Jordan and was led by the Spirit in the wilderness, where for forty days he was tempted by the devil. He ate nothing at all during those days, and when they were over, he was famished. The devil said to him, 'If you are the Son of God, command this stone to become a loaf of bread.' Jesus answered him, 'It is written, one does not live by bread alone.'"

The second temptation is most clearly related to the borrowing of power at the cost of spiritual integrity: "Then the devil led him up and showed him in an instant all the kingdoms of the world. And the devil said to him, 'To you I will give their glory and all this authority; for it has been given over to me, and I give it to anyone I please. If you, then, will worship me, it will all be yours.' Jesus answered him, 'It is written, Worship the Lord your God, and serve only him.'"

On offer is power that Jesus would surely use wisely, well, and for good. He is understood to be the most deeply good person ever. Yet he declines power that would position him to perfect the world. What are we to make of the Adversary's contention that the glory and authority of all the kingdoms of the world belong to him? What would it mean for Jesus to participate in the Adversary's business, to share in his imagination, to adopt his understanding of glory and authority, just like "all the kingdoms of the world"?

Finally, the Adversary invites Jesus to leverage his relationship with God to extract himself from the human condition: "Then the devil took him to Jerusalem, and placed him on the pinnacle of the temple, saying to him, 'If you are the Son of God, throw yourself down from here, for it is written, "He will command his angels concerning you, to protect you," and "On their hands they will bear you up, so that you will not dash your foot against a stone."' Jesus answered him, 'It is said, "Do not put the Lord your God to the test."'"

To make things more useful—stones into bread; to gain (or maintain) power to accomplish good; to avoid the pain—broken hearts and broken bodies—that comes with being human: we call these "the temptations in the wilderness." But to a man who has had no food for forty days, who feels in his heart every suffering and wound of injustice and carelessness, and who will die alone and in pain, they must have felt more like invitations. That is how temptation works: it doesn't call itself temptation; it calls itself a solution, an opportunity. And so unlike Jesus, who returns in his teaching again and again to the theme of staying awake, who stays awake and prayerful on the last night of his life, we fall asleep. We are like the disciples who argue about power, avoiding the costly reality that Jesus confronts when he turns his face toward Jerusalem. Like the disciples who cannot stay awake with Jesus on the last night of his life, we too fall asleep and tumble effortlessly into "just the way things are." Intent on making the world more useful, better, safer, we do the most awful things and tell the people we hurt that it is for their own good. But stones are stones, not bread. The power the Adversary offers will contribute nothing to the cause of God. There is no way to present God to the world without making ourselves vulnerable and risking the breaking of our hearts and bodies.

In Chapter 4, Valerie Michaelson writes of "the lies that have shaped us," and reminds us that those lies are deep and pervasive in their impact. Those lies are not new; their authority is rooted in our tacit submission to them as "just the way things are." Mark MacDonald (Chapter 1) invites us to recognize the systemic evil that underwrites both colonialism and the residential schools. In seeking to understand how the associated lies make themselves attractive, how that systemic evil can seem normal and even good, I invite the churches, and all who care for the common good, to recognize that robust spiritual traditions offer an alternative imagination, a healing of human purpose, and the power to unmask the principalities and powers as neither good nor inevitable.

In the binding of Isaac, surely the archetypal narrative of divinely sanctioned violence against children, the divine name changes partway through the narrative. It is Elohim who demands the death of Isaac, and YHWH who provides an alternative. "Elohim" is a generic name, translated in English as "God," but also meaning "a god" or "the gods." YHWH is translated "the Lord." In his troubling work, *Why Abraham Killed Isaac*,[10] Hebrew scholar Tzemah Yoreh invites us to consider how the text of this narrative developed. He proposes the strong possibility that the original text (in which the divine name is Elohim) ends with the completion of Isaac's death, with Abraham returning alone to his young men at the foot of Moriah. He notes that Isaac never appears again in a text in which the divine name is Elohim.

He speculates that the death of Isaac is necessary because he is not the son of Abraham and Sarah but of Abimelech and Sarah, conceived during Sarah's brief sojourn in the house of Abimelech. Would "the gods" of "just the way things are" have understood, perhaps even insisted, that Isaac, the offspring of this deceit, must die? Yoreh, who insists that "no-one has the authority to seal the gates of interpretation" does not argue that the narrative *must*, or even *should* be read in this way. He does argue clearly that it *may* be read in this way. Reading the text in that way, we come to understand that the God of Israel (YHWH) is distinct from the gods of "just the way things are" (Elohim). We come to see, early in the biblical narrative, that the God of Israel and of Jesus offers an alternative to "just the way things are," an alternative imagination that overcomes apparent "divine inevitability."

We have been reading the biblical narrative through a particular lens of imagination for so long that we have come to believe the lens's distortion is what the narrative actually means. We have believed in a God who demands that we punish our children because they are inherently sinful, and who equips and empowers us to know what is good for others and to impose that good on them. The motto was: "Christianity, Commerce, and Civilization." It doesn't require an evil culprit but a corrupt imagination, an ideology hiding behind a religious smokescreen of conversion. In the Finnish Museum of Mission in Helsinki, I saw "before and after" photos of a southwest African man. In the before photo, he was lightly covered on those parts that modesty might call for. After his conversion, he wore a three-piece suit, a collar and tie, oxfords, and a pith helmet. And he smoked a cigarette. This is what comes of imposing our ways on people "for their own good."

If, when an adult hits a child, we stop the film and see all of this, we will remove from our Criminal Code the excuse for that action and end the violence against children that both state and religion have sanctioned. We will see ahead of us a long road of healing and reconciliation for all the harm done by the awful and godless idea that some of us are equipped to know what is good for others and empowered to impose that good on them.

Notes

1 John E. Biersdorf, *Healing of Purpose: The Call to Discipleship* (Nashville: Abingdon, 1985).

2 Truth and Reconciliation Commission of Canada, *Honouring the Truth, Reconciling for the Future: Summary of the Final Report of the Truth and Reconciliation Commission of Canada* (Winnipeg: Truth and Reconciliation Commission of Canada, 2015), 2.

3 Truth and Reconciliation Commission of Canada, *The Survivors Speak: A Report of the Truth and Reconciliation Commission of Canada* (Winnipeg: Truth and Reconciliation Commission of Canada, 2015).

4 Amy Bombay, Kim Matheson, and Hymic Anisman, *Origins of Lateral Violence in Aboriginal Communities: A Preliminary Study of Student-to-Student Abuse in Residential Schools* (Ottawa: Aboriginal Healing Foundation, 2014), 62.

5 Bombay, Matheson, and Anisman, 63.

6 Ephesians 6:12, NRSV.

7 Truth and Reconciliation Commission of Canada, "Backgrounder" (Winnipeg: Truth and Reconciliation Commission of Canada, 2015), accessed 8 July 2018, http://www.trc.ca/websites/trcinstitution/File/pdfs/Backgrounder_E.pdf. This statement is often attributed to Deputy Minister of Indian Affairs Duncan Campbell Scott, who stated the following in relation to assimilation policies: "Our object is to continue until there is

not a single Indian in Canada that has not been absorbed into the body politic," as cited in Truth and Reconciliation Commission of Canada, *Honouring the Truth, Reconciling for the Future*, 2–3.

8 Marcus J. Borg and John Dominic Crossan, *The Last Week: What the Gospels Really Teach about Jesus's Final Days in Jerusalem* (San Francisco: HarperCollins, 2007).

9 This account of the temptations of Jesus is found in Luke 4:1–13.

10 Tzemah Yoreh, *Why Abraham Killed Isaac,* Kernel to Canon (Scotts Valley, CA: CreateSpace Independent, 2013).

18

HIDING, FINDING, AND BREAKING

One Man's Journey to Breaking the Intergenerational Cycle of Violence

CLARENCE HALE AND VALERIE E. MICHAELSON

Clarence Hale is the caretaker at St. James' Anglican Church in Kingston, Ontario. His great-aunt tells him he is of Indigenous heritage, Lakȟóta Sioux, they think.

Clarence was a part of the original vision of the project on which this book is based, and an integral participant in the forum that produced the *Theological Statement.* In this chapter, I (Valerie Michaelson) have drawn together pieces of several audio-recorded interviews—more accurately, long conversations over coffee—that Clarence and I had during the spring of 2018. With permission, I have rearranged and edited the interviews in order to shape a story. Every word in italics is Clarence's.

This is the story of how he broke the cycle of violence.

Hiding

When you've been close friends for twenty years, you don't bother with small talk. And Clarence is the most open person I know. He's very comfortable talking about hard things, and after all, our project is about corporal punishment. He talks about his childhood straight off.

My father used to hit me with his belt. He would take down my pants in front of people and whip me. I have had that happen, and that closed me down. But my anger was so high I would say, go ahead, I don't feel anything. That is what I would do at school. If the principal would give me the belt I would say, go ahead I don't feel it, and then they would get more mad and they would hit me harder. Yeah. It has happened many times to me.

I closed off. Fear closed me off, but I didn't want to show it. My father was very abusive and had a lot of anger. At six or seven years old, I would hide under my bed. I escaped every chance I could. I was protecting myself, you know? I didn't like what was going on around me. It was not a good picture, and I hid a lot. Everywhere. Every opportunity that I had. I used to jump out of my balcony that was ten feet high and take off. I would go anywhere—the woods, forest. It was a safe haven for me. I used to hide under my bed . . . in garbage cans . . . they never looked in the garbage . . . I lived in a lot of shame . . . I hid from shame.

By age twelve, alcohol had become another escape, and another place to hide.

I used to sneak it off my parents here and there. But this other guy that I hung around with, he and I stole twenty dollars off my mother, and we walked in town and got two guys to buy us two bottles of wine and we were twelve. And then we went down to the tracks and drank it and when I drank about half of it . . . I don't remember very much. And I don't know where he went.

"You could have died on the train tracks!" Perhaps unhelpfully, I point this out.

Oh yeah, I was about five feet from the tracks, drunker than a skunk. Twelve years old and sicker than a dog. I thought alcohol was just a normal thing. I saw my dad beat on my mother many times, and I watched it. And that is why I would hide. When I saw my mother being beat up with blackened eyes and everything, I escaped. But I was always afraid. It was a scary experience. Yeah. I lived in fear most of my life.

I have lost a lot of my old buddies. They are not here. They committed suicide. And a lot of them said that I was worse than them with my addiction. But a lot of them are gone.

Well, that was part of my life, being hit. Because of the sickness; it causes damage and it closed me up. I thought I knew how to act, but I didn't, and that is why I hurt a lot of people. That is why my relationships did not work out, because I ran. I ran from it. I got very angry inside and did not know how to deal with it. So, it came out in full force of rage where I could hurt someone.

That is what rage does and that is what put a lot of people in prison, because of their rage. And I could have been one of them. I went a different route. I didn't go to prison, but I went somewhere else. It is just like prison because it is all walls. Walls within. That is a big prison. Everyone in prison has made mistakes. Some make big mistakes. And I made big mistakes.

I had hit bottom and I didn't want to live anymore. I was sick and tired of being sick and tired. I couldn't go on much more. I was a black-out guy. I was lost, and I didn't know how to get found.

Finding

I remember the day that Clarence told me about his ancestry. It was an August morning in 2010, and we were setting up for the church Sunday school. My children were running around trying to get him to play with them, as they always did, and he told them he had just been to Nova Scotia, where he had talked with his aunt. "*I'm Native, girls,*" he said to them. "*I'm Indian!*" Their excitement drew me over. "I didn't know you were Indigenous," I said. "*Neither did I,*" he responded. Eight years later, we are talking about it again.

I didn't think that I was a white person anyway, because I was always called different names. I was called black or a nigger because I had dark skin back then. Especially in the summer. I was always outside and never home. I was darker than most others who I hung around with. So, I always thought I was different because of my skin colour. I didn't fit in and I felt that I wasn't a part of things.

But I didn't know I was Native. . . . You see, there was no communication at home. We came up from down east when I was four years old. I didn't grow up where I was born. We moved off to a different . . . to Kingston. So, Nova Scotia to Kingston. So, we grew up not really knowing our roots.

I never thought about my roots, to tell you the truth. In the past eight years probably, a lot of stuff came out from my mother's sister about this Native stuff. It came down through my mother's side, through North Dakota.

"Wait a minute," I interrupt. "When you first found out, I thought you told me you were Mi'kmaq, from Nova Scotia."

No, I was mixed up about that. So, they say that Rain-in-the-Face is my great-great-grandfather. My aunt has a couple of pictures of him at home. He is . . . from the States. North Dakota. Yeah. And he was in that ambush back with Custer and he was involved in that. I'm not really sure because we don't really know all the pieces, and I wish I did know. I don't know if I could ever really find out because it comes from my mother's aunt and she is dead now, and so is her cousin, the one that found out. So, I might never really know.

Later, I would look up Rain-in-the-Face on the internet. I would find out that he was also known as Itonagaju and that he was a chief of the Lakȟóta tribe. I would do some searching and find out that with Sitting Bull and Crazy Horse, he defeated General Custer and the U.S. 7th Cavalry Regiment at the 1876 Battle of Little Big Horn.[1] I would stare at my screen in stunned silence as I read the poem "The Revenge of Rain-in-the-Face." It is here I would learn that, at least by Henry Longfellow's account,[2] Rain-in-the-Face cut out the heart of the "White Chief with yellow hair," personally dispatching George Armstrong Custer.[3] And I would realize that there was a reasonable chance that Clarence is the great-great-grandson of a man who is recognized by some as one of the most fierce and heroic leaders in American history.

While Clarence is not certain about his ancestry, everything he is telling me makes sense. Why else would they have this family picture, hidden away in an attic for generations but marked with family names? Clarence is certainly not alone in having this kind of experience. Over and over, stories emerge of First Nations, Inuit, and Métis people in Canada who have lost all sense of their family history due to colonial-driven racism and shame. For now, all I know is what Clarence tells me about his great-great-grandfather. And he sounds proud:

He had to earn being a chief. His background was not anything like a chief's. He earned it by being a warrior. He was a brave warrior. And how he got his name was in a fight. He punched someone in the face and all the blood came on to him. And that is why they call him Rain-in-the-Face. It is true.

After I learn about Clarence's heritage, the racist and shaming tentacles of colonialism strike me deeply, in an entirely new way. I am left with a question I cannot get out of my mind. How is it that the great-great-grandson of one of the most renowned Indigenous heroes in the United States of America ended up growing up in Canada, with no idea he had any kind of Indigenous ancestry until he was nearly fifty years old? Clarence's ancestry is the stuff of poetry and legend. Yet growing up in Kingston, Canada, in the 1960s and '70s, he knew nothing about it and his skin colour caused him shame.

Breaking

Violence breeds violence. It launches a cruel cycle, and it is often hard to pinpoint where it starts. Clarence knows this well.

There was no communication in our house. It was all negative and abusive stuff. That is all they knew. And it causes issues in the future. I was in rage at times and blamed others. It was always someone else's fault, like my parents'. They got a lot of anger off of me. I used to bang my head on the floor and accuse them of everything. Oh yeah. I was there.

I had so much anger and rage. About the whole situation. Just about the way my life was. Deep down I know . . . I always wanted some love and someone to be there for me. But that was not the case. I just thought it was normal and was the way it was. But it wasn't normal. It is sick. And I became a sick person. I didn't realize it. It started at five years old for me when I closed off. I didn't allow anyone in and didn't trust anyone. So, I closed down.

But then our conversation takes a whole new turn.

I don't blame my parents today. I love my parents. It probably went generation from generation—back before my parents. We were sick, but it is not their fault. I have to deal with my own stuff.

I am just learning today that I am on a different life than I was back then. It has taken all this time for me to come and learn what I never learned, and I didn't know how back then. I didn't think that I was capable of doing it. I was crying out for help. That is what it was. I knew that I needed help. I was contemplating suicide. Yeah. I had it on my brain a lot of the time. I would get up and didn't want to get up anymore. So, I said, "I have had enough, and I can't go on." Well I went through a couple of rehabs and that has been helpful. AA [Alcoholics Anonymous] *has been really there for me.*

Getting away fishing helps me too. Fishing is the opposite of hiding. Fishing I enjoy, and I don't have to feel guilty about it. And I love what I am doing. Hiding is different. I don't want to be caught feeling guilt. And fear is the biggie. Fear is the one that made me hide a lot. I was afraid. I was used to being afraid. That was my whole life—it was about being afraid. So, I had to overcome being afraid.

Today, Clarence and his wife, Shirley, are raising their grandson free of violence. Everyone who knows them admires their collective determination, commitment, and gentleness. I listen with quiet admiration as Clarence tells me about this journey.

We're learning . . . it's not easy. Shirley and I communicate with each other. That is where it starts, agreeing with each other on discipline. We talk things out. And that has been good. The doctor and school have been helping us with that. They give us some direction on how to go about with our grandson wanting to be in control all the time. And I know that because I have been there. I wanted to be in control all the time.

We try to talk to him. We talk to him about what is right and wrong in our opinion. So, what the behaviour will do when you don't follow rules. I tell him, "You know what happened to Papa when he went to school, and he didn't do his homework? You know where it will get you, right?" And he says, "Oh yeah, Papa." He catches on. We try to tell him the best we know how. You know? Not by hitting or spanking. We don't do that. . . . I disagree on hitting because what I saw when I was a kid. It doesn't go over well. It can close a person up and they can get very angry.

I am grateful that he can come to me and still does. He comes and hugs me every day. "Oh, I need a hug, Papa," and that is very special to me. I never got that when I was a kid. It was the opposite. . . . You didn't get that back then.

Being there for someone else is the greatest gift on earth. When you can do that and sacrifice for others. It is a healing process, and that is what I try to do today. My grandson is way ahead of me from when I went to school. He is way ahead. He has caught up. I see a lot of good qualities in him and it is going to be okay. I have a lot of hope for him and that he is going to be okay.

Reconciling

Clarence and I now talk about the Truth and Reconciliation Commission (TRC) because after all, this is a book about reconciliation. First, we reflect on the *Theological Statement* (page 11).

It is a positive thing. The kids should come first in life. I saw it in my background and it wasn't a healthy one. It was a very painful life. So, we should be there for kids. I disagree with hitting kids. . . . That is a crime for me. It causes a lot of damage.

But for Clarence, it was not easy to be part of the forum:

When I was at the [forum], *it was emotionally draining for me. I was going through a lot of emotions and the real stuff was coming out and I didn't know how to handle it. I enjoyed* [the forum], *but there was a lot of pain and suffering that I was going through at that time. I was wrapped up in Clarence. And I apologize for that, but that is where I was at that time.*

When you got me to talk, I knew that it was a turning point for me. I was either going to live or die here. It was a crucial point for me. But it was meant to be because I am here today, and I am learning from it. So, what I had to say . . . it was very painful what I said. It was going down to the core of my childhood and that is where I was very stopped. I was going through a lot of . . . it was coming to the surface, all of that pain of my childhood. Because of my skin colour and I didn't fit in. I thought I was different. I felt that I wasn't a part of. . . . There was no one . . . when I came to Kingston, no one was Native where I was hanging around. I was the only one and I didn't realize that I was Native back then. I didn't know that I had Native in me, but I felt different. Now I know I am a Native and that it is my blood.

I remind Clarence of Bishop MacDonald's words (Chapter 1) about how reconciliation happens when people move from being victims to being survivors. "Does that resonate with you?" I ask.

It does. That is exactly what it is. Yep. I am a survivor from my past. The past reconciliation. I come to grips with it and I know who I am today. I am proud of who I am today. I'm not a victim anymore. People tell me that. I don't have to be in that darkness today. And I thank God for it. It is with help from a lot of people and I know that I couldn't do it alone. I tried all my life to do it on my own and it didn't work out.

What Clarence really wants to talk about is a different kind of reconciliation:

For me, it's about making amends . . . like forgiveness. I just did one not too long ago on a person who I did a lot of damage to. And . . . it was hard. It was the right time to tell this person that I apologize for the damage that I had caused. And I know that I caused a lot. I was not making excuses today for that. It was all because of what I had done, and I am very sorry for that. It was tough because I did a lot of damage to her.

I am getting freedom now. It is making amends which is part of me getting my freedom. I feel better about this incident because it was on my shoulders for a long time. I carried it for a long time. Oh yeah. It was finally the timing. I don't want to do it for wrong the reasons. It would stir up more stuff, and I don't want to do that. So, I felt that it was the right timing. The AA meetings helped. They gave me some direction and guidance. I have never had that. I had my own guidance and it was not that good.

I can go to bed at night knowing that I didn't hurt anyone today. And that is a good feeling. I try every day to do some good for someone else. That is right. You don't have to live the way I used to live. I don't have to be there today. And that is the bottom line and I am grateful for that. It was a hellhole back then. Oh yeah. Complete darkness. Blackness and no light. No light would shine. And I put myself there.

I am trying to break the pattern of what I knew, just being myself. Be the real me, be there for others. The disease will take everything from you, so you have to let it go in our recovery. And we have to pass on what we are learning to the others that come in the doors. So that is a good thing. So, knowing that I have something to give to someone else. Telling my story, telling the truth . . . it's all part of the healing. That's why I share.

I now try to make sense of this story, and the place of Christianity in particular.

I had a lot of prejudice toward God because of what happened to me. I didn't want nothing to do with it. But also, *I feel a lot of love at the church. I look for the love, not the negative.*

I find it complicated to think about the place of the church in this narrative. The same church that contributed to these colonial systems is one of the places where Clarence is finding healing today. I am awed by the depth of this man's forgiveness toward the forces that almost destroyed him, including his forgiveness of the church. And it is more than a little bit uncomfortable for me to recognize the many ways in which I have not only participated in but even benefitted from the system that was established at the expense of Indigenous people like my friend. This paradox presents me with an intellectual challenge. But, in effect, Clarence is asserting self-determination: having control over his own life and not being told by anyone else what to do, or think, or believe.

Clarence tells me about a picture of his great-great-grandfather and laughs.

I think I look like him. I was like him. I've had fights in bars . . . I don't know who I fought with. I had the same problem as him, with alcohol. I was on the run all the time. I was in the forest and I was good at it, like he was. He was a great warrior. I am too when I'm sober. I just feel like everything he's done, I've done that. The good and the bad. A lot of people loved him for bravery. You still have to be brave.

In his poem "The Revenge of Rain-in-the-Face," the American poet Longfellow wrote, "Whose was the right and the wrong? / Sing it, O funeral song, / With a voice that is full of tears. / And say that our broken faith / Wrought all this ruin and scathe, / In the Year of a Hundred Years."[4] In these short lines, Longfellow reflects on a century of dishonour. And as John Koster notes, even while treating the fallen troops as "tragic heroes,"[5] Longfellow blames the "ruin and scathe" on "our broken faith"—a reference to the violation of the Treaty of Fort Laramie in 1868.[6] Five generations have passed since then, but our history of broken treaties continues. Here in colonial Canada, the descendant of a hero can exist with no knowledge of his heritage. Clarence's self-knowledge has been thwarted by the same racism and systemic oppression that his great-great-grandfather experienced, and which many Indigenous people across Canada continue to experience today.

I think again of Bishop MacDonald's words about "the courage of survivors." Clarence has travelled along a long road to tell his truth and reclaim his true spirit. His life has been marked by transmission of violence across generations—violence that shares its roots with the racism that fuelled the residential schools. Corporal punishment has left him with emotional scars that are still not healed, even decades later. Like Clarence, many of the victims of the cycles of violence that were created through colonization continue to experience the harms that colonial ideologies and their resultant policies, attitudes, and behaviours have caused. And through no fault of their own, many lack the resources they need to break the cycle once and for all.

Clarence would never call himself a hero. But I would. Over the course of our long friendship, he has given me profound glimpses into the possibility of healing and forgiveness. I have observed first-hand that violence, hurt, and brokenness do not have to have the final word in a person's life. Some weeks, he goes to four AA meetings just to keep his sanity, just so he can get out of bed the next day. He tells me he goes to the church in the middle of the night and has long talks with God about the dark memories that haunt him still. He forgives with generosity. He lets go of grudges. He does not lay blame. He hugs his grandson, and he goes out in the woods to be quiet and to the lake to fish. This is how he has broken the cycle of violence.

I've changed big time. It's not about fear. . . . It's about . . . feeling good about Clarence. The good within myself. Not every day is a good day and I have my bad days. But today is a good day. I am here.

Notes

1 Shari Benstock, *No Gifts from Chance: A Biography of Edith Wharton*, vol. 5 (Austin: University of Texas Press, 2004); Frederick Whittaker, *A Complete Life of General George A. Custer: From Appomattox to the Little Big Horn*, vol. 2 (Lincoln: University of Nebraska Press, 1993).

2 Henry Wadsworth Longfellow, "The Revenge of Rain-in-the-Face," in *Longfellow's Poetical Works: With 83 Illustrations by Sir John Gilbert, RA, and Other Artists* (London: George Routledge and Sons, 1883), 479.

3 Hamlin Garland, *The Book of the American Indian* (Lincoln: University of Nebraska Press, 2002); M.A. Elliot, *Custerology: The Enduring Legacy of the Indian Wars and George Armstrong Custer* (Chicago: University of Chicago Press, 2008).

4 Longfellow, "The Revenge of Rain-in-the-Face," 479.

5 John Koster, "Right as Rain-in-the-Face: A Lakota Warrior Speaks about Little Bighorn," 4. HistoryNet. 25 December 2019, https://www.historynet.com/right-as-rain-in-the-face-a-lakota-warrior-speaks-about-little-bighorn.htm.

6 Koster, 2019.

19

Let Ours Be Hands That Bless

RISCYLLA SHAW

This work matters to me. It is personal; it is professional. It is in my ancestry, my family, my community, and my church. It is academic, theological, and experiential. For me, this project has been a groundbreaking and heart-expanding experience, challenging all of us to consider three distinct yet interconnected threads: corporal punishment, Christian theologies, and reconciliation. We have been called to reflect upon what it would look like if churches in Canada embraced the call to decolonize the discipline of children: the children of our hearts and bodies, the children of our neighbours, the children of our enemies and of our friends; young people who are fully human, made in the image of God, who, like older people, have a right to dignity, personhood, and participation in this life. They are co-creators of our life together.

For Christians in Canada, the truth-telling that flows from the Truth and Reconciliation Commission (TRC) must lead to repentance. It is both our responsibility and our opportunity to learn the whole truth of the residential schools, to dwell deeply in that pain, and to take a deep and sustained look at the way we in the church have historically treated children. This in turn can lead to the rediscovery of the grace that inspired the Christian movement. The TRC provides an enormous opportunity for churches to now live into the various apologies that we have made and, animated by faith, to move forward in true reconciliation.

Yet we cannot read this volume without being sobered by the damage that has been done to children, families, and communities in the name of Christian ministry. We are not alone in our experiences and in our failings. Regardless of whether or not they used corporal punishment, many who have gone before us had good intentions to raise children as cooperative, respectful, contributing members of society. Caring, well-meaning, and well-respected adults have made mistakes that have been and remain common in our cultural-religious context, where we have been taught that punishment and obedience are the *action* (punishment: spanking, strapping, slapping) and *outcome* (obedience: submission, meekness, "good behaviour") equation for harmonious relationships between children and their parents, church communities, and social worlds.

Jesus teaches us another way.

Re-Visioning Discipline as Belonging

A few years ago, I travelled to another city for an event held at a university, where the audience was mainly composed of graduate students and accomplished authors. It was advertised as open to the public—so, bottles of juice and sandwich bags in hand, I wandered in with my two little children. I set them up in the corner with food and crayons, praying that they would quietly blend into the background. What happened next was an education for me. Several Elders, some guests, and a few of the students came toward us, stood at a respectful distance, and said to my children, "We are glad you are here with us! Welcome!" "You are special to come with your mom to hear us. Thank you for being here." "Do you need anything? If you do, come and ask." What happened next? My children "behaved" better than they ever did in church (where we often shush and give the side-eye to our wee ones and their parents, meanwhile saying that we love having children in our services!). In fact, they behaved *as if they belonged*. When we belong, we are free to be our authentic selves. That is the core purpose of discipline: not to be "trained," but to know trust and belonging.

The importance of trust and belonging has been demonstrated throughout this volume. Martin Brokenleg (Chapter 9) writes that "the primary human experience is belonging." In his words, how a child is treated will "give them the experience of belonging." Consistent experiences of belonging will help children grow into stronger people. Shirley Tagalik (Chapter 10) also writes about belonging to the group as core to the Inuit concept of *inunnguiniq*, the developmental process which by a child grows into "a capable human being." For Marcia Bunge (Chapters 8 and 11), beyond belonging to the community, children belong to God. And no less than the very Reign of God belongs to them. These insights are not inconsistent with each other; belonging in all of these ways is core to the Christian life.

Tragically, the history of our land is one of persistence in destroying children's belonging: the destruction and disintegration of parent-child relationships resulting from colonial cultural, religious, and societal teachings (Chapter 1) interpreted within the context of the Doctrine of Discovery (Chapter 4). The tenaciously effective and insidious purpose of the Doctrine of Discovery was to abolish the culture, language, teachings, and ideologies of the peoples of the "undiscovered lands," replacing them with the institutional teachings and exploitative management and domination policies of the colonizers. It was the goal of the residential schools to "take the Indian out of the child"—to erase all elements of Indigenous cultures and ways, to replace them with "civilized" ways, namely conformity, complacency, and colonial convention. The outcomes of the Doctrine of Discovery have been so pervasive that to the detriment of us all, many Indigenous languages and cultural traditions, creation stories and environmental preservation practices have been suppressed, disrupted, and severely damaged. One price of these ideologies and related practices was paid in the damage done to basic *belonging*.

The Paradox of Reconciliation and the Church

There is a paradox—a contradiction—that runs throughout this entire project, and it is perhaps most obviously seen in our team. To move us toward reconciliation, settler church leaders from the very churches that ran the residential schools are drawing from the same canon of sacred texts that were used to oppress. Indigenous stakeholders who themselves and in their family histories have been harmed by colonization are leaders in the Christian church. Health researchers who have no affiliation with the Christian church at all are partners in this project. We are journeying together, seeking reconciliation.

This is not the first time I have experienced this kind of paradox. I once took an excellent class on Indigenous Knowledges. It was taught by a wise, respected, deeply spiritual Ojibway Elder who is known for his antagonism toward the historical church due to the legacy of the residential schools and European colonization of this land. The class had no formal introductions or conversations between the students and the professor—so the facts that my grandfather went to residential school and that I am Métis and clergy never came up.

A year later at a public reconciliation event, the Holy Spirit brought us together again—only this time, I was the Anglican clergy on duty, collar on. That same Elder was leading the prayers at the opening ceremonies in his language and tradition. When I went to thank him afterwards, for a very long moment he was speechless. He was staring at me as if I were a ghost—then he simply said, "I have never seen you in the collar before." By chance, later in the day, I came face to face with him again, and he said, "I am still getting used to you in the collar," accompanied by dead silence and a very intense gaze. It felt as if the weight of 500 years of history was on my shoulders. Recognizing the intensity of the situation, I was respectfully quiet and remained present in the moment.

Balancing in the tension of the unresolved, the message that I work to embody is that "the church" as an institution is willing and able to listen and learn. It recognizes mistakes made, has apologized, and is working very hard in many ways to restore right relationships. This wisdom, learning, and respect is deeply necessary in our church relationships with all of those who have been hurt by the colonial system, which Christianity has animated over centuries. Wearing a perceived sign of oppression and simultaneously bringing the liberating message of Jesus to all is integrating my identity as one who walks in both worlds.

In terms of this project on Call to Action 6, it is rightly an unsettling place for all of us. Yet God is with us in this place, unsettling us to leave behind the ways of injustice, broken treaties, and doctrines of domination that have harmed so many lives. The common thread holding us together is that we believe in—and are committed to—the hard work of reconciliation. We believe a new way forward is possible, and that churches in Canada have a role to play in becoming partners in a just and transformed land: a place in which all children are protected from every form of violence. May this small project be one piece.

Moving Forward in Reconciliation

Through the work of the TRC and the partnerships of parties to the Settlement Agreement (the Anglican, United, and Presbyterian Churches, and the Government of Canada), we are directed to examine the depths of darkness and pain in the family lives of our forebears. We must recognize the violence that was inflicted on children in the name of discipline, in the name of the Government of Canada, and in the name of God. In doing so, we are drawn to reflect on the pain that we ourselves have inflicted on children. This is not an easy task for any of us. But we are not alone in this because we are all Treaty People. Let us begin to renew our treaty responsibilities, and to "change our lives to fulfill the obligations and possibilities of our shared life together in this land."[1] It is incumbent upon each of us, with the help of God our Creator, to wrestle with the inheritance we have received. We must be intentional in reflecting upon the "moral wound," the "systemic evil," the inhumanity with which we have used corporal punishment to control and manipulate the smallest, most vulnerable members of our families and communities.

We as a church, as followers of Jesus, as proclaimers of the God of Love, are being called by our Life-Giver to identify the pernicious lies that perpetuate violence against children. Call to Action 6 has revealed these cruel lies and drawn attention to the ways that they have brought harm to so many children. As we respond to the TRC, may we be guided in our faith to name and reject any and all ageist, racist, colonial (and other) lies that prevent us from living as fully human together, all equally made in the image of God. May we be shown by the Holy Spirit how to articulate and disallow the cruel and racist lies that tear the fabric of our souls and that deny the dignity of our children.

In the church, we have the capacity to provide critical leadership in decolonizing discipline. We have the opportunity to dismantle the narratives that have grown from our own tradition and that have sustained the normalization of violence against children, and replace them with a new theological imagining of what "discipline" means. Ideas of what this vision might look like, ideas that are rooted in the sacred texts we hold dear, have been articulated throughout this book. As this volume has demonstrated repeatedly, positive discipline does not mean no discipline; it means teaching children about appropriate expectations, boundaries, and self-regulation in ways that honour their dignity as full human beings who bear God's image. Whether it is in our homes or in our churches, promoting positive approaches to discipline is a necessity for those of us in Christian ministry today.

This work is deeply faithful to who we are as Christians and as parents. It is liberating, redeeming, and healing to learn how to communicate with those closest to our hearts without inflicting physical or emotional pain. When we understand and accept that our children are born spiritually complete, made in the image of God, we build a different kind of relationship than when we believe they are not yet fully human. They do not need to be made into our adult image or made into an imagined image of perfection or completion. They have already arrived as blessed and loved by God, who loves our children as they are: not *more* because they behave a certain way, and certainly not *less* if they behave a certain way.

Throughout this book, Christian churches in Canada are charged to become champions of Call to Action 6 of the TRC, and to petition our government to ensure the full protection of children, which includes the repeal of Section 43 of the Criminal Code of Canada. This is the first of six recommendations that came out of the original forum, during which the *Christian Theological Statement in Support of the Truth and Reconciliation Commission's Call to Action 6* was written.

There is much more work to be done. At this same forum, we also called upon Christian churches to recognize the deep wounds that remain as a result of colonialism, and to actively address the ongoing, disproportionate physical, spiritual, and emotional harm experienced by Indigenous children and youth. We recognized the opportunity for our churches to increase awareness in our own communities of the impact of violence, including physical punishment, in homes, families, institutions, and communities. These are not simple quick fixes; they are fundamental and foundational changes that will take time to make and to build, and real commitment to sustain. Yet I believe this to be true: if all leaders and educators in Christian communities would commit to becoming active in the protection of children, and to work together in continuing to develop healthy, effective, and non-violent approaches to discipline in raising children and youth, lives would be changed.

For What Will We Be Remembered?

This volume began with Bishop MacDonald's call to the church to participate in the "creation of a society in which children are protected and flourish" and so to speak prophetically to the repeal of Section 43. And there is more to be done:

> *We are called to prophetically see, with the eyes of our hearts, the lasting outcomes of our actions, practices, and policies upon our children.*
>
> *We are called to reclaim life, healing, justice, strength, courage, and wisdom, and to protect especially those who are most vulnerable among us.*
>
> *We are called to live fully in freeing ways that honour the whole, of which we are a part.*
>
> *We are called to engage in the spiritual discipline of becoming fully human.*
>
> *We are called to live as people of hope: who hope and trust that reconciliation is possible, and who are willing to do the hard work not only to imagine but to create a shared future together.*

Let ours be a time remembered for the awakening of a new reverence for the mysteries of our parent-child relationships, gratitude for the gift of life, humility for our role and place in our children's worlds, and full engagement in the process of authentic reconciliation. By God's grace, may we be persuaded to use our prophetic imaginations and create our shared future so that all children may truly be protected and flourish.

May our hands no longer be associated with harm.
Let ours be hands that bless.

Notes

1 Jennifer Henry, "A Reflection on the United Nations Declaration on the Rights of Indigenous Peoples," KAIROS Canada, 2019, accessed 28 August 2019, https://www.kairoscanada.org/what-we-do/indigenous-rights/undrip-reflection.

BIBLIOGRAPHY

Aboriginal Legal Service of Western Australia. *Telling Our Story: A Report by the Aboriginal Legal Service of Western Australia on the Removal of Aboriginal Children from Their Families in Western Australia.* Western Australia: Aboriginal Legal Service of Western Australia, 1995.

Afifi, T.O., D. Ford, E.T. Gershoff, M. Merrick, A. Grogan-Kaylor, K.A. Ports, H.L. MacMillan, G.W. Holden, C.A. Taylor, S.J. Lee, and R.P. Bennett. "Spanking and Adult Mental Health Impairment: The Case for the Designation of Spanking as an Adverse Childhood Experience." *Child Abuse and Neglect* 71 (2017): 24–31.

Alderson, Priscilla, and Christopher Goodey. "Research with Disabled Children: How Useful Is Child-Centred Ethics?" *Children and Society* 10 no. 2 (1996): 106–16.

All Africa Conference of Churches (AACC-CETA). "The All Africa Conference of Churches (AACC)." Accessed 20 June 2018. http://aacc-ceta.org/en/about/10-about-aacc.

Andraos, Michel. "Doing Theology after the TRC." *Toronto Journal of Theology* 32, no. 3 (2017): 295–301.

Andraos, Michel, Lee Cormie, Néstor Medina, and Becca Whitla. "Decolonial Theological Encounters: An Introduction." *Toronto Journal of Theology* 33, no. 2 (2017): 259–60.

Anglican Church in Aotearoa, New Zealand and Polynesia. "Removing the Loophole: Anglican Bishops Support Repeal of Section 59." 1 May 2007. http://www.churches-fornon-violence.org/New%20Zealand%20Bishops%20statement.pdf.

Assembly of First Nations Environmental Stewardship Unit. *The Health of First Nations Children and the Environment: Discussion Paper.* Ottawa: Assembly of First Nations, 2008. Accessed 18 October 2018. https://www.afn.ca/uploads/files/rp-discussion_paper_re_childrens_health_and_the_environment.pdf.

Australian Government. Australian Institute of Health and Welfare. *Child Protection Australia 2014–15*. Canberra: Australian Institute of Health and Welfare, 2016. Accessed 20 May 2018. http://www.aihw.gov.au/publication-detail/?id=60129554728.

Australians Together. "About Us." Australians Together. Accessed 20 May 2018. https://www.australianstogether.org.au/about-us/.

———. "The Stolen Generations: The Forcible Removal of Indigenous Children from Their Families." Australians Together. Accessed 20 May 2018. https://australianstogether.org.au/discover/australian-history/stolen-generations.

Baidawi, Susan, Philip Mendes, and Bernadette Saunders. "Indigenous Young People Leaving Out of Home Care in Victoria: A Literature Review." *Indigenous Law Bulletin* 8, no. 7 (July/August 2013): 24–27.

Beckwith, Ivy. *Formational Children's Ministry: Shaping Children Using Story, Ritual, and Relationship*. Grand Rapids, MI: Baker Books, 2010.

Bengtson, Vern. *Families and Faith: How Religion Is Passed Down across Generations*. New York: Oxford University Press, 2013.

Bennett, John, and Susan Rowley, eds. *Uqalurait*. Montreal: McGill-Queen's University Press, 2004.

Benstock, Shari. *No Gifts from Chance: A Biography of Edith Wharton*. Vol. 5. Austin: University of Texas Press, 2004.

Bernstein, Richard. *Beyond Objectivism and Relativism: Science, Hermeneutics and Praxis*. Philadelphia: University of Pennsylvania Press, 1983.

Berryman, Jerome W. *Children and the Theologians: Clearing the Way for Grace*. New York: Morehouse Publishing, 2009.

———. *The Complete Guide to Godly Play*. Vol. 1. Denver: Living the Good News, 2002.

———. *Godly Play: An Imaginative Approach to Religious Education*. San Francisco: HarperSanFrancisco, 1991.

———. *Stories of God at Home: A Godly Play Approach*. New York: Church Publishing, 2018.

Best Start Resource Centre. *A Child Becomes Strong: Journeying through Each Stage of the Life Cycle*. Toronto: Best Start Resource Centre, 2010. Accessed 9 October 2018. www.beststart.org.

Biersdorf, John E. *Healing of Purpose: The Call to Discipleship*. Nashville: Abingdon Press, 1985.

Bohlin, N.E. "A Statistical Analysis of 28,000 Accident Cases with Emphasis on Occupant Restraint Value." *Society of Automobile Engineers (SAE) Transactions* 76, Section 4, Papers 670805–984 (1968): 2981–94.

Bombay, Amy, Kim Matheson, and Hymic Anisman. *Origins of Lateral Violence in Aboriginal Communities: A Preliminary Study of Student-to-Student Abuse in Residential Schools*. Ottawa: Aboriginal Healing Foundation, 2014.

Borg, Marcus J., and John Dominic Crossan. *The Last Week: What the Gospels Really Teach about Jesus's Final Days in Jerusalem*. San Francisco: HarperCollins, 2007.

Botterweck, G.J., H.J. Fabry, and H. Ringgren, eds. *The Theological Dictionary of the Old Testament*. Grand Rapids, MI: Eerdmans, 1998.

Bourassa, Carrie, Kim McKay-McNabb, and Mary Hampton. "Racism, Sexism and Colonialism: The Impact on the Health of Aboriginal Women in Canada." *Canadian Woman Studies* 24, no. 1 (2004): 23–29.

Bradt, Kevin M. *Story as a Way of Knowing*. London: Sheed and Ward, 1997.

Brendto, Larry, Martin Brokenleg, and Steve VanBockern. *Reclaiming Youth at Risk: Our Hope for the Future.* Bloomington, IN: Solution Tree, 1990.

Briggs, Jean L. *Never in Anger: Portrait of an Eskimo Family*. Cambridge, MA: Harvard University Press, 1970.

Briskman, Linda. "Beyond Apologies: The Stolen Generations and the Churches." *Children Australia* 26, no. 3 (2001): 4–8.

———. *Social Work with Indigenous Communities.* Sydney: Federation Press, 2014.

Brown, Stuart. *Play: How It Shapes the Brain, Opens the Imagination, and Invigorates the Soul.* New York: Penguin, 2009.

Brown, William P. "To Discipline without Destruction: The Multifaceted Profile of the Child in Proverbs." In *The Child in the Bible,* edited by Marcia J. Bunge, Terence E. Fretheim, and Beverly Roberts Gaventa, 63–81. Grand Rapids, MI: William B. Eerdmans, 2008.

Brueggemann, Walter. *Truth-Telling as Subversive Obedience.* Edited by K.C. Hanson. Eugene, OR: Cascade Books, 2011.

Bunge, Marcia J., ed. *The Child in Christian Thought.* Grand Rapids, MI: Eerdmans, 2001.

Bunge, Marcia J. "The Child, Religion, and the Academy: Developing Robust Theological and Religious Understandings of Children and Childhood." *Journal of Religion* 86, no. 4 (October 2006): 549–78.

———. "Conceptions of and Commitments to Children: Biblical Wisdom for Families, Congregations, and the Worldwide Church." In *Faith Forward,* vol. 3, *Launching a Revolution through Ministry with Children, Youth, and Families,* edited by D.M. Csinos, 94–112. Kelowna, BC: Wood Lake Publishing, 2018.

———. "The Dignity and Complexity of Children: Constructing Christian Theologies of Childhood." In *Nurturing Child and Adolescent Spirituality,* edited by Karen M. Yust, Aostre N. Johnson, Sandy E. Sasso, and Eugene C. Roehlkepartain, 53–68. Lanham, MD: Rowman and Littlefield, 2006.

———. "A More Vibrant Theology of Children." *Christian Reflection: A Series in Faith and Ethics* 8 (Summer 2003): 11–19.

Bunge, Marcia J., Terence E. Fretheim, and Beverly Roberts Gaventa, eds. *The Child in the Bible.* Grand Rapids, MI: William B. Eerdmans, 2008.

Bushnell, Horace. *Christian Nurture*. New York: Charles Scribner, 1861.

Buti, Antonio. "The Removal of Aboriginal Children: Canada and Australia Compared." *University of Western Sydney Law Review* 6 (2002): 25–37.

———. "The Removal of Indigenous Children From Their Families: U.S. and Australia Compared." *University of Western Sydney Law Review* 8 (2004): 125–52.

Caillou, Sharilyn. "Peacekeeping Actions at Home: A Medicine Wheel Model for a Peacekeeping Pedagogy." In *First Nations Education in Canada: The Circle Unfolds,* edited by Marie Battiste and Jean Barman, 47–72. Vancouver: UBC Press, 1995.

Canada. Parliament. Senate. "Bill S-206: An Act to Amend the Criminal Code (protection of Children against standard child-rearing violence)." 2nd sess., 41st Parliament,

October 16, 2013–August 2nd, 2015." Accessed 28 August 2019. https://www.parl.ca/LEGISINFO/BillDetails.aspx?billId=6273086&Language=E&Mode=1.

———. "Criminal Code: Bill to Amend—Second reading—Debate Continue." Debates of the Senate, Senate of Canada, 1st sess., 42nd Parliament, vol. 150, no. 102 (March 7 2017): 2498–500.

Canada Without Poverty. "Just the Facts." Canada Without Poverty. Accessed 11 April 2018. http://www.cwp-csp.ca/poverty/just-the-facts/.

Canadian Broadcasting Corporation. "Mennonite Child Abuse Arrests Have Community Reeling." CBC News, 21 June 2013. https://www.cbc.ca/news/canada/manitoba/mennonite-child-abuse-arrests-have-community-reeling-1.1373140.

Canadian Council of Motor Transport Administrators. *National Occupant Restraint Program 2010: Annual Monitoring Report 2008*. Ottawa: CCMTA, 2010. Accessed 30 September 2018. https://ccmta.ca/images/publications/pdf//norp_report10.pdf.

Carlo, G., G.P. Knight, M. McGinley, and R. Hayes. "The Roles of Parental Inductions, Moral Emotions, and Moral Cognitions in Prosocial Tendencies among Mexican American and European American Early Adolescents." *Journal of Early Adolescence* 31 (2011): 757–81.

Castellano, Marlene Brant, Linda Archibald, and Mike DeGagné. Conclusion to *From Truth to Reconciliation: Transforming the Legacy of Residential Schools*, 403–10. Aboriginal Healing Foundation Research Series. Ottawa: Aboriginal Healing Foundation, 2008. Accessed 28 August 2019. http://www.ahf.ca/downloads/truth-to-reconciliation.pdf.

Cavalletti, S. *The Religious Potential of the Child*. New York: Paulist Press, 1983.

Chrysostom, St. John. *On Marriage and Family Life*. Translated by Catherine P. Roth and David Anderson. Crestwood, NY: St. Vladimir's Seminary Press, 1986.

Church of Scotland. "General Assembly Calls for Law Amendment to Protect Children." Church of Scotland: News and Events, 24 May 2016. http://www.churchofscotland.org.uk/news_and_events/news/2016/general_assembly_calls_for_law_change_to_protect_children.

Churches' Network for Non-violence. "What Can Christians Do towards Ending Corporal Punishment of Children?" Churches' Network for Non-violence. Accessed 9 July 2018. http://churchesfornon-violence.org/wp/wp-content/uploads/2012/02/Handbook-posters.pdf.

Churches' Network for Non-violence and Global Initiative to End All Corporal Punishment of Children. *Ending Corporal Punishment of Children: A Handbook for Worship and Gatherings*. Nottingham: CNNV, 2005.

———. *Ending Corporal Punishment of Children: A Handbook for Multi-Religious Gatherings*. Nottingham: CNNV, Global Initiative to End Violence against Children, and Save the Children, 2016.

Clines, D.J.A., ed. *The Dictionary of Classical Hebrew*. Sheffield: Sheffield Phoenix, 2011.

Coker, Joe L. *Liquor in the Land of the Lost Cause: Southern White Evangelicals and the Prohibition Movement*. Lexington: University Press of Kentucky, 2007.

Coles, R. *The Spiritual Life of Children*. Boston: Houghton Mifflin, 1990.

Comenius, Johannes Amos. *The School of Infancy*. 1663. Edited by Ernest M. Eller. Chapel Hill: University of North Carolina Press, 1956.

Crenshaw, James L. *Old Testament Wisdom: An Introduction.* Rev. ed. Louisville, KY: Westminster John Knox, 1998.

Crenshaw, Kimberle. "Mapping the Margins: Intersectionality, Identity Politics, and Violence against Women of Color." *Stanford Law Review* 43, no. 6 (1991): 1241–99. https://doi.org/10.2307/1229039.

Csikszentmihalyi, Mihaly. *Finding Flow: The Psychology of Engagement with Everyday Life.* New York: Basic Books, 1997.

Cyprian. "Letter 64.3." In *Letters*, translated by Sister Rose Bernard Donna. Washington, DC: Catholic University of America Press, 1964.

Davidov, M., and J.E. Grusec. "Untangling the Links of Parental Responsiveness to Distress and Warmth to Child Outcomes." *Child Development* 77 (2006): 44–58. https://doi.org/10.1111/j.1467-8624.2006.00855.x.

de Leeuw, Sarah, Margo Greenwood, and Nicole Lindsay. "Troubling Good Intentions." *Settler Colonial Studies* 3, no. 3–4 (2013): 381–94.

Denham, S.A., K.A. Blair, E. DeMulder, J. Levitas, K. Sawyer, S. Auerbach-Major, and P. Queenan. "Preschool Emotional Competence: Pathway to Social Competence?" *Child Development* 74 (2003): 238–56.

Denis, Jeffrey S., and Kerry A. Bailey. "'You Can't Have Reconciliation without Justice': How Non-Indigenous Participants in Canada's Truth and Reconciliation Process Understand Their Roles and Goals." In *The Limits of Settler Colonial Reconciliation*, edited by Sarah Maddison, Tom Clark, and Ravi de Costa, 137–58. Singapore: Springer, 2016.

Dobson, James. *The New Dare to Discipline.* Rev. ed. Carol Stream, IL: Tyndale Momentum, 2001.

Doriani, Daniel M. "A Response to William J. Webb." In *Four Views on Moving beyond the Bible to Theology*, edited by Stanley N. Gundry and Gary T. Meadors, 255–61. Grand Rapids, MI: Zondervan, 2009.

Dorpat, Theodore L. *Crimes of Punishment: America's Culture of Violence.* New York: Algora Publishing, 2007.

Dunn, J. "Moral Development in Early Childhood and Social Interaction in the Family." In *Handbook of Moral Development*, edited by M. Killen and J.G. Smetana, 331–50. Mahwah, NJ: Erlbaum, 2006.

Durrant, Joan, E. *Positive Discipline in Everyday Parenting.* 4th ed. Stockholm: Save the Children Sweden, 2016.

Durrant, Joan E., Ron Ensom, and Coalition on Physical Punishment of Children and Youth. *Joint Statement on Physical Punishment of Children and Youth.* Ottawa: Coalition on Physical Punishment of Children and Youth, 2004. Accessed 28 August 2019. Available through http://www.cheo.on.ca/en/physicalpunishment.

Durrant, J., D. Plateau, C. Ateah, G. Holden, L. Barker, A. Stewart-Tufescu, A. Jones, G. Ly, and R. Ahmed. "Parents' Views of the Relevance of a Violence Prevention Program in High, Medium, and Low Human Development Contexts." *International Journal of Behavioral Development* 41, no. 4 (June 2017): 523–31.

Eisenberg, N., A. Cumberland, and T.L. Spinrad. "Parental Socialization of Emotion." *Psychological Inquiry* 9 (1998): 241–73.

Elliot, M.A. *Custerology: The Enduring Legacy of the Indian Wars and George Armstrong Custer.* Chicago: University of Chicago Press, 2008.

Ellison, C.G., and M. Bradshaw. "Religious Beliefs, Sociopolitical Ideology, and Attitudes toward Corporal Punishment." *Journal of Family Issues* 30, no. 3 (2009): 320–40. https://doi.org/10.1177/0192513X08326331.

Engel, Madeline H., Norma Kolko Phillips, and Frances A. DellaCava. "Indigenous Children's Rights: A Sociological Perspective on Boarding Schools and Transracial Adoption." *International Journal of Children's Rights* 20, no. 2 (2012): 279–99.

Eshet, Dan. *Stolen Lives: The Indigenous Peoples of Canada and the Indian Residential Schools.* Facing History and Ourselves, 2015. Accessed 15 September 2019. https://www.facinghistory.org/sites/default/files/publications/Stolen_Lives_1.pdf.

Fabes, R.A., S.A. Leonard, K. Kupanoff, and C.L. Martin. "Parental Coping with Children's Negative Emotions: Relations with Children's Emotional and Social Responding." *Child Development* 72, no. 9 (2001): 907–20.

Fedio, Chloe. "TRC Report Brings Calls for Action, Not Words." CBC News, 2 June 2015. Accessed 15 September 2019. https://www.cbc.ca/news/politics/truth-and-reconciliation-report-brings-calls-for-action-not-words-1.3096863.

Fitzgerald, John T. "Proverbs 3:11–12, Hebrews 12:5–6, and the Tradition of Corporal Punishment." In *Scripture and Traditions: Essays in Early Judaism and Christianity in Honor of Carl R. Holladay,* edited by P. Gray and G.R. O'Day, 291–318. Leiden: Brill, 2008.

Fitz-Gibbon, Jane Hall. *Corporal Punishment, Religion, and United States Public Schools.* Ithaca, NY: Palgrave Macmillan, 2017.

Focus on the Family. "Questions about Spanking." Focus on the Family. Accessed 21 April 2018. https://www.focusonthefamily.com/family-q-and-a/parenting/questions-about-spanking.

Forget, André. "Church's Knowledge of Doctrine of Discovery 'Woefully Inadequate.'" *Anglican Journal,* 28 August 2015. https://www.anglicanjournal.com/articles/church-s-knowledge-of-doctrine-of-discovery-woefully-inadequate/.

Fowler, James W. *Stages of Faith: The Psychology of Human Development and the Quest for Meaning.* New York: HarperCollins, 1981.

Fox, Michael V. *Proverbs 1–9: A New Translation with Introduction and Commentary.* The Anchor Bible 18A. New Haven, CT: Yale University Press, 2008.

———. *Proverbs 10–31: A New Translation with Introduction and Commentary.* The Anchor Bible 18B. New Haven, CT: Yale University Press, 2009.

Freeman, Michael. "Children Are Unbeatable." *Children and Society* 13, no. 2 (1999): 130–41.

Friesen, John D. "Rituals and Family Strength." *Direction* 19, no. 1 (1990): 39–48. www.directionjournal.org/19/1/rituals-and-family-strength.html.

Gardner, Matt. "Vision Keepers: Primate's Council of Indigenous Elders and Youth Holds First Meeting." Anglican Church of Canada. Accessed 28 August 2019. https://www.anglican.ca/news/vision-keepers-primates-council-indigenous-elders-youth-holds-first-meeting/30019491/.

Garland, Hamlin. *The Book of the American Indian.* Lincoln: University of Nebraska Press, 2002.

Garvey, Catherine. *Play: The Developing Child.* Enlarged ed. Cambridge, MA: Harvard University Press, 1990.

Geisst, Charles R. *Beggar Thy Neighbor: A History of Usury and Debt.* Philadelphia: University of Pennsylvania, 2013.

Gershoff, Elizabeth Thompson. "Corporal Punishment by Parents and Associated Child Behaviours and Experiences: A Meta-Analytic and Theoretical Review." *Psychological Bulletin* 128, no. 4 (2002): 539–79. https://doi.org/10.1037//0033-2909.128.4.539.

Gershoff, E.T., and A. Grogan-Kaylor. "Spanking and Child Outcomes: Old Controversies and New Meta-Analyses." *Journal of Family Psychology* 30, no. 4 (2016): 453–69. https://doi.org/10.1037/fam0000191.

Gershoff, Elizabeth T., Andrew Grogan-Kaylor, Jennifer E. Lansford, Lei Chang, Arnaldo Zelli, Kirby Deater-Deckard, and Kenneth A. Dodge. "Parent Discipline Practices in an International Sample: Associations with Child Behaviors and Moderation by Perceived Normativeness." *Child Development* 81, no. 2 (2010): 487–502. https://doi.org/10.1111/j.1467-8624.2009.01409.x.

Gingrich, Wilbur F., and Frederick W. Danker. *A Greek-English Lexicon of the New Testament and Other Early Christian Literature.* 2nd ed. Revised and augmented from Walter Bauer's 5th ed. Chicago: University of Chicago Press, 1979.

Global Initiative to End All Corporal Punishment of Children and Global Movement for Children in Latin America and the Caribbean. *Prohibiting Corporal Punishment of Children in the Caribbean: Progress Report 2012.* London: Global Initiative to End All Corporal Punishment of Children, 2012.

Gray, Peter. *Free to Learn: Why Unleashing the Instinct to Play Will Make Our Children Happier, More Self-Reliant, and Better Students for Life.* New York: Basic Books, 2013.

Gray, S. *The Northern Territory Intervention: An Evaluation.* Melbourne: Castan Centre for Human Rights Law, 2015.

Grogan-Kaylor, A. "Corporal Punishment and the Growth Trajectory of Children's Antisocial Behavior." *Child Maltreatment* 10, no. 3 (2005): 283–92.

Gryczkowski, Michelle R. "An Examination of Potential Moderators in the Relations between Mothers' and Fathers' Parenting Practices and Children's Behavior." PhD diss., University of Southern Mississippi, 2011.

Haig-Brown, Celia. *Resistance and Renewal: Surviving the Indian Residential School.* Vancouver: Arsenal Pulp Press, 1988.

Hartup, W.W. "Peer Relations in Early and Middle Childhood." In *Handbook of Social Development: A Lifespan Perspective,* edited by V.B. Van Hasselt and M. Hersen, 257–81. New York: Plenum Press, 1992.

Hay, David, and Rebecca Nye. *The Spirit of the Child.* London: Fount, 1998.

Hay, David, K. Helmut Reich, and Michael Utsch. "Spiritual Development: Intersections and Divergence with Religious Development." In *The Handbook of Spiritual Development in Childhood and Adolescence,* edited by Eugene C. Roehlkepartain, Pamela E. King, Linda M. Wagener, and Peter L. Benson, 46–59. Thousand Oaks, CA: Sage, 2006.

Hebb, D. *The Organization of Behavior: A Neuropsychological Theory.* New York: Wiley, 1940.

Henry, Jennifer. "A Reflection on the United Nations Declaration on the Rights of Indigenous Peoples." KAIROS Canada, 2019. Accessed 28 August 2019. https://www.kairoscanada.org/what-we-do/indigenous-rights/undrip-reflection.

Hiltz, Fred, Mark MacDonald, and Michael Thompson. "There Was Nothing Good: An Open Letter to Canadian Senator Lynn Beyak." Anglican Church of Canada, 30 March 2017. https://www.anglican.ca/news/nothing-good-open-letter-canadian-senator-lynn-beyak/30018179/.

Hodgins, J.G., and Department of Education, Ontario. *Documentary History of Education in Upper Canada (Ontario), from the Passing of the Constitutional Act, 1791 to the Close of Ryerson's Administration of the Education Department in 1876*. Toronto: Warwick Bros. and Rutter, 1900.

Holden, G.W. *Parenting: A Dynamic Perspective*. Thousand Oaks, CA: Sage, 2015.

Huizinga, Johan. *Homo Ludens: A Study of the Play Element in Culture*. London: Routledge and Kegan Paul, 1949.

Human Rights and Equal Opportunity Commission. *Bringing Them Home*. Sydney: Commonwealth of Australia, 1997.

Ingram, Chip. "What the Bible Says about Discipline." Focus on the Family. Accessed 9 October 2018. www.focusonthefamily.com/parenting/effective-biblical-discipline/effective-child-discipline/what-the-bible-says-about-discipline.

Initiatives of Change Australia. "Reflecting on the National Apology to Australia's Stolen Generation." Accessed 9 January 2019. Initiatives of Change Australia. https://au.iofc.org/reflecting-national-apology-australia's-stolen-generations.

KAIROS. "History of the Blanket Exercise." KAIROS Canada, 2019. Accessed 27 September 2019. https://www.kairosblanketexercise.org/about/#history.

Kaiser, Walter, Jr. "A Response to William J. Webb." In *Four Views on Moving beyond the Bible to Theology*, edited by S.N. Gundry, 249–54. Grand Rapids, MI: Zondervan, 2009.

Karetak, Joe, Frank Tester, and Shirley Tagalik, eds. *Inuit Qaujimajatuqanit—What Inuit Have Always Known to Be True*. Halifax: Fernwood Press, 2017.

Katz, L.F., A.C. Maliken, and N.M. Stettler. "Parental Meta-Emotion Philosophy: A Review of Research and Theoretical Framework." *Child Development Perspectives* 6 (2012): 417–22. https://doi.org/10.1111/j.1750-8606.2012.00244.x.

Khondkar, L., C. Ateah, and F. Milon. "Implementing 'Positive Discipline in Everyday Parenting' among Ethnic Minorities, Urban Slums, and Brothel Areas of Bangladesh." Presentation at the International Society for the Prevention of Child Abuse and Neglect. Calgary, AB, August 2016.

Kochanska, G. "Children's Temperament, Mothers' Discipline, and Security of Attachment: Multiple Pathways to Emerging Internalization." *Child Development* 66 (1995): 597–615.

Kochanska, G., and N. Aksan. "Children's Conscience and Self-Regulation." *Journal of Personality* 74, no. 6 (1995): 1587–1617.

Kochanska, G., and R.A. Thompson. "The Emergence and Development of Conscience in Toddlerhood and Early Childhood." In *Parenting and Children's Internalization of Values*, edited by J.E. Grusec and L. Kuczynski, 53–77. New York: Wiley, 1997.

Köstenberger, Andreas J. *God, Marriage, and Family: Rebuilding the Biblical Foundation*. Wheaton, IL: Crossway, 2010.

Koster, John. "Right as Rain-in-the-Face: A Lakota Warrior Speaks About Little Bighorn." HistoryNet. Accessed 25 December 2019. https://www.historynet.com/right-as-rain-in-the-face-a-lakota-warrior-speaks-about-little-bighorn.htm.

Land, Richard, and Barrett Duke. "The Christian and Alcohol." *Criswell Theological Review* 5, no. 2 (2008): 19–38.

Lemnos, T.M. "Did the Ancient Israelites Think Children Were People?" *Bible History Daily* (blog). Biblical Archeology Society. Accessed 16 March 2018. https://www.biblicalarchaeology.org/daily/biblical-topics/bible-interpretation/ancient-israel-children-personhood/.

Lerner, R.M., C. Brentano, E.M. Dowling, and P.M. Anderson. "Positive Youth Development: Thriving as a Basis of Personhood and Civil Society." *New Directions for Youth Development* 95 (2002): 11–34.

Lewis, Clive Staples. *The Lion, the Witch and the Wardrobe*. London: Geoffrey Bless, 1950.

Lindenberger, J.M. "The Words of Ahiqar." In *The Old Testament Pseudepigrapha,* vol. 2, edited by James H. Charlesworth, vi, 3–5, 498. Garden City, NY: Doubleday, 1985.

Long, Thomas G. "The First Commandment with a Promise: Recent American Preaching on 'Honor Your Father and Your Mother.'" *Journal of Law and Religion* 31, no. 2 (2016): 169–82. https://doi.org/10.1017/jlr.2016.14.

Longfellow, Henry Wadsworth. "Revenge of Rain-in-the-Face." In *Longfellow's Poetical Works: With 83 Illustrations by Sir John Gilbert, RA, and Other Artists*, 479. London: George Routledge and Sons, 1883.

Luther, Martin. *The Large Catechism of Dr. Martin Luther, 1529: The Annotated Luther Study Edition*. Edited by Kirsi Stjerna. Minneapolis: Fortress Press, 2016.

———. *Luther's Large Catechism*. Translated by F.S. Janzow. St. Louis, MO: Concordia, 1978.

MacDonald, David. "A Call to the Churches: You Shall Be Called the Repairer of the Breach." In *From Truth to Reconciliation: Transforming the Legacy of Residential Schools*, prepared for the Aboriginal Health Foundation by Marlene Brant Castellano, Linda Archibald, and Mike DeGagné, 343–58. Ottawa: Aboriginal Healing Foundation, 2008. Accessed 28 August 2019. http://www.ahf.ca/downloads/truth-to-reconciliation.pdf.

MacDonald, Mark. "Spiritual Struggle, Systemic Evil." *Anglican Journal*, 28 February 2018. https://www.anglicanjournal.com/articles/spiritual-struggle-systemic-evil/.

Mason, Jan, and Jan Falloon. "Some Sydney Children Define Abuse: Implications for Agency in Childhood." In *Conceptualizing Child-Adult Relations*, edited by Leena Alanen and Beryy Mayall, 110–27. London: Routledge Falmer, 2001.

Mayer, J.D., and P. Salovey. "What Is Emotional Intelligence?" In *Emotional Development and Emotional Intelligence: Educational Implications,* edited by J.D. Mayer and P. Salovey, 3–31. New York: Basic Books, 1997.

Michaelson, Valerie, Peter Donnelly, William Morrow, Nathan King, Wendy Craig, and William Pickett. "Violence, Adolescence, and Canadian Religious Communities." *Journal of Interpersonal Violence* (May 2018): 1–25 https://doi.org/10.1177%2F0886260518775160.

Middleton, Richard. *The Liberating Image: The Imago Dei in Genesis 1*. Grand Rapids, MI: Brazos Press, 2005.

Miller, Lisa. *The Spiritual Child: The New Science on Parenting for Health and Lifelong Thriving.* London: Picador, 2015.

Miller-McLemore, Bonnie J. "'Let the Children Come' Revisited: Contemporary Feminist Theologians on Children." In *The Child in Christian Thought*, edited by Marcia J. Bunge, 446–73. Grand Rapids, MI: Eerdmans, 2000.

Milloy, J.S. "'Suffer the Little Children': The Aboriginal Residential School System 1830–1992." Submitted to the Royal Commission on Aboriginal Peoples, May 1996.

Mohler, Albert. "Commentary: Should Spanking Be Banned? Parental Authority under Assault." Albert Mohler, personal website. 24 June 2004. Accessed 19 October 2018. https://albertmohler.com/2004/06/22/should-spanking-be-banned-parental-authority-under-assault/.

Moltmann, Jürgen. *Theology of Play.* New York: HarperCollins, 1972.

Moore, Tim P. "Children and Young People's Views on Institutional Safety: It's not Just Because We're Little." *Child Abuse and Neglect* 74 (December 2017): 73–85. https://doi.org/10.1016/j.chiabu.2017.08.026.

Morrow, William S. "Toxic Religion and the Daughters of Job." *Studies in Religion* 27, no. 3 (1998): 263–76.

———. "Violence and Religion in the Christian Tradition." In *Teaching Religion and Violence*, edited by Brian K. Pennington, 94–117. Oxford: Oxford University Press, 2012.

Mouton, Elna. "Reimagining Ancient Household Ethos? On the Implied Rhetorical Effect of Ephesians 5:21–33." *Neotestamentica* 48, no.1 (2014): 163–85.

Mulvaney, M.K., and C.J. Mebert. "Parental Corporal Punishment Predicts Behavior Problems in Early Childhood." *Journal of Family Psychology* 21, no. 3 (2007): 389–97.

Naselli, Andy D. "Training Children for Their Good." *Journal of Discipleship and Family Ministry* 3, no. 2 (2013): 48–64.

National Collaborating Centre for Aboriginal Health (NCCAH). *Inuit Qaujimajatuqangit: The Role of Indigenous Knowledge in Supporting Wellness in Inuit Communities in Nunavut.* NCCAH and the Public Health Agency of Canada, 2009–10. https://www.ccnsa-nccah.ca/docs/health/FS-InuitQaujimajatuqangitWellnessNunavut-Tagalik-EN.pdf.

———. *Inunnguiniq: Caring for Children the Inuit Way.* NCCAH and the Public Health Agency of Canada, 2009–10.

———. *Inutsiaqpagutit: That Which Enables You to Have a Good Life: Supporting Inuit Early Life Health.* NCCAH and the Public Health Agency of Canada, 2010.

Newbigin, Lesslie. *Foolishness to the Greeks: The Gospel and Western Culture.* Grand Rapids, MI: Eerdmans, 1980.

———. *The Open Secret: An Introduction to the Theology of Mission.* Rev. ed. Grand Rapids, MI: Eerdmans, 1995.

Nye, Rebecca. *Children's Spirituality: What It Is and Why It Matters.* London: Church House Publishing, 2009.

Ohene, S.A., M. Ireland, C. McNeely, and I.W. Borowsky. "Parental Expectations, Physical Punishment, and Violence among Adolescents Who Score Positive on a Psychosocial Screening Test in Primary Care." *Pediatrics* 117 (2006): 441–47.

Osborne, Grant R. *The Hermeneutical Spiral: A Comprehensive Introduction to Biblical Interpretation.* Downers Grove, IL: InterVarsity, 1991.

Pastorelli, Concetta, Jennifer E. Lansford, Bernadette Paula Luengo Kanacri, Patrick S. Malone, Laura Di Giunta, Dario Bacchini, Anna Silvia Bombi, et al. "Positive Parenting and Children's Prosocial Behavior in Eight Countries." *Journal of Child Psychology and Psychiatry* 57, no. 7 (2016): 824–34.

Pate, Matthew, and Laurie A. Gould. *Corporal Punishment around the World.* Santa Barbara: Prager, 2012.

Penninga, Mark. "Spanking Does Have a Place in Canada." *Reformed Perspective: A Magazine for the Christian Family*, 10 February 2017. http://reformedperspective.ca/its-still-legal-to-use-physical-discipline-and-it-should-remain-so/.

Pinheiro, Paulo Sérgio. "Speech of the Independent Expert United Nations Secretary-General's Study on Violence against Children." General Segment United Nations Human Rights Council, Palais des Nations, Geneva, 22 June 2006.

———. *World Report on Violence against Children.* Geneva: United Nations Secretary-General's Study on Violence Against Children, 2006.

Postman, Neil. *The Disappearance of Childhood.* New York: Delacorte Press, 1982.

Powell, Kara, Brad Griffin, and Cheryl Crawford. *Sticky Faith: Youth Worker Edition.* Grand Rapids, MI: Zondervan, 2011.

PREVNet. "Bullying: What We Know and What We Can Do." PREVNet. Last modified 2015. http://www.prevnet.ca/bullying/facts-and-solutions.

Punch, Samantha. "Research with Children: The Same or Different from Research with Adults?" *Childhood* 9, no. 2 (2002): 321–41. https://doi.org/10.1177%2F0907568202009003005.

Qaujigiartiit Health Research Centre (QHRC). *Inunnguiniq Parenting Curriculum.* Iqaluit, NU: QHRC, 2013.

Qitsualik, Rachel, ed. "The Inuit Educational Concept." Special issue, *Ajurnarmat*, no. 4 (Nov. 1979). Inuit Cultural Institute.

Queen's University Truth and Reconciliation Commission Task Force. *Yakwanastahentéha Aankenjigemi Extending the Rafters: Truth and Reconciliation Commission Task Force Final Report.* Kingston, ON: Queen's University, Office of the Provost, 2017.

Rabson, Mia. "Pope Won't Personally Apologize for Catholic Church's Role in Residential Schools," *Globe and Mail*, 27 March 2018. Accessed 15 September 2019. https://www.theglobeandmail.com/canada/article-pope-wont-personally-apologize-for-catholic-churchs-role-in/.

Regev, E., N. Gueron-Sela, and N. Atzaba-Poria. "The Adjustment of Ethnic Minority and Majority Children Living in Israel: Does Parental Use of Corporal Punishment Act as a Mediator?" *Infant and Child Development* 21 (2012): 34–51.

Religions for Peace. *A Multi-Religious Commitment to Confront Violence against Children.* Adopted at the Religions for Peace VIII World Assembly, Kyoto, Japan, 28 August 2006. http://churchesfornon-violence.org/wp/wp-content/uploads/2012/02/Violence-Against-Children-.pdf.

Religions for Peace and UNICEF. *From Commitment to Action: What Religious Communities Can Do to Eliminate Violence against Children.* New York: UNICEF and Religions for Peace, 2010.

Road Safety Observatory. *Seat Belts.* United Kingdom: Road Safety Observatory, 2013. Accessed 30 September 2018. http://www.roadsafetyobservatory.com/Summary/vehicles/seat-belts.

Roberto, John, Kathie Amidei, and Jim Merhaut. *Generations Together: Caring, Praying, Learning, Celebrating, and Serving Faithfully*. Naugatuck, CT: LifelongFaith Associates, 2014.

Roehlkepartain, Eugene C., Pamela E. King, Linda M. Wagener, and Peter L. Benson, eds. *The Handbook of Spiritual Development in Childhood and Adolescence.* Thousand Oaks, CA: Sage, 2006.

Romano, E., R.E. Tremblay, B. Boulerice, and R. Swisher. "Multilevel Correlates of Childhood Physical Aggression and Prosocial Behavior." *Journal of Abnormal Child Psychology* 33, no. 5 (2005): 565–78.

Ruckstaetter, J., J. Sells, M.D. Newmeyer, and D. Zink. "Parental Apologies, Empathy, Shame, Guilt, and Attachment: A Path Analysis." *Journal of Counseling and Development* 95, no. 4 (2017): 389–400.

Runyan, Desmond, Corrine Wattam, Robin Ikeda, Fatma Hassan, and Laurie Ramiro. "Child Abuse and Neglect by Parents and Other Caregivers." In *World Report on Violence and Health*, edited by Etienne G. Krug, Linda L. Dahlberg, James A. Mercy, Anthony B. Zwi, and Rafael Lozano, 57–81. Geneva: World Health Organization, 2002.

Samuel, Vinay, and Chris Sugden. *Mission as Transformation.* Oxford: Regnum, 1999.

Saunders, Bernadette J. "'Because There's a Better Way Than Hurting Someone': An Exploratory Study of the Nature, Effects and Persistence of 'Physical Punishment' in Childhood." PhD diss., Monash University, 2005.

———. "Ending Corporal Punishment in Childhood: Advancing Children's Rights to Dignity and Respectful Treatment." In *Law and Society: Reflections on Children, Family, Culture and Philosophy*, edited by Alison Diduck, Noam Peleg, and Helen Reece, 243–71. Leiden: Brill Nijhoff, 2015.

———. "Ending the Physical Punishment of Children by Parents in the English-Speaking World: The Impact of Language, Tradition and Law." *International Journal of Children's Rights* 21, no. 2 (2013): 278–304.

Saunders, Bernadette J., and Chris Goddard. *Physical Punishment in Childhood: The Rights of the Child.* Chichester, UK: John Wiley and Sons, 2010.

Schreiner, Thomas. Review of *Corporal Punishment in the Bible*, by William J. Webb. The Gospel Coalition, 12 September 2011. https://www.thegospelcoalition.org/reviews/corporal_punishment_in_the_bible/.

Schreiter, Robert J. *Ministry of Reconciliation: Spirituality and Strategies*. Ossining, NY: Orbis Books, 2015.

———. *Reconciliation: Mission and Ministry in a Changing Social Order*. Ossining, NY: Orbis Books, 2015.

Search Institute. "Developmental Assets." Search Institute.. Accessed 17 October 2018. https://www.search-institute.org/our-research/development-assets/.

Shupak, Nili. *Where Can Wisdom Be Found? The Sage's Language in the Bible and in Ancient Egyptian Literature*. Orbis Biblicus et Orientalis 130. Fribourg: Universitätsverlag; Göttingen: Vandenhoeck & Ruprecht, 1993.

Sinclair, Murray, Senator. "My Challenge." At *Indian Horse* (film), official website. Accessed 28 August 2019. https://next150.indianhorse.ca/challenges/94-calls-to-action.

Smith, Carly Parnitzke, and Jennifer J. Freyd. "Institutional Betrayal." *American Psychologist* 69, no. 6 (2014): 575–87.

Smith, Christian, and Melinda L. Denton. *Soul Searching: The Religious and Spiritual Lives of American Teenagers*. Oxford: Oxford University Press, 2005.

Southern African Catholic Bishops' Conference (SACBC), Parliamentary Liaison Office. Submission by the Southern African Catholic Bishops' Conference Parliamentary Liaison Office on "The Use of Corporal Punishment in the Home," 2013. Accessed 4 February 2020. http://www.cplo.org.za/wp-content/uploads/downloads/2013/06/Corporal-Discipline-in-the-Home-June-2013.pdf.

Southern Baptist Convention. *On Alcohol Use in America*. Southern Baptist Convention, Greensboro, NC, 2006. Accessed 19 October 2018. http://www.sbc.net/resolutions/1156.

Spellman, Ched. "The Drama of Discipline: Toward an Intertextual Profile of *Paideia* in Hebrews 12." *Journal of the Evangelical Theological Society* 59, no. 3 (2016): 487–506.

Sterling, Shirley. *My Name Is Seepeetza.* Toronto: Groundwood, 2008.

Stewart-Tufescu, Ashley, and R. Aljawi. "Transporting a Violence Prevention Parenting Program to a Conflict Setting: Positive Discipline in Everyday Parenting in the Palestinian Territories." Presentation at the International Society for the Prevention of Child Abuse and Neglect, Prague, Czechoslovakia, September 2018.

Stewart-Tufescu, A., C. Ateah, D. Plateau, and T. Sudrajat. "Evaluating the Positive Discipline in Everyday Parenting Facilitator Training Program with Community Health Workers in Indonesia." Presentation at the International Society for the Prevention of Child Abuse and Neglect, Prague, Czechoslovakia, September 2018.

Stonehouse, Catherine, and Scottie May. *Listening to Children on the Spiritual Journey: Guidance for Those Who Teach and Nurture*. Grand Rapids, MI: Baker Academic, 2010.

Straus, M.A., Sugarman, D.B., and J. Giles-Sims. "Spanking by Parents and Subsequent Antisocial Behavior of Children." *Archives of Pediatrics and Adolescent Medicine* 151, no. 8 (1997): 761–67.

Strommen, Merton P., and Richard Hardel. *Passing on the Faith: A Radical New Model for Youth and Family Ministry*. Winona, MN: St. Mary's Press, 2000.

Tagalik, Shirley. "The Arviat Language Research Project: Language Beliefs as an Influencing Factor in the Quality of Oral Language in Arviat. " M.A. thesis, McGill University, 1998.

———. "Inuit Knowledge Systems, Elders and Determinants of Health—Harmony, Balance and the Role of Holistic Thinking." In *Determinants of Indigenous Peoples' Health in Canada: Beyond the Social*, edited by Margo Greenwood, Sarah de Leeuw, Nicole Lindsay, and Charlotte Reading, 25–32. Toronto: Canadian Scholars' Press, 2015.

Tagalik, Shirley, and J. Joyce. *Relationality and Its Importance as a Protective Factor for Indigenous Youth*. Arviat, NU: Centre of Excellence for Children and Adolescents with Special Needs, 2005.

Taylor, Charles. *A Secular Age*. Cambridge MA: Belknap, 2007.

Taylor, Z.E., N. Eisenberg, T.L. Spinrad, N.D. Eggum, and M.J. Sulik. "The Relations of Ego-Resiliency and Emotional Socialization to the Development of Empathy and Prosocial Behavior across Early Childhood." *Emotion* 13 (2013): 822–31.

Thira, Darien. "Beyond Colonization: Canadian Aboriginal Context: A Post-Colonial Perspective." Thira Consulting, 2008. https://thira.ca/thira-tools/papers-articles/.

Trothen, Tracy J. *Shattering the Illusion: Child Sexual Abuse and Canadian Religious Institutions*. Waterloo, ON: Wilfrid Laurier University Press, 2012.

Truth and Reconciliation Commission of Canada. "Backgrounder." Winnipeg: Truth and Reconciliation Commission of Canada, 2015. Accessed 8 July 2018. http://www.trc.ca/assets/pdf/mroom_Backgrounder_E.pdf.

———. *Canada's Residential Schools: The History, Part 1: Origins to 1939.* Vol. 1 of *The Final Report of the Truth and Reconciliation Commission of Canada.* Kingston, ON: McGill–Queen's University Press, 2015.

———. *Canada's Residential Schools: The History, Part 2: 1939–2000.* Vol. 1 of *The Final Report of the Truth and Reconciliation Commission of Canada.* Kingston, ON: McGill–Queen's University Press, 2015.

———. *Honouring the Truth, Reconciling for the Future: Summary of the Final Report of the Truth and Reconciliation Commission.* Winnipeg: Truth and Reconciliation Commission of Canada, 2015. Accessed 18 October 2018. http://www.trc.ca/assets/pdf/Honouring_the_Truth_Reconciling_for_the_Future_July_23_2015.pdf.

———. *The Survivors Speak: A Report of the Truth and Reconciliation Commission of Canada.* Winnipeg: Truth and Reconciliation Commission of Canada, 2015. Accessed 9 January 2019. http://www.trc.ca/assets/pdf/Survivors_Speak_English_Web.pdf.

———. *The Truth and Reconciliation Commission of Canada: Calls to Action.* Winnipeg: Truth and Reconciliation Commission of Canada, 2015. Accessed 18 October 2018. http://trc.ca/assets/pdf/Calls_to_Action_English2.pdf.

Turkle, Sherry. *Reclaiming Conversation: The Power of Talk in a Digital Age.* New York: Penguin Books, 2015.

UN General Assembly. *Convention on the Rights of the Child*, 20 November 1989. United Nations, Treaty Series, vol. 1577, p. 3. Accessed 19 October 2018. http://www.refworld.org/docid/3ae6b38f0.html.

———. *United Nations Declaration on the Rights of Indigenous Peoples: Resolution / Adopted by the General Assembly*, 2 October 2007, A/RES/61/295. Accessed 21 January 2020. https://www.refworld.org/docid/471355a82.html.

UNICEF. *Declaration: Conference on the Role of Religions and Religious Leaders in Confronting Corporal Punishment of Children in the Family and Educational Settings*, 20 October 2011. Accessed 19 October 2018. https://jliflc.com/resources/declaration-qom-iran-2011-the-role-of-religions-and-religious-leaders-in-confronting-corporal-punishment-of-children-in-the-family-and-educational-settings/.

———. *Partnering with Religious Communities for Children*. New York: UNICEF, 2012. https://www.unicef.org/eapro/Partnering_with_Religious_Communities_for_Children.pdf.

UNICEF and World Council of Churches. *Churches' Commitments to Children: Churches Uniting for Children in the Pilgrimage of Justice and Peace*. Geneva: World Council of Churches, 2017.

United Church of Canada. "The Apologies." United Church of Canada. Accessed 15 September 2019. https://www.united-church.ca/social-action/justice-initiatives/apologies.

———. "Church Leaders: Make C-262 Unanimous." United Church of Canada, 12 March 2019. Accessed 28 August 2019. https://www.united-church.ca/news/church-leaders-make-c-262-vote-unanimous.

———. "United Church Reconciliation Journey to Australia." United Church of Canada, 30 March 2019. Accessed 28 August 2019. https://www.united-church.ca/news/united-church-reconciliation-journey-australia.

United Church of Canada Archives. "Alberni Indian Residential School." Residential School Archives Project: Children Remembered. Accessed 6 July 2018. http://thechildrenremembered.ca/school-locations/alberni/#ftn22.

United Church of Canada British Colombia Conference Archives. "Fonds-Alberni Indian Residential School." MemoryBC. Last modified 28 January 2015. https://www.memorybc.ca/alberni-indian-residential-school-fonds.

Valeri, Mark. "The Christianization of Usury in Early Modern Europe." *Interpretation* 65, no. 2 (2011): 142–52.

Van Kirk, Sylvia. *Many Tender Ties: Women in Fur-Trade Society, 1670–1870.* Norman: University of Oklahoma Press, 1980.

Vermeulen, Keith. "Resolutions from the 9th All Africa Conference of Churches' General Assembly: Developments in Africa." *Article 19* 5, no.1 (2009): 9–11. https://hdl.handle.net/10520/EJC21044.

von Rad, Gerhard. *Wisdom in Israel.* London: SCM, 1972.

WCC (World Council of Churches) Executive Committee. "Statement on the Doctrine of Discovery and Its Enduring Impact on Indigenous Peoples." World Council of Churches, 17 February 2012. Accessed 17 October 2018. https://www.oikoumene.org/en/resources/documents/executive-committee/2012-02/statement-on-the-doctrine-of-discovery-and-its-enduring-impact-on-indigenous-peoples.

Webb, Elspeth. "Discrimination against Children." *Archives of Disease in Childhood* 89, no. 9 (2004): 804–8. https://adc.bmj.com/content/archdischild/89/9/804.full.pdf.

Webb, William J. *Corporal Punishment in the Bible: A Redemptive-Movement Hermeneutic for Troubling Texts.* Downers Grove, IL: InterVarsity Press, 2011.

Webb, William J., and Gordon K. Oeste. *Bloody, Brutal, and Barbaric? Wrestling with Troubling War Texts.* Downers Grove, IL: InterVarsity Press, 2019.

Wegner, Paul D. "Discipline in the Book of Proverbs: 'To Spank or Not to Spank.'" *Journal of the Evangelical Theological Society* 48, no. 4 (2005): 720–28.

Wenger-Nabigon, Annie. "The Cree Medicine Wheel as an Organizing Paradigm of Theories of Human Development." *Native Social Work Journal* 7 (November 2010): 139–61.

White, Keith J. "'He Placed a Little Child in the Midst': Jesus, the Kingdom and Children." In *The Child in the Bible,* edited by Marcia J. Bunge, Terence E. Fretheim, and Beverly Roberts Gaventa, 253–74. Grand Rapids, MI: William B. Eerdmans, 2008.

Whittaker, Frederick. *A Complete Life of General George A. Custer: From Appomattox to the Little Big Horn.* Vol. 2. Lincoln: University of Nebraska Press, 1993.

Wink, Walter. *Engaging the Powers: Discernment and Resistance in a World of Domination.* Minneapolis: Ausburg Fortress Press, 1992.

World Council of Churches. *Putting Children at the Center*. Accessed 8 November 2013. http://churchesfornon-violence.org/wp/wp-content/uploads/2012/02/Putting-Children-at-the-Center.pdf.

———. "Resources and Tools Available for the Implementation of Churches' Commitments to Children." Oikoumene.org, last modified 2018. https://www.oikoumene.org/en/resources/documents/wcc-programmes/public-witness/rights-of-children/resources-available-to-support-member-churches-in-the-implementation-of-each-principle.

———. "WCC Develops Digital Map for Churches' Commitments to Children." Oikoumene.org, 19 October 2017. https://www.oikoumene.org/en/press-centre/news/wcc-develops-digital-map-for-churches-commitments-to-children.

Wuthnow, Robert. *Growing Up Religious: Christians and Jews and Their Journeys of Faith.* Boston: Beacon Press, 1999.

Yaconelli, Mike. *Dangerous Wonder: The Adventure of Childlike Faith.* 3rd ed. Colorado Springs, CO: NavPress, 2003.

Yoreh, Tzemah. *Why Abraham Killed Isaac.* Kernel to Canon. Scotts Valley, CA: CreateSpace Independent, 2013.

Yust, Karen M., Aostre N. Johnson, Sandy E. Sasso, and Eugene C. Roehlkepartain, eds. *Nurturing Child and Adolescent Spirituality: Perspectives from the World's Religious Traditions*. Lanham, MD: Rowman and Littlefield, 2006.

CONTRIBUTORS

The Reverend Canon Dr. Martin Brokenleg, OSBCn, is a member of the Rosebud Sioux Tribe and practises the culture of his Lakȟóta people. He holds a doctorate in psychology, is a graduate of the Episcopal Divinity School in Cambridge, Massachusetts, and is a retired priest of the Anglican Church of Canada. He is the founder of the Anglican Canon Communities of St. Benedict and prior of the Community of St. Aidan in Victoria, BC. He was a co-founder of the Circle of Courage and continues to provide training worldwide for individuals who work on behalf of Reclaiming Youth International. Brother Brokenleg is an enrolled member of the Rosebud Sioux Tribe of South Dakota, and also a member of the Kyaanuuslii Raven House of the Haida First Nation.

Dr. Marcia J. Bunge is Professor of Religion and the Droll and Adeline Bernhardson Distinguished Chair of Lutheran Studies at Gustavus Adolphus College in St. Peter, Minnesota, and Extraordinary Research Professor at North West University, South Africa. She has published five volumes on religious conceptions of children, including *The Child in Christian Thought* (Eerdmans, 2001), and is a prominent leader in international conversations about religion, theology, and child protection. She was a theological contributor to the Joint Statement on Child Protection Issues by the World Council of Churches and UNICEF (2016) and a Kempe-Haruv Fellow for the International Initiative on Child Protection (sponsored by the Kempe Center of the University of Colorado and the Haruv Institute of Hebrew University). She seeks to promote child well-being through her scholarship and advocacy and currently serves on the editorial board of the *International Journal on Child Maltreatment.*

The Reverend Amy Crawford is the Team Leader for Faith Formation and Congregational Mission with the United Church of Canada. Amy has been in ministry with children, youth, and their families for over twenty-five years. She is a Godly Play teacher and trainer and has been instrumental in bringing Godly Play to Canada, as well as training teachers and trainers around the world. With Amy's leadership, the United Church of Canada was one of the early endorsers of the *Joint Statement on Physical Punishment of Children and Youth* issued by the Coalition on Physical Punishment of Children and Youth.

Chris Dodd is a co-founder of the Churches' Network for Non-violence (CNNV), which was formed in 2006 to bring faith communities into discussions about law reform to end all corporal punishment of children and other cruel and humiliating forms of violence against children. This has included working with others to develop a network of support, creating practical resources and information, and encouraging religious communities to play an active role in the global movement for law reform. She also worked as faith-based advocacy coordinator for the Global Initiative to End All Corporal Punishment of Children from 2015 to 2017. Her background is in early childhood development and public health.

Kacey Dool holds a master's degree in Religious Studies from the School of Religion at Queen's University in Kingston, Ontario. Her research has led her to an exploration of the circumstances and outcomes of the Indian residential school system and has led to the unearthing of her own disrupted and disjointed Métis heritage, which was known among her family but rarely discussed. Through her involvement with the gathering that led to this book and through dialogue with family members, Kacey has expanded her understanding of her own Indigenous heritage and has begun to discover her own place in the tenuous process of reconciliation.

Dr. Joan E. Durrant is a child-clinical psychologist and Professor of Community Health Sciences at the University of Manitoba. For three decades, her academic work has focused on the multi-faceted issue of corporal punishment of children. She served on the Research Advisory Committee of the *United Nations Secretary-General's Study on Violence against Children* and is the co-author of the Canadian *Joint Statement on Physical Punishment of Children and Youth* (Coalition on Physical

Punishment of Children and Youth, 2004). She partnered with Save the Children to create *Positive Discipline in Everyday Parenting*, a program designed to help parents adopt a non-punitive, collaborative approach to discipline that is being implemented around the world.

Clarence Hale tragically died shortly before this book was published. Clarence grew up in Ontario and Nova Scotia. As a child, he experienced the cycle of violence and was taught to be ashamed of his heritage, even though he didn't know much about it. He spent his life in a process of deep healing which, in part, he found through the Christian church. At the time of his death, he had begun a discovery of his rich Lakȟóta heritage and was navigating the complexities of colonialism in his own life and family. He and his wife, Shirley, were raising their grandson and working together to break the intergenerational cycle of violence and bring health and wholeness to the next generation.

Charlene Hallett is a Métis woman of the Sabe clan, with Nêhiyawak and French ancestry, who grew up in the north end of Winnipeg. In the spring of 2020, she completed her degree within the University of Manitoba's Family Social Sciences Program, specializing in Child and Youth Development and Family Violence, with a minor in Native Studies. She is the recipient of a University of Manitoba Emerging Leader Award, an UMSU Award for Indigenous Community Leaders, and most recently, a University of Manitoba Graduate Fellowship, after being accepted into the Master's of Science program in the Community Health Sciences Department for the fall of 2020. Charlene is a cultural educator, a mentor with the Neechiwaken Indigenous Peer Mentorship Program, a member of the Manitoba Métis Federation's Bison Local, and the student representative on the Manitoba Collaborative Indigenous Education Blueprint steering committee. She participates in Sundance, Sweatlodge, Full Moon, and other ceremonies.

Ken Letander is a First Nation artist from Manitoba's Treaty 1 territory who worked with Canada's Truth and Reconciliation Commission, hearing and documenting the stories of Indian Residential School survivors.

The Most Reverend Mark MacDonald was elected Archbishop of the newly formed self-determining Indigenous church within the Anglican Church of Canada in July 2019. Before that, he served for twelve years as National Indigenous Bishop to the Anglican Church of Canada. He has spoken extensively about the way Indigenous concerns are woven into the fabric of Canadian life and continues to be very involved in the Truth and Reconciliation process. Having Indigenous ancestry through both his mother and father, growing up among the Ojibway people, and also having a pastoral relationship with Canada's Indigenous Anglican church over the last decade, Bishop MacDonald has first-hand experience of the impact of the Indian residential schools on the lives of Canadians.

Dr. Valerie E. Michaelson is Professor in the Department of Health Sciences at Brock University. Her academic work relates to decolonization and reconciliation, and she is particularly focused on examining social and cultural norms that rationalize harmful health behaviours and attitudes, and that lead to poor child health outcomes. Between 2013 and 2019, she was a postdoctoral researcher at Queen's University, cross-appointed between the Department of Public Health Sciences and the School of Religion. This interdisciplinary appointment provided an ideal platform to initiate the project reflected in this volume. Before completing her doctoral studies, she served as an ordained Anglican priest in Kingston, Canada.

The Reverend Dr. William S. Morrow is Professor Emeritus of Hebrew and Hebrew Scriptures in the School of Religion at Queen's University in Kingston, Canada. An expert in methods of biblical interpretation, he has spent much of his professional life teaching candidates for Christian ministry as well as students in religious studies, and is active in church circles as an ordained minister (formerly Presbyterian) and priest (currently Anglican). Dialogue between church and academy has been an intrinsic part of his career. His research has particularly focused on questions of law and violence as they manifested themselves in the communities that created and transmitted biblical literature, and as they continue to manifest themselves in contemporary experiences of religiously motivated violence.

The Reverend Dr. Peter Robinson teaches theology at Wycliffe College at the University of Toronto, where he is Professor of Proclamation, Worship and Ministry. He is also an ordained priest in the Anglican Church of Canada and has a particular interest in the working relationship between the church and the academy, spiritual formation, catechism, and practical theology.

Dr. Bernadette J. Saunders is Senior Lecturer and Coordinator of the Master of Social Work program in the Faculty of Medicine, Nursing and Health Sciences at Monash University in Melbourne, Australia. She has professional qualifications in social work and education. Her PhD research focused upon the physical punishment of children and the intergenerational transmission of punitive violence. Her academic publications largely focus upon injustices resulting from law, language, and culture that impact disadvantaged groups, especially children. She teaches in the areas of human rights, law, ethics, and child maltreatment.

The Right Reverend Riscylla Shaw is a Bishop in the Anglican Diocese of Toronto (Trent-Durham), where she has also served as Ambassador for Reconciliation. As a Métis woman and parent to two teenagers, she sees her role of promoting reconciliation and justice for marginalized peoples as a priority. Inspired by Archbishop Desmond Tutu in South Africa, she continues to interpret the findings of the Truth and Reconciliation Commission to the church and the broader community by building bridges ecumenically and culturally. Bishop Shaw is a member of the Métis Nation of Ontario.

The Reverend Canon Dr. Andrew Sheldon is a priest of the Diocese of Toronto, and an adjunct faculty member of Trinity College Faculty of Divinity. He has taught numerous pastoral theology courses, including Beyond Religious Education: The Implications of the Spirituality of Children for Theory and Practice. He is a Godly Play practitioner and trainer, and currently holds the position of Godly Play Advocate for International Development. Andrew serves as Associate Priest in a local parish, where he also assists in providing chaplaincy to the independent day school attached to the church. At church and at school, he sits in weekly circles of children sharing and wondering about the stories of the Christian faith.

Dr. Ashley Stewart-Tufescu holds bachelor's degrees in forensic archaeology and social work, a master's degree in family social sciences with a focus on family violence, and a PhD in applied health sciences. She has worked in child protection, crisis counselling, and public education. Her research has focused on the implementation of parenting support initiatives in diverse cultural and religious settings, as well as children's perceptions of health and well-being. Currently, she is a post-doctoral fellow in the Departments of Community Health Sciences and Psychiatry and teaches in the Faculty of Social Work at the University of Manitoba.

Shirley Tagalik is Principal Consultant for Inukpaujaq Consulting and a research associate at Qaujigiartiit Health Research Centre in Iqaluit, Nunavut. Her main areas of research have been Inuit youth mental health, the design of an Indigenous Health Framework, and the applications of an

Inuit world view to health and education. She is also interested in early childhood/maternal health, heritage language revitalization, and curriculum development to promote an Inuit world view. She has published widely; some of her work is available through the National Collaborating Centre for Indigenous Health. Ms. Tagalik has been raising her children and grandchildren in an Inuit community over many decades.

Soon to retire from his work as General Secretary of the Anglican Church of Canada (2001–2020), **Michael Thompson** has served in educational, administrative, and pastoral ministry for almost forty years. His most recent position has led to a growing awareness of the historic injustices of colonialism, especially in its continuing impact on Canadian First Nations, Inuit, and Métis communities. He lives in Kingston and Toronto, and has served parishes in Edmonton and Wetaskiwin (Alberta) and Toronto and Oakville (Ontario), as well as at Trinity College, (University of Toronto, 1988-1992) and as Principal Secretary to former Primate of the Anglican Church of Canada, Archbishop Michael Peers (2001-2004).

Dr. William J. Webb is married to Marilyn, and together they have three grown children (Jonathan, Christine, and Joel) and a dog (Cindy Lou). He received his PhD from Dallas Theological Seminary and currently teaches as an adjunct professor at Tyndale Seminary in Toronto, Canada. In addition to conference speaking, Bill has published several articles and books, including *Returning Home: New Covenant and Second Exodus as the Context for 2 Corinthians 6.14-7.1* (Sheffield Press, 1993), *Slaves, Women, and Homosexuals: Exploring the Hermeneutics of Cultural Analysis* (InterVarsity Press, 2001), *Four Views on Moving beyond the Bible to Theology* (one view and responses; Zondervan, 2009), *Corporal Punishment in the Bible: A Redemptive Hermeneutic for Troubling Texts* (InterVarsity Press, 2011), and *Bloody, Brutal and Barbaric? Wrestling with Troubling War Texts* (InterVarsity Press, 2019).

The Reverend Dr. John H. Young is Executive Minister, Theological Leadership, for the United Church of Canada. Previously he served in congregational ministry in Nova Scotia and in Ontario and taught for twenty-five years in the theology program of the School of Religion at Queen's University in Kingston, Ontario. He is the author of a number of articles and book chapters, and co-author with the Reverend Dr. Catherine MacLean of *Preaching the Big Questions: Doctrine Isn't Dusty* (United Church Publishing House, 2015).